Anthropology Matters!

Anthropology Matters!

SHIRLEY A. FEDORAK

UTP

Originally published by Broadview Press 2007

LIBRARY AND ARCHIVES CANADA CATALOGUING IN PUBLICATION

Fedorak, Shirley
    Anthropology matters! / Shirley A. Fedorak.

Includes bibliographical references and index.
ISBN 978-1-44260-108-6
(Previous ISBN 978-1-55111-761-4)

    1. Anthropology. I. Title.

GN25.F43 2007   301   C2007-900517-9

We welcome comments and suggestions regarding any aspect of our publications—please feel free to contact us at the addresses below or at:
news@utphighereducation.com/www.utphighereducation.com

Higher Education University of Toronto Press acknowledges the financial support of the Government of Canada through the Book Publishing Industry Development Program (BPIDP) for our publishing activities.

Cover & Interior Design by Michel Vrána, Black Eye Design.
Printed in Canada

10 9 8 7 6 5 4 3 2 1

North America
5201 Dufferin Street, North York
Ontario, Canada, M3H 5T8
2250 Military Road, Tonawanda
New York. USA. 14150
Tel: (416) 978-2239
Fax: (416) 978-4738
customerservice@utphighereducation.com

UK, Ireland and continental Europe
Plymbridge Distributors Ltd.
Estover Road, Plymouth PL6 7PY, UK
tel: 44 (0) 1752 202300;
fax order line: 44 (0) 1752 202330;
enquiries@nbninternational.com

This book has been printed on 100% post consumer waste paper, certified Eco-logo and processed chlorine free.

FSC   Recycled
Supporting responsible use
of forest resources
www.fsc.org Cert no. SGS-COC-003153
© 1996 Forest Stewardship Council

TO MY STUDENTS, WHO HAVE ASKED THESE QUESTIONS

Contents

THEMATIC GUIDE TO CONTENT   IX

AUTHOR PROFILE   XVII

ACKNOWLEDGEMENTS   XVIII

TO THE INSTRUCTOR   XIX

INTRODUCTION   XXIV

PART ONE: HOW DOES ANTHROPOLOGY WORK?   1

CHAPTER ONE: What are the Challenges in Ethnographic Fieldwork?   3

CHAPTER TWO: What is Culture Shock and How Does it Affect People Living, Studying, and Working Abroad?   15

CHAPTER THREE: Of What Use is Anthropology to the Business World? The Anthropology of Shopping   31

PART TWO: WHY DOES ANTHROPOLOGY MATTER?   45

CHAPTER FOUR: What are the Underlying Reasons Behind Ethnic Conflict, and the Consequences of these Conflicts?   47

CHAPTER FIVE: What Challenges Do Immigrants in Canada Face?   69

CHAPTER SIX: How Has the Push for the Perfect Body Impacted on the Self-Image, Health, and Comfort of Women?   91

CHAPTER SEVEN: Is Female Circumcision a Violation of Human Rights or a Cherished Cultural Tradition?   105

CHAPTER EIGHT: What Does it Mean to Grow Old?   123

CHAPTER NINE: What Impact Has Missionism Had on Indigenous Cultures?   143

CHAPTER TEN: Is the Practice of Purdah and Wearing the Hijab Oppressive to Women or an Expression of Their Identity?   155

CHAPTER ELEVEN: How Do Anthropologists View Same-Sex Marriages and Changing Family Structure? How Do We Define Marriage?   173

CHAPTER TWELVE: Has the Medium of Television Changed Human Behaviour and World Views?   191

CONCLUSION: Anthropology Matters!   207

GLOSSARY   211

SOURCES   221

INDEX   223

Thematic Guide
to Content

CROSS-CULTURAL COMPARISON

CHAPTER FOUR: What are the Underlying Reasons Behind Ethnic Conflict, and the Consequences of these Conflicts?   47

CHAPTER SIX: How Has the Push for the Perfect Body Impacted on the Self-Image, Health, and Comfort of Women?   91

CHAPTER SEVEN: Is Female Circumcision a Violation of Human Rights or a Cherished Cultural Tradition?   105

CHAPTER EIGHT: What Does it Mean to Grow Old?   123

CHAPTER NINE: What Impact Has Missionism Had on Indigenous Cultures   143

CHAPTER TEN: Is the Practice of Purdah and Wearing the Hijab Oppressive to Women or an Expression of Their Identity?   155

CHAPTER ELEVEN: How Do Anthropologists View Same-Sex Marriages and Changing Family Structure? How Do We Define Marriage?   173

CHAPTER TWELVE: Has the Medium of Television Changed Human Behaviour and World Views?   191

CULTURE CHANGE

CHAPTER FIVE: What Challenges Do Immigrants in Canada Face?   69

CHAPTER SIX: How Has the Push for the Perfect Body Impacted on the Self-Image, Health, and Comfort of Women?   91

CHAPTER SEVEN: Is Female Circumcision a Violation of Human Rights or a Cherished Cultural Tradition?   105

CHAPTER NINE: What Impact Has Missionism Had on Indigenous Cultures?   143

CHAPTER TEN: Is the Practice of Purdah and Wearing the Hijab Oppressive to Women or an Expression of Their Identity?   155

CHAPTER ELEVEN: How Do Anthropologists View Same-Sex Marriages and Changing Family Structure? How Do We Define Marriage?   173

CHAPTER TWELVE: Has the Medium of Television Changed Human Behaviour and World Views?   191

CULTURAL IMPERIALISM

CHAPTER FOUR: What are the Underlying Reasons behind Ethnic Conflict, and the Consequences of these Conflicts?   47

CHAPTER FIVE: What Challenges Do Immigrants in Canada Face?   69

CHAPTER SIX: How Has the Push for the Perfect Body Impacted on the Self-Image, Health, and Comfort of Women?   91

CHAPTER SEVEN: Is Female Circumcision a Violation of Human Rights or a Cherished Cultural Tradition?   105

CHAPTER NINE: What Impact Has Missionism Had on Indigenous Cultures?   143

CHAPTER TEN: Is the Practice of Purdah and Wearing the Hijab Oppressive to Women or an Expression of Their Identity?   155

CHAPTER ELEVEN: How Do Anthropologists View Same-Sex Marriages and Changing Family Structure? How Do We Define Marriage?   173

CHAPTER TWELVE: Has the Medium of Television Changed Human Behaviour and World Views?   191

CULTURAL RELATIVISM

CHAPTER ONE: What are the Challenges in Ethnographic Fieldwork?   3

CHAPTER TWO: What is Culture Shock and How Does it Affect People Living, Studying, and Working Abroad?   15

CHAPTER FOUR: What are the Underlying Reasons Behind Ethnic Conflict, and the Consequences of these Conflicts?   47

CHAPTER FIVE: What Challenges Do Immigrants in Canada Face?   69

CHAPTER SEVEN: Is Female Circumcision a Violation of Human Rights or a Cherished Cultural Tradition?   105

CHAPTER NINE: What Impact Has Missionism Had on Indigenous Cultures?   143

CHAPTER TEN: Is the Practice of Purdah and Wearing the Hijab Oppressive to Women or an Expression of Their Identity?   155

CHAPTER ELEVEN: How Do Anthropologists View Same-Sex Marriages and Changing Family Structure? How Do We Define Marriage?   173

CULTURE SHOCK

CHAPTER ONE: What are the Challenges in Ethnographic Fieldwork? 3

CHAPTER TWO: What is Culture Shock and How Does it Affect People Living, Studying, and Working Abroad? 15

CHAPTER FIVE: What Challenges Do Immigrants in Canada Face? 69

DIFFUSION

CHAPTER THREE: Of What Use is Anthropology to the Business World? The Anthropology of Shopping 31

CHAPTER SIX: How Has the Push for the Perfect Body Impacted on the Self-Image, Health, and Comfort of Women? 91

CHAPTER SEVEN: Is Female Circumcision a Violation of Human Rights or a Cherished Cultural Tradition? 105

CHAPTER NINE: What Impact Has Missionism Had on Indigenous Cultures? 143

CHAPTER TEN: Is the Practice of Purdah and Wearing the Hijab Oppressive to Women or an Expression of Their Identity? 155

CHAPTER ELEVEN: How Do Anthropologists View Same-Sex Marriages and Changing Family Structure? How Do We Define Marriage? 173

CHAPTER TWELVE: Has the Medium of Television Changed Human Behaviour and World Views? 191

ENCULTURATION

CHAPTER TWO: What is Culture Shock and How Does it Affect People Living, Studying, and Working Abroad? 15

CHAPTER FIVE: What Challenges Do Immigrants in Canada Face? 69

CHAPTER SIX: How Has the Push for the Perfect Body Impacted on the Self-Image, Health, and Comfort of Women? 91

CHAPTER EIGHT: What Does it Mean to Grow Old? 123

CHAPTER TEN: Is the Practice of Purdah and Wearing the Hijab Oppressive to Women or an Expression of Their Identity? 155

CHAPTER TWELVE: Has the Medium of Television Changed Human Behaviour and World Views? 191

ETHICS IN ANTHROPOLOGY

CHAPTER ONE: What are the Challenges in Ethnographic Fieldwork? 3

CHAPTER THREE: Of What Use is Anthropology to the Business World? The Anthropology of Shopping 31

CHAPTER SEVEN: Is Female Circumcision a Violation of Human Rights or a Cherished Cultural Tradition? 105

ETHNICITY

CHAPTER FOUR: What are the Underlying Reasons Behind Ethnic Conflict, and the Consequences of these Conflicts? 47

CHAPTER FIVE: What Challenges Do Immigrants in Canada Face? 69

CHAPTER SIX: How Has the Push for the Perfect Body Impacted on the Self-Image, Health, and Comfort of Women? 91

CHAPTER SEVEN: Is Female Circumcision a Violation of Human Rights or a Cherished Cultural Tradition? 105

CHAPTER EIGHT: What Does it Mean to Grow Old? 123

CHAPTER NINE: What Impact Has Missionism Had on Indigenous Cultures? 143

CHAPTER TEN: Is the Practice of Purdah and Wearing the Hijab Oppressive to Women or an Expression of Their Identity? 155

ETHNOCENTRISM AND DISCRIMINATION

CHAPTER TWO: What is Culture Shock and How Does it Affect People Living, Studying, and Working Abroad? 15

CHAPTER FOUR: What are the Underlying Reasons Behind Ethnic Conflict, and the Consequences of these Conflicts? 47

CHAPTER FIVE: What Challenges Do Immigrants in Canada Face? 69

CHAPTER SIX: How Has the Push for the Perfect Body Impacted on the Self-Image, Health, and Comfort of Women? 91

CHAPTER SEVEN: Is Female Circumcision a Violation of Human Rights or a Cherished Cultural Tradition? 105

CHAPTER NINE: What Impact Has Missionism Had on Indigenous Cultures? 143

CHAPTER TEN: Is the Practice of Purdah and Wearing the Hijab Oppressive to Women or an Expression of Their Identity? 155

CHAPTER ELEVEN: How Do Anthropologists View Same-Sex Marriages and Changing Family Structure? How Do We Define Marriage? 173

ETHNOGRAPHIC FIELDWORK

CHAPTER ONE: What are the Challenges in Ethnographic Fieldwork? 3

CHAPTER TWO: What is Culture Shock and How Does it Affect People Living, Studying, and Working Abroad? 15

CHAPTER THREE: Of What Use is Anthropology to the Business World? The Anthropology of Shopping 31

CHAPTER FIVE: What Challenges Do Immigrants in Canada Face? 69

CHAPTER SEVEN: Is Female Circumcision a Violation of Human Rights or a Cherished Cultural Tradition? 105

CHAPTER EIGHT: What Does it Mean to Grow Old? 123

CHAPTER TEN: Is the Practice of Purdah and Wearing the Hijab Oppressive to Women or an Expression of Their Identity? 155

CHAPTER ELEVEN: How Do Anthropologists View Same-Sex Marriages and Changing Family Structure? How Do We Define Marriage? 173

FAMILY AND KINSHIP

CHAPTER FIVE: What Challenges Do Immigrants in Canada Face? 69

CHAPTER EIGHT: What Does it Mean to Grow Old? 123

CHAPTER TEN: Is the Practice of Purdah and Wearing the Hijab Oppressive to Women or an Expression of Their Identity? 155

CHAPTER ELEVEN: How Do Anthropologists View Same-Sex Marriages and Changing Family Structure? How Do We Define Marriage? 173

CHAPTER TWELVE: Has the Medium of Television Changed Human Behaviour and World Views? 191

FEMINIST ANTHROPOLOGY

CHAPTER SIX: How Has the Push for the Perfect Body Impacted on the Self-Image, Health, and Comfort of Women? 91

CHAPTER SEVEN: Is Female Circumcision a Violation of Human Rights or a Cherished Cultural Tradition? 105

CHAPTER TEN: Is the Practice of Purdah and Wearing the Hijab Oppressive to Women or an Expression of Their Identity? 155

GENDER

CHAPTER ONE: What are the Challenges in Ethnographic Fieldwork? 3

CHAPTER THREE: Of What Use is Anthropology to the Business World? The Anthropology of Shopping 31

CHAPTER SIX: How Has the Push for the Perfect Body Impacted on the Self-Image, Health, and Comfort of Women? 91

CHAPTER TEN: Is the Practice of Purdah and Wearing the Hijab Oppressive to Women or an Expression of Their Identity? 155

CHAPTER ELEVEN: How Do Anthropologists View Same-Sex Marriages and Changing Family Structure? How Do We Define Marriage? 173

CHAPTER TWELVE: Has the Medium of Television Changed Human Behaviour and World Views? 191

GLOBALIZATION

CHAPTER FOUR: What are the Underlying Reasons Behind Ethnic Conflict, and the Consequences of these Conflicts? 47

CHAPTER FIVE: What Challenges Do Immigrants in Canada Face? 69

CHAPTER SIX: How Has the Push for the Perfect Body Impacted on the Self-Image, Health, and Comfort of Women? 91

CHAPTER SEVEN: Is Female Circumcision a Violation of Human Rights or a Cherished Cultural Tradition? 105

CHAPTER TWELVE: Has the Medium of Television Changed Human Behaviour and World Views? 191

LANGUAGE AND COMMUNICATION

CHAPTER ONE: What are the Challenges in Ethnographic Fieldwork? 3

CHAPTER TWO: What is Culture Shock and How Does it Affect People Living, Studying, and Working Abroad? 15

CHAPTER FIVE: What Challenges Do Immigrants in Canada Face? 69

PARTICIPANT OBSERVATION

CHAPTER ONE: What are the Challenges in Ethnographic Fieldwork?   3

CHAPTER THREE: Of What Use is Anthropology to the Business World? The Anthropology of Shopping   31

CHAPTER FIVE: What Challenges Do Immigrants in Canada Face?   69

CHAPTER SEVEN: Is Female Circumcision a Violation of Human Rights or a Cherished Cultural Tradition?   105

CHAPTER EIGHT: What Does it Mean to Grow Old?   123

PATRIARCHY

CHAPTER FIVE: What Challenges Do Immigrants in Canada Face?   69

CHAPTER SEVEN: Is Female Circumcision a Violation of Human Rights or a Cherished Cultural Tradition?   105

CHAPTER EIGHT: What Does it Mean to Grow Old?   123

CHAPTER NINE: What Impact Has Missionism Had on Indigenous Cultures?   143

CHAPTER TEN: Is the Practice of Purdah and Wearing the Hijab Oppressive to Women or an Expression of Their Identity?   155

POPULAR CULTURE

CHAPTER THREE: Of What Use is Anthropology to the Business World? The Anthropology of Shopping   31

CHAPTER SIX: How Has the Push for the Perfect Body Impacted on the Self-Image, Health, and Comfort of Women?   91

CHAPTER TWELVE: Has the Medium of Television Changed Human Behaviour and World Views?   191

SEXUALITY

CHAPTER SIX: How Has the Push for the Perfect Body Impacted on the Self-Image, Health, and Comfort of Women?   91

CHAPTER SEVEN: Is Female Circumcision a Violation of Human Rights or a Cherished Cultural Tradition?   105

CHAPTER TEN: Is the Practice of Purdah and Wearing the Hijab Oppressive to Women or an Expression of Their Identity?   155

CHAPTER ELEVEN: How Do Anthropologists View Same-Sex Marriages and
Changing Family Structure? How Do We Define Marriage? 173

STRATIFICATION

CHAPTER THREE: Of What Use is Anthropology to the Business World?
The Anthropology of Shopping 31

CHAPTER FOUR: What Are the Underlying Reasons Behind Ethnic
Conflict, and the Consequences of these Conflicts? 47

CHAPTER EIGHT: What Does it Mean to Grow Old? 123

CHAPTER TEN: Is the Practice of Purdah and Wearing the Hijab
Oppressive to Women or an Expression of Their Identity? 155

Author Profile

Shirley A. Fedorak has taught socio-cultural anthropology and archaeology at the University of Saskatchewan since 1991. In the 1990s she worked on several curriculum projects, including "People in Their World. A Study of First Nations Peoples on the Plains," sponsored by the Saskatoon Public School Board. She has also written and developed multimedia courses in anthropology and archaeology for the University of Saskatchewan Extension Division. Recently, she discovered the value of Web-based resources, and has designed her own Web page, entitled "Anthropology and You" (http://anthropology.dyndns.org/).

In addition to serving as lead author for the first and second Canadian editions of William A. Haviland's *Cultural Anthropology* (2002, 2005), Shirley Fedorak has co-authored a Canadian supplement for archaeology and biological anthropology courses, *Canadian Perspectives on Archaeology and Biological Anthropology* (2002), and the first Canadian edition of William A. Haviland's *Human Evolution and Prehistory* (2005). Her most recent publication is *Windows on the World: Case Studies in Anthropology* (2006).

She currently lives in Cairo, Egypt, where she is researching and writing two new books and immersing herself in Egyptian culture.

Shirley Fedorak considers socio-cultural anthropology to be one of the most valuable forms of education in today's rapidly changing world: "Of all the disciplines we teach at university, socio-cultural anthropology is the one where students actually learn about what it means to be citizens of the world."

Acknowledgements

Over the years when students approached me with a concern, or searched for the answers to troubling questions, it became increasingly apparent to me that anthropology is much more than an academic discipline. Therefore, I wish to extend my heartfelt thanks to my students, who have grappled with difficult questions and turned to anthropology for at least part of their answers. To the young people who shared their experiences with immigrating to Canada and China, or expressed their opinions regarding several topics in this book, I am very grateful for your assistance. I would like to extend a very special thank you to my research assistants, Fiona Robertson, Joshua Alm, and Alana Conway, for cheerfully marking countless assignments, and relentlessly searching for the right resources so that I could focus on writing.

I would like to thank Anne Brackenbury, Broadview Acquisitions Editor, for recognizing the value of this text. Her enthusiasm and willingness to let me find the direction this book would take are greatly appreciated, as is all the help Keely Winnitoy, Editorial Assistant, has provided. I also wish to thank developmental editor Laura Cardiff for all her hard work, and Elizabeth Phinney for her diligent copy editing of the text. I would like to extend my heartfelt appreciation to the reviewers of the first draft of *Anthropology Matters!* Their kind words of encouragement are much appreciated, and their many helpful suggestions greatly enhanced the quality of this book.

I would also like to thank William A. Haviland, a man I consider my mentor even though we have never personally met. His introductory anthropology texts provided me with valuable insights, and taught me what the world of anthropology could mean to me, my community, and the global community. As well, the research and fieldwork experiences of many dedicated anthropologists are featured in this book; their wisdom and insights have proven invaluable.

Some very special people have assisted me with this project. My son Kris and his partner, Rachel, helped me understand the social structure of modern China as they led me through that magnificent country. My son Cory, as always, kept the computer equipment running smoothly, and my daughter Lisa provided information and assistance with several of the chapters. I wish to thank my brother Herb and my sister Deb for providing photos for the chapter on the anthropology of shopping, and my friend Janna Cadieux for photographing her Barbie collection. Finally, I would like to thank my husband, Rob. Over the years he has played sounding board, editorial critic, bibliographer, librarian, subject specialist, instructional designer, and cheerleader with all of my writing projects.

To the Instructor

Many instructors now use anthropology courses to prepare students for their future roles in society, rather than only as an academic field of study. To that end, *Anthropology Matters!* will provide instructors and students with two avenues for discussing anthropology's relevance. First, the research methods, perspectives, and application of anthropology will be examined to determine how anthropologists acquire their knowledge. Second, some of the contemporary and often controversial issues that influence people's lives and the way they deal with the world around them will be explored using an anthropological perspective.

Pedagogical Value

This book is written primarily for first- or second-year students and is designed to supplement introductory anthropology textbooks. *Anthropology Matters!* is an attempt to make anthropology more accessible to its audience by linking concepts commonly discussed in anthropology classes to contemporary issues and practices:

- *participant observation and fieldwork challenges;*
- *enculturation and culture shock;*
- *applied economic anthropology and consumer habits;*
- *religion and ethnic conflict;*
- *ethnocentrism and immigration;*
- *cultural diffusion and body image;*
- *cultural relativism and female circumcision;*
- *cross-cultural comparison and aging;*
- *cultural imperialism and missionism;*
- *gender stratification and purdah;*
- *inequality and same-sex marriage; and,*
- *popular culture and the media.*

Anthropology Matters! will address these timely and socially relevant topics from a global perspective to generate class discussions about the relevance of anthropology in understanding our modern world.

Anthropology Matters! offers students the opportunity for cross-cultural comparative studies. For example, students will compare differing interpretations of human rights by examining the practice of purdah and female circumcision. They may investigate the underlying reasons for ethnic and religious intolerance and the ensuing conflicts in several regions of the world. Global variations in the ideal body image, media influence, attitudes about aging, the impact of missionism, and same-sex marriages also lend themselves to a comparative approach.

Anthropology does not exist in isolation. Anthropologists rely on the knowledge and expertise of scholars from many disciplines (e.g., history, religion, economics, sociology, psychology, medicine, gender studies, law and politics, and indigenous studies). This multidisciplinary approach allows students to gain a broader understanding of the questions posed in *Anthropology Matters!* On several occasions *Anthropology Matters!* presents the opinions and narrative of anthropologists native to the group being studied. Their perspective offers a higher level of credibility to anthropological work, providing an insider's view. For example, Sierra Leone anthropologist Fuambai Ahmadu was circumcised; thus she offers both an anthropological and participant's viewpoint on the practice. The insights of my students are also presented in this work. They are not trained anthropologists, nor do they have much experience "out in the real world," but what they do possess is a sense of clarity not yet clouded with confusing and conflicting theory. Their candour is often refreshing and eye-opening.

The selected topics in *Anthropology Matters!* complement the subjects covered in general anthropology textbooks. Instructors may assign readings from *Anthropology Matters!* that correspond to topics covered in class. Some of the topics were chosen because of their interest quotient for students: body image is a current issue of particular importance to young people, yet most of us do not recognize the political, cultural, and economic machinations at work in perceptions of an ideal body. Other topics were chosen because of their current social or political implications, such as the debate concerning same-sex marriage raging in many industrial nations. Some topics, such as aging, were chosen to encourage students to examine a subject seldom considered by young people.

Anthropology Matters! enables instructors to draw on a variety of instructional tools to expand their students' comprehension. The Questions for Consideration in each chapter are designed to encourage critical thinking and group discussions, and will challenge students to apply the knowledge they have gained to compare, analyze, and interpret the material. The questions may also guide students in identifying major themes and anthropological concepts found in each chapter. Many of the chapters include maps of the cultural groups studied, and where applicable, personal narratives from anthropologists or individuals within a cultural group are included. The References at the end of each chapter list various sources used in the research, including chosen ethnographies, and the Suggested Readings list offers students the opportunity to investigate the subject matter in greater detail. Bolded terms throughout the text highlight key anthropological concepts that are then defined in the comprehensive Glossary at the end of the book.

Organization of the Text

Anthropology Matters! is divided into two main sections: anthropological research, and contemporary issues viewed through an anthropological lens. Part One contains three methods chapters and Part Two contains nine issues chapters. The content and organization of most of these chapters is not standardized; those topics most relevant to the discussion are emphasized. However, a basic template is followed in most chapters, including a list of key terms, an introduction, an investigation of anthropology's connection to the issue, a discussion of the issue, and a conclusion.

Part One, "How Does Anthropology Work?" investigates the relevance of anthropology as a discipline—how anthropologists go about acquiring their understanding of human behaviour. We begin with a look at the challenges of anthropological fieldwork, followed by one of the common side effects of fieldwork (or living in a foreign environment)—culture shock. In the anthropology of shopping, students will encounter a case of applying anthropological principles and research methods in the business world. These three topics are designed to introduce students to the "doing" of anthropology, while also linking the world of anthropology to their everyday lives. Key concepts, such as participant observation, enculturation, culture shock, and applied anthropology are featured in this opening section of *Anthropology Matters!*

The research methods of anthropology, in particular participant observation, are examined in Chapter 1, "What are the Challenges in Ethnographic Fieldwork?" Here, the challenges faced by anthropologists when "in the field" are considered. This chapter provides students with a basic understanding of anthropological research methods and their efficacy, as well as problems associated with qualitative research.

We learn our culture from birth through the process of enculturation, which helps us to predict the behaviour of members of our culture. The difficulties that may arise when we are no longer able to predict the behaviour of others, or comprehend how we should behave in given circumstances can lead to culture shock. Chapter 2, "What is Culture Shock, and How Does it Affect People Living, Studying, and Working Abroad?" investigates the feelings of disorientation, confusion, and insecurity that may affect us (and this includes anthropologists) when we move into an unfamiliar cultural environment. Examining culture shock from an anthropological perspective will hopefully prepare students to meet people who are "different" than they are—who speak a different language, or who look, believe, and behave differently. The material on culture shock draws heavily on the insights of specialists in other fields, such as psychology, and provides several examples of anthropologists who have dealt with culture shock.

Anthropology is the study of humankind, yet until recently anthropologists have focused on exotic, small-scale cultures, and ignored their own and other industrial societies. In Chapter 3, "Of What Use is Anthropology to the Business World? The Anthropology of Shopping," we consider the relevance of anthropology in the world of business. Our case study features "anthropology in action" as applied anthropologists study marketing and consumer habits in North American shopping malls.

In Part Two, "Why Does Anthropology Matter?" socially relevant issues, such as immigration, are discussed from an anthropological perspective. This section challenges students to re-evaluate their media-shaped positions and helps diminish ill-conceived stereotypes. Several key concepts, including cultural relativism, ethnocentrism, cultural diffusion, gender, and cultural imperialism provide interrelated themes running through this section. The importance of cultural relativism, and the controversy associated with this fundamental principle of anthropology is examined throughout Part Two, as is the harm caused by ethnocentrism and cultural imperialism.

Ethnic and religious intolerance is rampant the world over. In Chapter 4, "What are the Underlying Reasons Behind Ethnic Conflict, and the Consequences of These Conflicts?" the economic, political, social, and religious reasons behind these conflicts are addressed. Ethnic conflict is not just a political issue; it creates human victims known as refugees. Their plight is examined from an anthropological perspective. This discussion will reinforce the fact that cultural institutions are integrated, and that anthropologists cannot understand such a complex issue in isolation from the other systems of culture.

Chapter 5, "What Challenges Do Immigrants in Canada Face?" investigates the experiences of immigrants moving to a new country, in this case, Canada. This discussion will emphasize the importance of cultural retention, and the harmful effects of ethnocentrism.

Chapter 6, "How Has the Push for the Perfect Body Impacted on the Self-Image, Health, and Comfort of Women?" provides an opportunity to investigate the diffusion of Western ideas, in this case, regarding the ideal body, to the rest of the world via the media, and the powerful influence media has on shaping our world view. The value of cross-cultural comparisons when studying issues such as body image is reinforced in this chapter.

Chapter 7, "Is Female Circumcision a Violation of Human Rights or a Cherished Cultural Tradition?" lends itself to a discussion of ethics in anthropology and the problems with maintaining a neutral, culturally relativistic stance while conducting research on contentious issues. In this chapter, the voices of the women who value this custom, as well as those who oppose it, will be heard. With such a sensitive topic, on which people have such strong feelings, acquiring the knowledge of anthropologists who have spent their careers studying female circumcision assists in developing a relativistic, inclusive perspective.

In Chapter 8, "What Does it Mean to Grow Old?" the discussion on the "culture of oldness" addresses the importance of using ethnographic fieldwork and participant observation to gain an in-depth and comparative understanding of the human condition. Students will learn that the way old age is viewed and the treatment of elderly people varies considerably from one cultural environment to another.

In Chapter 9, "What Impact Has Missionism Had on Indigenous Cultures?" the discussion provides an opportunity to discuss cultural and or religious imperialism and the impact of cultural change stemming from missionary actions.

Chapter 10, "Is the Practice of Purdah and Wearing the Hijab Oppressive to Women or an Expression of Their Identity?" offers a cross-cultural comparison of differing, and oftentimes contradictory, opinions on purdah and hijab. This chapter is designed to dispel some of the misconceptions that many people in the West hold about women and women's status in Muslim societies, yet also addresses the volatility of gender stratification and the very real possibility of gender oppression.

The discussion in Chapter 11, "How Do Anthropologists View Same-Sex Marriages and Changing Family Structure? How Do We Define Marriage?" lends itself to an examination of different types of marriage, including same-sex marriage, as the institution is viewed and defined cross-culturally. This discussion may help students make some sense of the debate over same-sex marriage raging in many Western countries today.

Chapter 12, "Has the Medium of Television Changed Human Behaviour and World Views?" discusses the impact of media (and technology) on cultural behaviour. In this chapter we briefly examine the power of popular culture, and take the opportunity to examine ourselves from the "outside in."

Obviously, the questions posed in *Anthropology Matters!* will not be answered in any definitive way, but they will be probed, analyzed, and critiqued to the point where readers will gain a broader, balanced, and comprehensive sense of the complexity of these issues. *Anthropology Matters!* was written for anyone interested in the anthropological study of humankind and the issues that have meaning for students and other readers. This is not a theoretical discourse; rather, much like the field of anthropology, *Anthropology Matters!* challenges readers to rise above their current level of understanding—to think outside and beyond the box.

Introduction

KEY TERMS: anthropology, applied anthropology, participant observation, holistic approach, cross-cultural comparison, culture, cultural relativism, human rights, ethnocentrism, cultural imperialism.

What good is anthropology, anyway? This is a question I have been asked on several occasions—the first time when I was an undergraduate student struggling to absorb the basic concepts of anthropology. The person asking had little experience with academia or the world outside her community, and I had even less experience with answering such a complex question. Later, as an instructor, I asked my students a similar question: "Of what relevance is anthropology—to you, to your community, and to the global community?" The answer to this question is the subject of *Anthropology Matters!* We will examine why anthropology matters and why anthropology is relevant in our everyday lives.

What Is Anthropology?

ANTHROPOLOGY is the study of humankind. Anthropologists seek to explain human behaviour, and understand the diverse ways people organize their lives. Although anthropologists have traditionally studied small-scale, non-Western cultures, today they are also interested in the lives and behaviour of people in modern, industrialized societies. This is why *Anthropology Matters!* examines contemporary issues, such as body image, same-sex marriage, immigration, and ethnic conflict.

Although anthropologists have gathered ethnographic information on many cultural groups, anthropology is far more than a receptacle for cultural knowledge. In the field of **APPLIED ANTHROPOLOGY**, the knowledge and methods of anthropologists are put to practical use to help solve or alleviate some of the societal problems humans face. Applied anthropology may invoke images of intrepid anthropologists bravely marching into a crisis situation and saving the day, yet more often the knowledge and insights that anthropologists possess regarding human culture are what is of value when considering the myriad problems and concerns of humankind. Anthropology is approached from an applied perspective in *Anthropology Matters!* although it is not the practice of anthropology, but the principles of anthropology and the way these principles can assist us in understanding people that is stressed.

The Relevance of Anthropology

Anthropology, like most other disciplines, is being increasingly challenged to justify its existence and its relevance in contemporary society. Anthropology can successfully meet these challenges. The underlying philosophies of anthropology, if applied to our everyday lives, can provide fascinating insights into human behaviour. By this I mean, if we look at the world in the same way as an anthropologist, and if we deal with the issues and concerns of the world around us from an anthropological perspective, we may be surprised at the value of this discipline. Beyond the academic, theoretical, ethnographic, and even the applied, anthropology speaks to the heart of humankind. Anthropology is relevant because anthropologists attempt to answer questions such as "Who are we?" and "Why do we behave in the way we do?" As Conrad Philip Kottak (1990: 17) so succinctly states, anthropologists have "a lot to tell the public."

Anthropology's role as an educator is equally important. Eminent anthropologist Franz Boas encouraged his colleagues to recognize the uniqueness and validity of every cultural group. This is a laudable sentiment, one that anthropologists attempt to pass on to the general public. By increasing cultural awareness and appreciation of cultural diversity, anthropology teaches us to recognize that regardless of "difference" we all share the same basic humanity. *Anthropology Matters!* repeatedly emphasizes this stance by promoting the value of other world views and other ways of living.

Contemporary students live in a world mired in conflict and inequalities. Through the media they are exposed to human problems and contentious issues at home and abroad that cause them great concern, and they know that in the very near future they will have to step into that world and make some sense of it. *Anthropology Matters!* addresses contemporary issues and global concerns, such as immigration and inequalities based on gender, sexuality, religion, and ethnicity, and exposes the false notions of gender, racial, or cultural superiority. Topics of special interest to students, such as the influence of mass media, and dealing with culture shock when living and travelling in foreign environments, are also discussed.

Methods of Anthropology

Attempting to quantify human behaviour and reduce this behaviour to a set of statistics is difficult and often proves meaningless. Anthropologists more often rely on qualitative research—interviewing, observing, and participating in the daily lives and activities of the people they are studying. This is known as **PARTICIPANT OBSERVATION**. The value of participant observation cannot be overstated. Living in close proximity to the study group, learning their language, and participating in their lives enables anthropologists to develop a much deeper understanding of the range of human behaviour. The adage "See me as I do, not as I say" is remarkably accurate when studying human behaviour. Whether as anthropologists or the general public, trying to understand other people through listening, observing, and even participating goes a long way toward dispelling some of the stereotypes and intolerance we hold for other ways of living. *Anthropology Matters!* relies on the information anthropologists have gathered during their field research using participant observation.

Participant observation has also become an integral research method in other fields that study human behaviour. Educators, sociologists, and human geographers, to name only a few, now spend more time in the setting they are studying, rather than relying only on surveys and questionnaires that at best provide superficial information. For example, educational psychology students work in clinics to gain first-hand experience counselling students who are dealing with death or divorce in the family. Economists now regularly employ ethnographic research methods in the market and design industry. In my own research on the relevance of archaeology in education, I spent 18 months working as part of a curriculum development team, and later as an observer and participant in the pilot project to introduce archaeology into elementary social studies classes. This form of research gave me an in-depth understanding of archaeology's place in an educational setting that I could not have achieved without participant observation. As the relevance of anthropological research methods becomes better known, likely many more research projects in diverse fields of human study will adopt some form of participant observation.

Anthropologists face many ethical dilemmas in their practice. For example, how involved should they become in the community they are studying, and should they interject with suggestions for the "betterment" of the community? At what point does advice become interference? In the following chapters you will encounter many examples of this challenge, for example, the ancient practice of purdah, which elicits strong and often negative reactions from people outside the cultures that follow this custom. The ethical questions that anthropologists face are significant because they also reflect the struggles that occur between different cultural groups in our increasingly pluralistic societies.

Approaches in Anthropology

Anthropologists approach their research from three interrelated perspectives: holism, cross-cultural comparison, and cultural relativism. Each culture is composed of integrated cultural systems (e.g., economic, social, political, and religious) that interact and influence the others; thus, if one system of culture is interfered with or destroyed, such as religious beliefs and practices through missionism, then the other systems of that culture will also be affected. This means anthropologists must consider the influence of these systems on each other. For example, acceptable marriage practices in a cultural group will likely be influenced or even controlled by religious beliefs; if the religious beliefs change, then likely so will the marriage customs. In light of this reality, anthropologists take a **HOLISTIC APPROACH**—examining the culture as a whole, rather than as discrete parts.

Many of the issues discussed in *Anthropology Matters!* use ethnographic information from a **CROSS-CULTURAL COMPARISON**. This means a custom or practice common to humans, for example, exchange, is compared from one culture to another, although we should never think of comparison as a means of determining the superiority of one custom over another. Rather, anthropologists gather significant data to make generalizations about human behaviour. As an example, cross-cultural comparison of growing old has shown that aging is viewed in diverse ways among cultural groups, yet there also appears to be a shared sentiment among elderly people the world over that they need to feel useful and part of their community.

Anthropology has always been "global" in that the groups studied have come from all over the world. Today, however, anthropologists themselves originate in many regions of the world, and provide diverse voices and interpretations of culture. The quest to understand other people is a paramount goal of any anthropologist; thus, this pluralistic perspective adds a new dimension to the cross-cultural study of humankind.

The third approach in anthropology, cultural relativism, is an approach so fundamental to anthropology and so contentious because of conflicting ideas and human rights issues, that it will be discussed in some detail in the following section.

Key Concepts and Issues in Anthropology

In *Anthropology Matters!* we will be examining several contemporary issues from an anthropological perspective. This requires an under-standing of key concepts in anthropology that will be addressed in the discussions, including the concepts of culture, cultural relativism, human rights, ethnocentrism, cultural imperialism, and genocide.

CULTURE may be defined as "the shared ideals, values, and beliefs that people use to interpret, experience, and generate behaviour" (Haviland et al. 2005), or in other words, "the whole way of life." All cultural groups determine the most effective way of making a living given their environmental circumstances. Culture includes social organization that facilitates the formation of conjugal (marital) bonds, family units, and kinship networks. Cultural groups express their religious beliefs through ritual traditions and practices, develop systems for maintaining social order within and between societies, and communicate symbolically through dress and decoration, art, music, and language.

Anthropologists attempt to understand other cultures through their practices, ethics and values, and their world view—what Overing (1985) calls their moral universe. In other words, they are trying to understand a cultural group based on how the people understand themselves and the world around them. This approach, known as CULTURAL RELATIVISM, acknowledges that the way "others" see the world is as valid as the way we see the world. Thus, anthropologists do not set out to disprove anyone's beliefs, customs, or traditions, although they certainly form their own opinions. Rather, their goal is to understand the reasons behind these practices within the context of that culture. Not to belabour the point, but to do anything else would make anthropology irrelevant.

Cultural relativism is a fundamental principle in anthropology that has helped shape the discipline. However, this principle is not with-out controversy, especially when it concerns customs that threaten the well-being of individuals. Nor has a consensus ever been reached as to what cultural relativism truly means. Simply put, cultural relativism is the belief that all cultures are equally valid in their own right. This suggests, for some, that the beliefs and traditions of cultural groups must be accepted, regardless of whether they fit into everyone's idea of acceptable behaviour. For others, the issue of human rights and equality supersedes cultural traditions: If a practice has the potential to harm, either physically or emotionally, a member of that culture, then it should be stopped, regardless of its cultural value or lengthy history.

HUMAN RIGHTS is a difficult concept to clearly define—it is vague, contradictory, and often misused. On its most basic level, human rights refers to "reasonable demands for personal security and basic well-being" (Messer 1993: 222). Depending on the agency, human rights may also include political and civil rights, socio-economic and cultural rights, development rights, and indigenous rights. However, what is or is not considered a human right differs from one nation to another. For example, is the requirement for women to follow purdah and wear the hijab a form of oppression or an expression of collective human rights? Is the practice of placing elderly North Americans in seniors' residences a form of elder abuse or a protection of their human right to safety and dignity? Why is male circumcision considered acceptable by Westerners while female circumcision is labelled a violation of human rights? The role of anthropologists in these debates is to serve as a conduit for voices from the culture that would otherwise go unheard, and if appropriate, anthropologists may also express their own positions on the issues. Although at times extremely difficult, anthropologists, and indeed all reflective people, must attempt to strike a balance between cultural relativism and human rights.

The concept of cultural relativism elicits fear in some people, including some anthropologists, because it calls into question, and even rejects their own sense of, what is right and wrong. Much of this fear can be traced to a misunderstanding of the basic tenets of cultural relativism. It is not that all ideas are true, but rather that all ideas deserve consideration. Cultural relativism is not about "anything goes," it is about *respect*—respect for other ways of living, believing, and practising, and respect for the rights of all cultural groups to self-determination.

Cultural relativism serves to counter **ETHNOCENTRISM**, the belief that one's own culture and way of life is superior to all others—an attitude all too prevalent in the West. If we fail to recognize that there are other world views, and other ways of living, then there is a very real danger of **CULTURAL IMPERIALISM** taking over. This is particularly evident in the West, where our economic, political, and military power has been used to "blackmail" other nations into adopting Western values, beliefs, and customs, and giving up their traditional way of life.

Critics often focus on extreme behaviours of the past to point out the weaknesses in cultural relativism. Hitler's extermination of Jews during World War II is often cited as an example of cultural relativism taken too far. What they mean is, for too long, the West stood by and "allowed" Hitler to kill Jews, rather than interfere and take a stand against it. However, extermination of a group of people is *not* a cultural tradition; it is a crime against humanity, as are all acts of genocide—and the West's failure to act in time is an example of apathy, not relativism. Thus, in any discussion of the merits or limitations of cultural relativism, the difference between a cultural tradition and deviant or criminal behaviour must be considered.

Anthropologists also recognize that as outsiders, we may never fully understand another culture and its practices, nor can anthropologists remain completely objective or value-free given the "cultural baggage" and social identities that we all possess. It is extremely difficult to reach the level of impartiality expected of anthropologists. This will become apparent as we examine complex issues such as female circumcision. Indeed, as Ginsburg (1991: 17) suggests, the practice of female circumcision presents one of the "strongest challenges to anthropology's central tenet of cultural relativism."

As should be evident, we will be discussing some rather contentious and complex issues in *Anthropology Matters!* It is not the goal of this text to solve these issues, but to investigate them from an anthropological perspective. Thus, throughout *Anthropology Matters!* we will consider the question "What good is anthropology, anyway?"

References

GINSBURG, F. (1991). What do women want? Feminist anthropology confronts clitoridectomy. *Medical Anthropology Quarterly*, 5(1), 17–19.

HAVILAND, W.A., FEDORAK, S., CRAWFORD, G., & LEE, R.B. (2005). *Cultural anthropology* (2nd Cdn. ed.). Toronto: Thomson Nelson Learning.

KOTTAK, C.P. (1990). *Prime time society: An anthropological analysis of television and culture.* Belmost, CA: Wadsworth Publishing Company.

MESSER, E. (1993). Anthropology and human rights. *Annual Review of Anthropology, 22*, 221–249.

OVERING, J. (Ed.). (1985). *Reason and morality.* New York: Tavistock Publications.

PART ONE

How Does Anthropology Work?

Anthropology has an exotic reputation—those unfamiliar with the discipline still carry images of intrepid, bespectacled scientists trekking through the dense forest in search of a "lost" tribe, then single-mindedly studying them to gain some insight into "primitive" man. Sound familiar? I have, on numerous occasions, encountered people who carry such misconceptions about anthropologists—or that we study dinosaurs. Although it may be true that early anthropologists focused on exotic cultures hidden away in distant lands, today anthropologists are interested in all things human, including those things modern—they may study the reciprocity system of men on skid row (Hauch 1992); shopping habits in large suburban malls (Underhill 1999); the AIDS epidemic in contemporary Africa (Lee 2005), mock wedding traditions on the Canadian prairies (Taft 2005), social control at Disneyland (Shearing & Stenning 1987), or behaviour in a hospital setting (Murphy 1987). All of these topics and many more are of interest to anthropologists as they endeavour to comprehend and explain the human condition.

In this first section of *Anthropology Matters!* the way in which anthropologists approach their research in the field, the challenges they face living among strangers in a strange land, and a particularly apt example of anthropological research methods applied to a business project are presented. In Chapter 1, "What are the Challenges in Ethnographic Fieldwork?" we will examine the nature of anthropological research. Since fieldwork is often viewed as a rite of passage that turns a student of anthropology into a bona fide anthropologist, this chapter emphasizes, through examples and narrative, the goals, methods, and trials of "doing fieldwork."

Although Chapter 1 introduces students to some of the challenges and issues that anthropologists face in the field, Chapter 2, "What is Culture Shock and How Does it Affect People Living, Studying, and Working Abroad?" presents a more detailed look at culture shock, a very real concern for anthropologists in the field. This chapter is designed to familiarize students, who often travel, work, or study abroad, to the condition of culture shock, which will undoubtedly afflict them at least for a short time. Several anthropologists share their experiences with culture shock and the way they have dealt with the condition. The featured narrative in this chapter is from a young man who has lived in China for the last two years, and still suffers occasional bouts of culture shock.

Finally, as emphasized in the introduction to *Anthropology Matters!*, anthropology is not just an academic endeavour. Anthropologists also put their research methods and skills to practical use, as is the case with Paco Underhill's study of the synthesis of consumer habits and shopping malls in Chapter 3, "Of What Use is Anthropology to the Business World? The Anthropology of Shopping." Readers may find the many considerations that go into planning a shopping mall interesting, as well as Underhill's astute dissemination of the habits we as consumers unconsciously share.

Part One, then, demonstrates how anthropology works, and also sets the stage for Part Two, which examines several contemporary issues on which anthropologists, through their ethnographic research, have developed unique perspectives.

References

HAUCH, C. (1992). Reciprocity on skid row. In J. Chodkiewicz (Ed.), *Peoples of the past and present. Readings in anthropology* (pp. 295–302). Toronto: Harcourt Brace.

LEE, R.B. (2005). Original Study. Health and disease in one culture: The Ju/'hoansi. In W.A. Haviland, S. Fedorak, G. Crawford, & R.B. Lee, *Cultural anthropology* (2nd Cdn. Ed., pp. 434–436). Toronto: Thomson Nelson Learning.

MURPHY, R.F. (1987). *The body silent*. New York: Henry Holt Co.

SHEARING, C.D., & STENNING, P.C. (1987). Say "Cheese!" The Disney order that is not so Mickey Mouse. In C.D. Shearing & P.C. Stenning (Eds.), *Private policing* (pp. 317–323). Newbury Park: Sage Publications, Inc.

TAFT, M. (2005). Original Study. The mock wedding folk drama in the prairie provinces. In W.A. Haviland, S. Fedorak, G. Crawford, & R.B. Lee, *Cultural anthropology* (2nd Cdn.. ed., pp. 296–400). Toronto: Thomson Nelson Learning.

UNDERHILL, P. (1999). *Why we buy: The science of shopping*. New York: Simon & Schuster.

CHAPTER ONE

What are the Challenges in Ethnographic Fieldwork?

Introduction

Fieldwork is a humbling experience. This statement, admitted by so many anthropologists, holds true today as much as it did 50 years ago. Anthropologists are seldom fully prepared for what they encounter in the field, and the onslaught of new sights, sounds, and smells can be overwhelming. Despite the romantic images some people have of fieldwork, the work is tedious and fraught with frustrations, culture shock, and loneliness.

    Fieldwork is often called a **RITE OF PASSAGE**—the time when an anthropologist learns to survive in a foreign environment, and in the process learns to face the personal and moral challenges of fieldwork. In this chapter we will address some of these challenges using anecdotal accounts from "seasoned" anthropologists who have spent considerable time in the field. As anthropologists struggle to understand the many nuances and meanings attached to the daily lives of their study group, they are also learning a great deal about their own ideals and cultural upbringing. This learning process will also be considered.

KEY TERMS: rite of passage, ethnographer, fieldwork, socio-cultural anthropology, qualitative research, quantitative research, key informants, gender, ethics, ethnography

Anthropologists and Fieldwork

Anthropologists and fieldwork go hand in hand. The field anthropologist, also known as an **ETHNOGRAPHER,** is a stranger in a strange place. Unaware of the local customs and expected behaviour, an ethnographer lives in constant fear of behaving inappropriately, and embarrassing him or herself and others, despite the best of intentions. This is what Annette Weiner encountered early in her fieldwork with the Kiriwini culture of the Trobrianders of New Guinea. While learning the values and norms of the Kiriwina, she also had to let go of her cultural assumptions about work, power, death, family, and friends. According to Weiner (1987: 1), "Walking into a village at the beginning of fieldwork is entering a world without cultural guideposts." Anthropologists must learn to be flexible, adaptable, and creative. In other words, anthropologists must learn "to go with the flow."

Fieldwork is a journey of discovery for the anthropologist, not only about the cultural group in question, but personally. According to James Clifford (1997) "sojourning somewhere else, learning a language, putting oneself in odd situations and trying to figure them out can be a good way to learn something new, simultaneously about oneself and about the places one visits" (White & Tengan 2001: 381). To that end, ethnographers are strongly influenced by practical, personal, and participatory experiences they have in the field. The role of an ethnographer is to learn and understand as best he or she can the symbols and concepts that have meaning to members of a culture, and then convey this understanding to others. Alice Reich considers the people anthropologists study as the real teachers (Kutsche 1998). Indeed, most anthropologists return from the field with a new sense of self, a new-found confidence in their abilities, and an expanded worldview. Knauft (2005: 37) sums up his fieldwork experience in Papua New Guinea: "We came to see cultural anthropology as a kind of dialogue—a conversation between Gebusi meanings and our own understandings."

> Fieldwork is best described as the ultimate learning experience, as you begin like a child and gradually absorb knowledge—and wisdom and insight if all goes well—which matures you in the eyes of your teachers and, ideally, wins you their approval ... the good things have heavily outweighed the bad.
>
> Anthropologist
> Robert Tonkinson (1991: 18)

A Discussion of Fieldwork

In anthropology, **FIELDWORK** is the process of collecting descriptive data on a specific culture through extended periods of living with members of the culture. Fieldwork is essential to anthropology; indeed, Whitehead and Conaway (1986) suggest that anthropology is shaped by fieldwork, and that anthropologists are shaped by field experiences. This shaping lends itself to more personal and first-hand accounts about the study group—a hallmark of **SOCIO-CULTURAL ANTHROPOLOGY.** As such, fieldwork defines anthropology and gives it a distinctive identity.

The most common and useful form of fieldwork is participant observation, which involves living with a cultural group for an extended period of time, and interacting with the people on a daily basis. This is where the humbling experience begins. Indeed, Alice Reich calls participant observation "a time honoured tradition of making a fool of oneself for a point" (Kutsche 1998: 5).

Although anthropological fieldwork is inherently **QUALITATIVE**, in some cases **QUANTITATIVE** research is also necessary. When Jon D. Holtzman (2000: 11) studied Nuer immigrants in Minnesota, he administered quantitative surveys to compile a community profile that included demographics, such as "age, gender, tribal and clan affiliation, education and work experiences, and basic outlines of the Nuer refugee experience." Despite structured research methods such as those discussed above, true ethnographic fieldwork relies primarily on personal conversations and interviews, as well as on interacting and participating in the daily lives of the study group (participant observation). Holtzman did not rely solely on his quantitative data, he also conducted life history research, in-depth structured interviews, and created detailed case studies.

KEY INFORMANTS, who are experts in the social complexities of their culture, provide the basis for understanding the culture's experience and meaning. When Robert Anderson (2005: 3) studied the ghosts of Iceland, he joined seance groups to observe and record conversations between the living and dead, and he regularly attended lectures at spiritist schools and spirit society coffee klatches. These informal participatory activities enabled him to better grasp their day-to-day beliefs.

Fieldwork, and in particular participant observation, is a unique method for learning about people and their behaviour. As mentioned in the introduction to the text, the efficacy of this research method has not gone unnoticed in other disciplines, such as psychology, geography, and education. These disciplines and others have "borrowed" participant observation and incorporated this research method into their studies.

> "I continue to believe that anthropology is the quintessential liberal arts discipline because it is about meaningful human life, not as a set of answers, but as a series of engaged conversations."
>
> ANTHROPOLOGIST ALICE REICH QUOTED IN KUTSCHE (1998: 4)

CHALLENGES OF FIELDWORK

Anthropologists face many challenges when first entering the field, beginning with the viability of their research proposal and a review by an ethics board, learning the language, dealing with personal and professional uncertainty, developing a rapport with community members, gender issues, and coping with health and safety issues and personal discomforts.

More than one anthropologist has been forced to scrap their original research project when they arrived in the community. Jean L. Briggs was placed in the unenviable position of seeing her research project fall apart when she arrived at Chantrey Inlet in the Arctic in 1963 (Briggs 1970). Planning to study the traditional shamanistic practices of the Utku Inuit, Briggs discovered that missionaries had converted the Utku to Christianity three decades earlier. Briggs' ability to adapt saved her

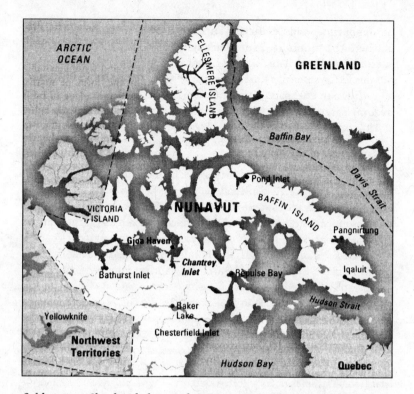

Utku Inuit Territory

field season. She decided to study Inuit emotional expression and their incredible emotional restraint. The Utku ability to express their hostile feelings in non-hostile ways, such as joking, fascinated Briggs, partly because she never quite mastered the art.

Annette Weiner (1987) did not plan to focus her research on the Trobriander women of New Guinea, but on her first day she happened upon women distributing bundles of dried banana leaves to other women as a way of commemorating the death of a villager. This chance encounter piqued Weiner's interest in women's economic roles, and her research has added considerably to our knowledge of women's wealth and their role in the economic, social, and political systems of the Trobrianders.

The most difficult challenge for the field ethnographer is learning the language—and not just the vocabulary and grammar, but the nuances and perhaps some colloquialisms. Most important of all, ethnographers must learn the non-verbal communication—body language, tone, use of space, and extraneous vocalizations that convey important messages and cues. The Knaufts spent the first six months of their fieldwork learning the Gebusi language by listening closely and trying to distinguish sounds, making endless lists of Gebusi words and phrases, and learning the tense and grammar (Knauft 2005: 36).

Ethnographers must deal with constant uncertainty, both personal and professional. When Robert Tonkinson (1991) arrived in the Gibson Desert in Western Australia to study the Mardu Aborigines, he was plagued with self-doubt and constantly second-guessed his behaviour. When offered some chewing tobacco, Tonkinson worried, "Will refusal offend? Is this what our teachers meant when they said rapport must be established at all costs?" (Tonkinson 1991: 16). This is an example of the insecurity that comes from not understanding the behaviour patterns of a group of people.

In a situation that may seem humorous now, Bruce Knauft (2005) found himself in a difficult and unusual quandary. The issue of human sexuality is always a delicate subject; indeed, anthropologists have been negligent in elaborating on the sexual practices in various cultures, partly because it is such a sensitive subject. Knauft hoped to rectify this weakness in his research with the Gebusi of Papua New Guinea. He knew that Gebusi men took part in homosexual acts during spirit seances and other festivities, but did not know the extent of the practice. One night at a spirit seance, when Bruce Knauft's wife Eileen was away from the village, a Gebusi man propositioned him. Knauft was caught off guard: If he refused, would he lose the trust of the Gebusi men and their willingness to include him in male activities? Would they be angry and insulted? Yet, participant observation only goes so far. Knauft handled the situation remarkably well, telling the man that although some men in his culture did have sex with other men, this was not his custom. Fortunately, the Gebusi man understood, since the same held true for his culture—some did, some did not.

Overcoming culture shock[1] is a long process filled with setbacks, but if the anthropologist is fortunate enough to develop friendships with some members of the community, the sense of isolation and disorientation may ease more quickly. Although ethnographers do not go into the field expecting to be welcomed with open arms, sometimes very special relationships do develop. When Richard B. Lee was adopted by a Ju/'hoan family, his relationship and position among the Ju/'hoansi

"I wanted to know what had gone wrong in my relationships with my Inuit family, so that I could restore those relationships.... Then, trying to explain why my improper expressive behavior was so extremely upsetting to Inuit, I began to notice the social meanings and values they placed on emotions like happiness and anger—meanings and values that were different from mine. For them a happy person was a good person, a safe person; anger was mindless, childish, also dangerous; an angry person might kill. For Inuit, social order did not derive merely from following rules of expression, it depended on feeling the culturally appropriate emotions. As they saw it, emotions motivated behavior."

ANTHROPOLOGIST JEAN L. BRIGGS AS QUOTED IN IVAN MUZYCHKA (N.D.)

Location of Gebusi in Papau New Guinea

Ethnographer Bruce Knauft participates in a Gebusi ritual.

changed from that of an outsider looking in, to a full member of the Dobe Ju/'hoansi community (Lee 2003). His responsibilities also changed as he was now expected to fulfill the roles of a Ju/'hoan son.

Holtzman (2000) slowly developed a rapport with the Nuer immigrants in Minnesota, USA, as he became involved in their lives and helped them settle in their new homes. He gradually became friends with some of the Nuer. These friendships can last a lifetime and, while in the field, offer a support network that can mean the difference between success and failure.

Moving into a strange environment requires courage and determination, and a certain amount of optimism. This was true of anthropologist Jean L. Briggs when she conducted fieldwork in the Arctic (Briggs 1970). For Briggs, a major challenge was bringing her temperament into line with the Utku Inuit outlook on appropriate behaviour. To the Inuit, showing open hostility is taboo. Briggs' difficulty with quelling her natural temperament led to countless incidents and frustrating confrontations with the Utku, and eventually her ostracization from the Utku Inuit and her adoptive family.

GENDER is one of the determining factors in field experiences. Hazel Weidman (1970) found her field experience difficult because she was a single woman, and single women did not live alone in Burma, especially given the high crime rate. As a consequence, she had difficulty finding a village willing to take responsibility for her. Indeed, she found her fieldwork experience to be a "struggle from beginning to end" (Whitehead & Conaway 1986 from Weidman 1970: 242).

Many ethnographers have come from societies where gender equality is at least a strived-for goal. This may not be the case when they are out in the field, and when confronted with situations where gender inequality is obvious, ethnographers are placed in a moral quandary. Bruce Knauft (2005) found himself unsure of how to deal with his own sense of morality, ethics, gender, and justice in the face of Gebusi patriarchy. The women of Gebusi society endured a great deal of gender inequality and male domination according to Knauft. They were excluded from spirit seances and other festive activities, their productive work (e.g., gardening, cooking) was not openly appreciated, and wife beating was fairly common. Knauft had to reconcile his sense of gender rights and roles with those of the community he was living in—an example of cultural relativism at work. If he had tried to interfere, his fieldwork would likely have ended right there. Yet, as discussed in the introduction to the text, the desire to step in and help is almost overwhelming.

Ethnographers also have to deal with research limitations due to gender. Male anthropologists have difficulty crossing gender barriers and discussing "women's issues" with the women, either because the women are unwilling or the men will not allow it. So, too, female ethnographers are often relegated to the women's side of society, and refused entry into the man's world. Knauft's wife, Eileen, found herself barred from male activities in the village even though she was an outsider—her gender, not her nationality, established her rights or lack thereof (Knauft 2005). Yet, there is a suggestion that older, single women may in fact have an easier time gaining access to field sites to study both male and female activities than others, mainly because of their age and academic status.

Nuisance problems also have a way of impacting the field research experience. Tonkinson (1991) had to deal with wild dingo dogs stealing whatever they could and, most annoying of all, millions of flies that got into everything, including his mouth, nose, and ears. Knauft (2005: 33) and his wife Eileen suffered malaria, digestive disorders, intestinal worms, skin lesions, boils, rashes, and jungle rot in all the wrong places. Heat and humidity, and swarms of insects were the most annoying daily problem. These little problems and chronic discomforts can become a "big deal" over the course of an extended field season.

Anthropologists have learned the hard way that taking the advice of the locals is usually wise. When Richard B. Lee was first setting up his camp near the Dobe Ju/'hoansi of the Kalahari Desert in Africa, he ignored the advice of the Ju/'hoan men and pitched his tent under a grove of trees on the edge of a rocky area. His choice was fine during the dry season, but once the rains started, Lee awoke in ankle-deep water to the sounds of the Ju/'hoan men laughing (Lee 2003).

Although it may seem a trivial point, food is an important issue in fieldwork. Refusing to eat the same food as other members of the community could be construed as an insult. Thus, anthropologists must make every effort to eat the traditional foods. The ensuing intestinal discomforts are part of the fieldwork experience. Food can also be perceived as a symbolic gift that establishes future relations, and food sharing establishes a support network that the anthropologist may dearly need.

A second seemingly trivial problem is toilet facilities and personal hygiene. Many an anthropologist has had to make do with non-existent toilet facilities, and the opportunity to bathe, except in a nearby stream, may be remote. Lack of cleanliness undoubtedly leads to various medical problems, such as skin lesions and infections.

The challenge of living and working with the Gebusi turned our own lives into something of an extreme sport. But in the crucible of personal experience, the Gebusi became not only human to us but also, despite their tragic violence, wonderful people. With wit and passion, they lived rich and festive lives. Vibrant and friendly, they turned life's cruellest ironies into their best jokes, and its biggest tensions into their most elaborate fantasies. Their humor, spirituality, deep togetherness, and raw pragmatism made them, for the most part, great fun to be with. I have never felt more included in a social world. And what personalities! To lump them together as simply "Gebusi" is as bland as it would be to describe David Letterman, Michael Jordan, Arnold Schwarzenegger, and Hilary Rodman Clinton as simply "American." The Gebusi were not simply "a society" or "a culture;" they were an incredible group of individuals.

Anthropologist
Bruce Knauft (2005: 3–4)

The climate may also be a source of extreme discomfort. Ethnographers often find themselves living in environments with scorching heat and intense humidity, or freezing cold. A tropical rainforest is considerably different from a North American metropolis, just as an Arctic environment is very different from both of these. Jean L. Briggs (1970) quickly realized she could not survive on her own; rather she had to rely on the benevolence of her Utku family. Tonkinson (1991) had to endure the harsh Australian desert weather, ranging from blistering heat in the summer to freezing cold in the winter.

Oftentimes, ethnographers are called upon to perform other duties while conducting their research; some have become teachers, others offer medical services. In Tonkinson's (1991) case, he was able to serve as an interpreter for the government welfare patrols that visited Mardu camps. When Jon D. Holtzman (2000) began his research into Nuer immigrants in Minnesota, he set out to ease their adjustment to American life. He helped organize a household-goods drive through a local church, drove Nuer men to job interviews, and developed a mentorship/friendship program between Nuer and American youths.

Anthropologists struggle with the need to find a balance in their fieldwork. They must remain neutral and objective, report what they learn, and maintain a culturally relativistic perspective by not passing judgment or interfering in the lives of the study group. Yet, Knauft (2005) wonders, at what point do we draw a line between appreciation of cultural diversity and critiquing some of the cultural practices and beliefs that are obviously harmful to at least some members of the community? In the case of the Gebusi, although Knauft saw the richness and vibrancy of their culture, he also saw the underside—the male dominance and subjugation of women, and the sorcerer accusations that often ended in the murder of an innocent person.

One of the valuable lessons of fieldwork is experiencing, even for a short time, what it feels like to be a minority person. Most ethnographers have come from Western societies where people of European descent are the "mainstream" and enjoy the highest position in society. To become the object of curiosity, the "odd" one, is an eye-opening experience that can fundamentally change the way we view ourselves and others, and should increase our cultural sensitivity.

FIELDWORK AND ETHICS

Ethical guidelines are an important part of ethnographic research. Anthropologists owe their allegiance first and foremost to the people they are studying—without their trust, an anthropologist's work becomes difficult if not impossible. Anthropologists endeavour to take every possible measure to protect the privacy and dignity of their study group (Fedorak 2006).

Regarding **ETHICS**, several areas deserve some further consideration. First, confidentiality is a concern. Some of the information anthropologists gather may be sensitive or even present some danger for the key informants. For example, will governments use information on a minority group to suppress their activism? Second, who is this research benefiting? The old joke "The anthropologists are coming! The anthropologists are coming!" is not so funny. Ethnographers have studied virtually every cultural group in existence and certainly the knowledge they have gained is academically valuable, but is that enough? This is where applied anthropology comes into play. As discussed in the introduction, applied anthropology makes anthropology relevant in the real world. It is putting to practical use the knowledge hiding in ethnographies. Anthropologists such as Harvey Feit, who, after completing his PhD research, worked with the James Bay Cree in their struggle to stop construction of a hydroelectric dam on their traditional hunting grounds was giving something back to the community (Feit 1995), as was Victoria J. Baker, who served as the schoolteacher in a Sinhalese village she was studying in Sri Lanka (Baker 1998).

Anthropologists are not always studying exotic cultures in far, distant places; sometimes the research is in their own backyard. American anthropologist William R. Ury studied conflict resolution at a Kentucky coal mine for his PhD. Since then he has helped resolve conflict in several high-profile cases, including the ongoing mediation of peace between the Russians and Chechens (Integral Naked 2004). Employing an anthropological perspective learned through years of experience with first-hand fieldwork (participant observation), Ury's work is becoming increasingly relevant in a world mired in conflict.

It is not the mandate of anthropologists to change a community, yet many anthropologists have found it exceedingly difficult to turn away when there is an obvious need. However, by whose definition is there a need? Gender inequalities and protection of children present a particularly difficult dilemma.[2] Another challenge, though not often mentioned, is the difficulty of navigating ethics review boards at universities, which at the very least may have a tremendous impact on what the anthropologist is allowed to study.

The culmination of months, even years, in the field is the **ETHNOGRAPHY**—a detailed descriptive account of the daily lives of a cultural group. The ethnography is written when the anthropologist returns home, compiled from copious field notes written in leather-bound crumpled journals, or more likely today, saved to a compact disk. Here, issues of voice, objectivity, and the validity of the information concern the anthropologist the most. As study groups have increasingly demanded their voices be heard, anthropologists have become recorders as well as interpreters of cultural data. Narratives from the people themselves may offer another level of information, but at all times, anthropologists must struggle to ensure the validity and objectivity

"Those encounters with my grandfather totally and fundamentally changed my understanding. They made me realize that I should live my life knowing that I will live on in an afterlife. Knowing that life goes on after death is a reality with enormous implications for how one should live this life in an earthly body."

PERSONAL NARRATIVE OF MAGNUS SKARPHEDINS-SON (ANDERSON 2005: 11)

of not only their interpretations but also their informants. Anderson (2005) gave voice to his key informants, who, through their personal narratives, spoke for themselves.

Interestingly, some anthropologists have turned the rigours of their fieldwork into literature as well.[3] These accounts provide a window into the experiences of the ethnographer. Diamond Jenness (1959), one of the most prestigious Canadian anthropologists, wrote *People of the Twilight*, which contains many personal accounts of his fieldwork experiences.

Conclusion

As we have seen, ethnographic fieldwork is a complex endeavour, fraught with pitfalls and challenges. Yet, as anthropologists such as Bruce Knauft readily point out, this struggle is not without its rewards. The relevance of ethnographic fieldwork becomes particularly evident when ethnographers become involved in the community they are studying, whether this is by providing interpreter or education services, or serving as advocates for the needs of "their" culture.

Most anthropologists see their fieldwork, at least in hindsight, as a rite of passage, a time when they became real anthropologists. Fieldwork is the foundation of anthropological studies, and is the source of cultural data and discussions that will be presented in the following chapters of *Anthropology Matters!* So important is fieldwork to anthropology that British anthropologist C.G. Seligman proclaimed, "Field research in anthropology is what the blood of the martyrs is to the church" (Lewis 1976: 27).

Questions for Consideration

1.   Outline a strategy for preparing for fieldwork. What preparations do you consider most important for your personal well-being? For your professional efficacy? For the reassurance of your study group?

2.   Discuss the ethics of anthropology. What measures can an ethnographer take to ensure the privacy of his or her study group?

3.   Anthropologists live with a study group and observe their daily lives. Imagine yourself as part of a study group. If an anthropologist moved into your community (be it your hometown, university dorm, or so on), how would you respond to this person's continuing presence in your life? What types of questions and topics would you be willing to discuss, and what aspects of your life would be considered too private to discuss with a stranger? Would the gender or age of the anthropologist make any difference to you?

4. Design a fieldwork project. Choose to study a "culture scene" close to home (e.g., your church group, the local Goth club, skateboarders, a Tupperware party, etc.).

NOTES

1 See Chapter 12 in this volume for a detailed discussion of culture shock, including the experiences of several anthropologists.

2 See Chapter 7 on female circumcision for an extensive discussion of this ethical dilemma.

3 See *The Naked Anthropologist* (1992) by Philip R. DeVita for personal accounts of fieldwork.

References

ANDERSON, R. (2005). *The ghosts of Iceland*. Belmont, CA: Thomson Wadsworth.

BAKER, V.J. (1998). *A Sinhalese village in Sri Lanka: Coping with uncertainty*. Toronto: Harcourt Brace·College Publishers.

BRIGGS, J.L. (1970). *Never in anger. Portrait of an Eskimo family*. Cambridge, MA: Harvard University Press.

DEVITA, P.R. (1992). *The naked anthropologist. Tales from around the world*. Belmont, CA: Wadsworth Publishing Co.

FEDORAK, S. (2006). *Windows on the world: Case studies in anthropology*. Toronto: Thomson Nelson Learning.

FEIT, H.A. (1995). Hunting and the quest for power: The James Bay Cree and Whitemen in the 20th century. In R.B. Morrison & C.R. Wilson (Eds.), *Native peoples: The Canadian experience* (2nd ed.). Toronto: McClelland & Stewart.

HAVILAND, W.A., FEDORAK, S., CRAWFORD, G., & LEE, R.B. (2005). *Cultural anthropology* (2nd Cdn. ed.). Toronto: Thomson Nelson Learning.

HOLTZMAN, J.D. (2000). *Nuer journeys, Nuer lives. Sudanese refugees in Minnesota*. Toronto: Allyn and Bacon.

INTEGRAL NAKED. (2004). *Who is Bill Ury?* Retrieved March 27, 2006, from the World Wide Web at http://in.integralinstitute.org/contributor.aspx?id=71.

JENNESS, D. (1959). *People of the twilight*. Chicago: University of Chicago Press.

KNAUFT, B. (2005). *The Gebusi. Lives transformed in a rainforest world*. Toronto: McGraw-Hill.

KUTSCHE, P. (1998). *Field ethnography. A manual for doing anthropology*. Upper Saddle River, NJ: Prentice Hall.

LEE, R.B. (2003). *The Dobe Ju/'hoansi* (3rd ed.). Toronto: Nelson Thomson Learning.

LEWIS, I.M. (1976). *Social anthropology in perspective*. Harmondsworth, England: Penguin Books.

MUZYCHKA, I. (n.d.). *Briggs: Studying emotions*. Retrieved March 27, 2006, from the World Wide Web at http://www.mun.ca/marcomm/gazette/1994-95/March.23/news/n03-brig.

TONKINSON, R. (1991). *The Mardu Aborigines. Living the dream in Australia's desert* (2nd ed.). Toronto: Holt, Rinehart & Winston.

WEINER, A. (1987). *The Trobrianders of Papua New Guinea*. Toronto: Holt, Rinehart & Winston.

WEIDMAN, H.H. (1970). *On ambivalence and the field*. The Hazel Hitson Weidman Papers, Harvard University.

WHITE, G.M., & TENGAN, T.K. (2001, Fall). Disappearing worlds: Anthropology and cultural studies in Hawaii's and the Pacific. *The Contemporary Pacific*, 13(2), 381-416. Retrieved November 3, 2005, from the World Wide Web at http://www.infotrac.galegroup.com.

WHITEHEAD, T.L., & CONAWAY, M.E. (Eds.). (1986). Introduction. In *Self, sex, and gender in cross-cultural fieldwork*. Urbana & Chicago: University of Illinois Press.

Suggested Readings

BRIGGS, J.L. (1970). *Never in anger. Portrait of an Eskimo family*. Cambridge, MA: Harvard University Press.

Although slightly dated, Briggs' fieldwork experiences, more than any other ethnography, highlight the many challenges that anthropologists face in an alien and sometimes harsh environment.

DEVITA, P.R. (Ed.) (1992). *The naked anthropologist. Tales from around the world*. Belmont, CA: Wadsworth Publishing Co.

DeVita has put together a collection of stories that recount sometimes embarrassing, sometimes startling experiences of anthropologists in the field. Readers should gain an understanding of the challenges faced by anthropologists as they deal with their insecurities, ignorance, isolation, missteps, and happenstance.

KNAUFT, B. (2005). *The Gebusi: Lives transformed in a rainforest world*. Toronto: McGraw-Hill.

A refreshing ethnography on a previously little-known group of hunter–gatherers living in the rainforests of Papua New Guinea. This book provides students with an excellent example of the ethnographic experience.

CHAPTER TWO

What is Culture Shock and How Does it Affect People Living, Studying, and Working Abroad?

Introduction

Imagine moving to a new country where everything is strange. You have no friends or family members nearby, and you do not speak the language, except how to ask where the nearest bathroom is located. You do not even know how or what to order in a restaurant. As the days go by, you lose your sense of euphoria at being in a new country, and become increasingly anxious and disoriented. Depression sneaks in and ruins your days; even getting out of bed becomes a chore. This scenario is fairly realistic of the early symptoms of **CULTURE SHOCK**—a term first coined by Oberg (1960).

Nolan (1990: 2) defines culture as "a pattern of meaning, a way of defining the world" that enables us to survive. Each of us has a sense of the way things ought to be—this sense is deeply ingrained, and has

KEY TERMS: culture shock, enculturation, norm, communication, non-verbal cues, proxemics, cultural identity, biculturalism been learned since birth through the process of **ENCULTURATION**. Our ideals, values, and beliefs generate acceptable behaviour for a particular culture, but when we move to another culture, we leave our familiar world behind and enter another one that is difficult to understand since it operates under another set of rules that take time to learn. In this new environment, we are no long able to predict other people's behaviour. This unpredictability creates a sense of insecurity that can be debilitating and cause culture shock (Haviland et al. 2005).

Culture shock is a stress-related syndrome that causes feelings of confusion, hostility, disorientation, and depression (Nolan 1990). It occurs when we find ourselves in foreign environments, where the people are culturally diverse. We meet people who live in different ways, speak different languages, and hold different beliefs and values on such matters as the status of women. This "otherness" makes people uncomfortable and insecure.

Culture shock is generally not a permanent condition, nor does it strike people who are in a new place for only a short time. However, the more extended the stay, and the more different the host country, the more likely culture shock will strike. This means the casual tourist booked into a Club Med will likely not experience real culture shock, but the young backpacker away from home for six months will. The same holds true for anthropologists embarking on ethnographic field-work. Unfortunately, knowing that culture shock will strike does little to ease the unpleasantness.

In this chapter we will consider some of the problems individuals, including anthropologists, encounter in a foreign environment, and the coping strategies for dealing with the debilitating symptoms of culture shock. In keeping with the multidisciplinary nature of anthropology, the expertise and insights of psychologists in studying culture shock will also be drawn on. Throughout this chapter you will be introduced to anecdotal stories of anthropologists and the problems they have encountered that often lead to culture shock.

Anthropologists and Culture Shock

Despite their "insider" understanding of culture shock, anthropologists are not immune to the experience any more than other visitors to a foreign environment. When William C. Young headed into the field to study the Rashaayda Bedouin of Sudan in 1978, he found himself in a vastly different world from the one he left behind in the United States (Young 1996). Instead of cars, he rode a camel, and instead of cities with tall buildings, shops, restaurants, and freeways, he lived in a goat-hair tent in the middle of the empty desert. At first, Young felt awkward living in a close-knit and highly structured society, but gradually he became friends with his Rashaayda hosts and grew comfortable with

Ethnographer William Young with one of his Rashiidi hosts.

his new lifestyle. He learned the language, wore their traditional cloth-ing, and, most important of all, learned to think and live as a Rashiidi (Fedorak 2006). Before leaving home, Young had converted to Islam, hoping this would make him more acceptable to the Rashaayda and help him understand their world view. This was certainly a drastic step, and not one many anthropologists would be willing to take.

Once the excitement of making contact and getting established among the Mardu Aborigines of the Gibson Desert in western Austra-lia wore off, Robert Tonkinson (1991) experienced culture shock. He endured bouts of depression, a sense of inadequacy, frustration, anger, and even paranoia. Above all, he was consumed with a sense of being an outsider, regardless of how the Mardu welcomed him into their lives. Tonkinson credited the Mardu children with helping him overcome his culture shock. They welcomed him warmly, and accepted him into their midst. Both Young and Tonkinson moved into cultural groups that were very different from their own, which likely exacerbated the degree of culture shock they experienced.

One of the more stirring encounters with culture shock is the story of anthropologist Victoria J. Baker's experiences in a Sinhalese village in Sri Lanka (Baker 1998). At first Baker was enthralled with the exoticness of Sri Lanka, and the mixture of modern with traditional. On any given street in Colombo, she might encounter a jumble of three-wheeled carts, slow-moving ox carts, and luxury vehicles, only to see sari-clad women delicately picking their way through the noise, filth, and confusion. Signs of poverty were everywhere, yet Baker also spotted luxury hotels and restaurants, and private clubs with manicured lawns.

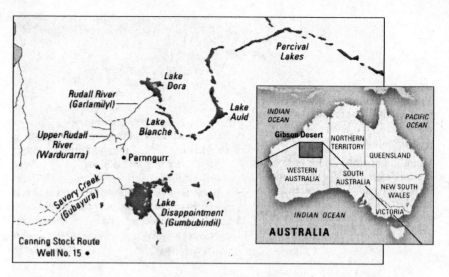

Location of Mardu Aborigines in Gibson Desert, Western Australia

The matter of offering a cup of tea in this land so famous for Ceylon tea was another situation that led to some mis-understandings when I first settled in my little house. Wanting to be the hospitable hostess, I bought tea sugar, milk powder, biscuits (cookies), even some fruit-drink syrup and bottled soft drinks to offer my guests. When they would come by for a visit, I would ask them, "Would you like a cup of tea?" ..."or a cool drink?" Inevitably they would refuse. "Epa, epa" (No, no I don't want any) they would repeatedly say. I would then ask, "Would you like a biscuit?" thinking they surely would not turn down cookies in this place of food shortages. I felt somewhat hurt by their refusal and even won-dered whether there might be a question of pollution and their not trusting the cleanliness of my kitchen. Only after relating the dilemma to my assistant some time later did the situa-tion become clear. In Sri Lanka, of course the guests want a cup of tea or a soft drink and some sweets. To ask them by question if they want it is like saying, "You don't want any, do you?" (BAKER 1998: 11)

Baker found Sri Lanka a sensory delight—what she called "naive anthropological gluttony"—when she first arrived to teach at Colombo University in 1983. However, disillusionment soon set in. The heat, transportation problems, the tendency of the Sri Lankans to forget or not show up for appointments, power outages, and equipment failure (e.g., telephones) all fuelled a growing frustration.

In 1984, Baker moved to a remote Sinhalese village called Suduwa-tura Ara to teach English and study the villagers. The villagers welcomed her warmly and did what they could to make her feel at home. Indeed, Baker grew to love the peaceful, lush rural setting of the isolated village. Eating a thick pancake served with chillies and onions for breakfast soon became delicious, and washing her clothes in the pond, normal.

Upon arrival Baker had to learn appropriate behaviour. For exam-ple, greetings such as "Good morning" were not a part of village social interaction; rather, when meeting someone they asked "Where are you going?" which startled Baker. Hospitality and generosity are a cultural **NORM** in Sri Lanka, and the Sinhalese thought it strange that Baker constantly thanked them for doing simple things that were expected. A smile would have been enough.

Communication was also a problem. Baker's urban Sinhalese inter-preter only lasted 12 days in the isolated village; her terror of poisonous snakes and distaste for the "primitiveness" of the village proved too much to bear. This left Baker with no one to translate, and a great deal of "conversation" was reduced to pantomime, dramatizing, and Baker's pidgin Sinhala. Besides the difficulties with conducting research, Baker also missed talking to someone. When her assistant and others came to visit, Baker talked their heads off.

Baker also had to deal with a feeling of cultural isolation. She was all too aware that her basic values, beliefs, perceptions, and practices were different than the Sinhalese. Symptoms of culture shock would

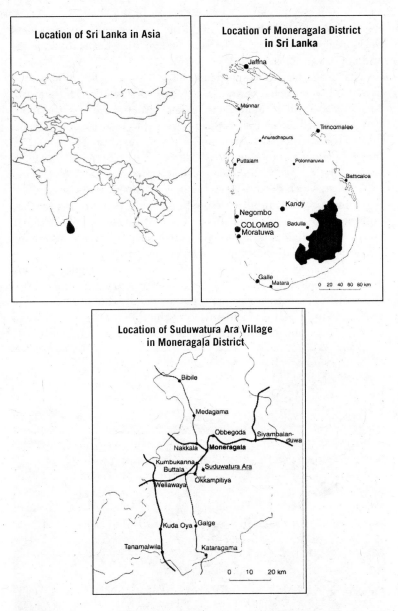

Location of Sri Lanka in Asia

Location of Moneragala District in Sri Lanka

Jaffna
Mannar
Trincomalee
Anuradhapura
Puttalam
Polonnaruwa
Batticaloa
Negombo
Kandy
COLOMBO
Badulla
Moratuwa
Galle
Matara
0 20 40 60 80 km

Location of Suduwatura Ara Village in Moneragala District

Bibile
Medagama
Obbegoda
Siyambalan-puwa
Nakkala
Moneragala
Kumbukanna
Buttala
Suduwatura Ara
Wellawaya
Okkampitiya
Kuda Oya
Galge
Tanamalwila
Kataragama
0 10 20 km

At times I consciously knew I was in some stage of culture shock, though I was powerless to shake off mild depressions and ethnocentric feelings, covering the profound to the most trivial: How can development take place when villagers go deep in debt to pay for Buddhist almsgiving ceremonies? How nice it would be to flick on a light switch, watch the news on TV, open a fridge, and have a cold drink. How incredible it is that no toilet paper can be bought in all of Moneragala District. (BAKER 1998: 14)

Location of Sinhalese village, Suduwatura, in Sri Lanka

wash over her: mild depression, ethnocentric feelings (e.g., why did people so poor spend everything they had to pay for Buddhist ceremonies?), and a desire to enjoy some of the niceties of back home (e.g., television, electricity and refrigeration, hamburgers, and toilet paper). Her Western values of privacy also created some stress. The Sinhalese visited when they felt like it, bringing fruit or sweets, and could not relate to Baker's need for occasional solitude.

Baker employed several coping strategies to ease her culture shock and sense of isolation: listening to tapes, writing letters, and reading novels. She also took advantage of the natural beauty and peacefulness of the region, often reading outside, enjoying the beautiful waterfall and pond, and trees dripping with fruit.

Baker also faced personal dangers. In Sri Lanka, wild animals, such as leopards and elephants, and Tamil terrorists threatened the safety of the Sinhalese and, by association, Baker. Although none of the above dangers caused Baker any problems directly, in the case of poisonous snakes, the situation was different. One day she discovered a snake crawling on her kitchen table. She chased it away with a broom, but still felt uneasy. The villagers cleared the brush around her hut and advised her to get a cat, which she did. Unfortunately the snakes still visited.

Obviously anthropologists must delve deeper into the reasons and mechanisms of culture shock. Most of the research to date has focused on individuals; however, Nolan (1990) believes that moving into a new cultural environment may be mediated by a group or organization, such as an exchange program, development agency, funding agency, and even the media. These groups may structure and control the transitional experience more than originally thought. According to Nolan (1990) more consideration of the role these groups play in cultural transition and culture shock may help us learn to manage it.

Contact with home and the "outside" world helps alleviate culture shock. Here ethnographer Victoria Baker receives mail from home.

A Discussion of Culture Shock

Culture shock involves several stages, beginning with a feeling of euphoria and fascination with the new culture, often called the honeymoon phase (Nolan 1990). These feelings of awe wear off after a few weeks and then the symptoms of the crisis phase of culture shock begin: sadness, crying bouts, homesickness and loneliness, insomnia or sleeping too much, loss of appetite, irritability, and feelings of inadequacy. Depending on personality and circumstances, more serious symptoms, such as depression, physical manifestations of illness, confusion, obsession with cleanliness, and unwillingness to interact with others, may develop (Guanipa 1998). Students studying abroad who exhibit these symptoms must also deal with academic pressures and the insecurity of entering a new school (Ward, Bochner, & Furnham 2001). Anthropologists who have experienced culture shock complain most about the inability to concentrate and carry on with their fieldwork.

In the second stage of culture shock, individuals may become frustrated with their inability to communicate and perform necessary tasks, such as finding a laundry, and they may begin to lose patience with their host country. Simple problems, such as not finding favourite foods (e.g., peanut butter) in local stores can create an outburst of irrational anger. They may also begin to feel a sense of loss for their home culture and way of life, often explained away as homesickness (Nolan 1990).

When anthropologist Ellen Holmes (1992) set out for American Samoa, she expected things to be much like the United States. On the surface this proved true; Samoa had hotels with air conditioning, electricity, telephones, banks, and supermarkets. Yet, it was different too. The interior of the island was poverty-stricken, banks were "limited" in their services, inter-island air service was unreliable, and the rats and geckos were too friendly. All of these concerns may seem trivial to us, but at the time overwhelmed Holmes. Culture shock struck in full force, reducing her to crying bouts, angry outbursts, depression, and constant frustration.

In the recovery phase, people become more comfortable with their surroundings and may begin to adopt some of the local lifestyle (Nolan 1990). Glitches in the daily routine do not bother them as much. They learn the social norms and behaviours of their new culture. As such, they have accomplished a degree of cultural transition. Nolan (1990) likens this cultural transition to a rite of passage. In the last few weeks of Holmes's research, even though she was on a much less developed island, Western Samoa, she found it easier to adjust, and events that would have frustrated her to the extreme when she first arrived in American Samoa, such as driving on a narrow road that ended up blocked by a fallen tree, no longer bothered her—she could now "go with the flow."

When a person returns to their home culture, they may experience reverse culture shock.[1] Setting aside everything they have learned and readjusting to their home culture can be challenging. Students returning home after completing their education often suffer severe reverse culture shock. Although anthropologists welcome rejoining their family and life, they may also experience anxiety about meeting with old friends and associates. They often express less satisfaction with life in their home country and a feeling of loss. When William Young (1996) returned from his two-year stay with the Rashaayda Bedouin in 1980, he experienced reverse culture shock. Using utensils to eat, wasting water on such things as cleaning floors, women dressed in immodest clothing, and a landscape full of tall buildings and rushing vehicles all seemed strange to him.

CHALLENGES OF LIVING IN A FOREIGN ENVIRONMENT

Because culture shock is a personal experience, and manifests itself in many ways depending on a person's personality, ability to adapt to new social norms, and previous experience in foreign settings, strategies for coping with culture shock can take many forms. In this section, we will examine some of the ways travellers and anthropologists have dealt with culture shock.

Even if the new culture is quite similar to our home country, there will be problems. Years ago, when my daughter lived in London, UK, during a telephone conversation she complained about the lack of good mustard in the supermarkets. The mustard was not the problem; her frustration with the difficulties she was experiencing in her daily life was the real issue. Becoming familiar with the neighbourhood, finding services and resources necessary to live comfortably, and "learning the culture" go a long way toward easing these petty frustrations.

Ward et al. (2001: 51) identifies culture learning as the "process whereby sojourners[2] acquire culturally relevant social knowledge and skills in order to survive and thrive in their new society." Living successfully in a foreign environment requires a great deal of determination, fortitude, and a bit of luck. Learning the language as soon as possible is of paramount importance. Being able to communicate is vital to a sense of well-being, and will help with daily tasks such as ordering food at a restaurant. Enrolling in language classes also provides opportunities to interact with other people in a similar situation. Linguistic problems create the most serious problems for students, academically and socially. Without sufficient command of the language, students have difficulty with course work, and lack the language skills to seek help from instructors or fellow students. They also experience difficulty making friends who might lessen their loneliness and help ease them into the cultural life of their host country.

Intercultural **COMMUNICATION** skills go beyond learning to speak the language. They also involve learning the conventions of a society, for example, **NON-VERBAL CUES**, such as appropriateness of gaze, **PROXEMICS** (personal space use), greetings, use of touch and gestures, responding to requests, and assertion of one's self (Ward et al. 2001). Forms of address also vary from one culture to another. On a recent visit to China, I was faced with the challenge of appropriately addressing the people I was visiting. In China, the surname has always come first and the given name last, which causes initial confusion for North Americans. While Canadians tend to address each other by first names, in China adults are usually addressed as Mr. and Mrs., although this is only a recent innovation. Until about 10 years ago, the Chinese of Shanghai addressed each other as "comrade," and Mr. and Mrs. was reserved for the wealthy and powerful.

Missing family and friends can be debilitating. When anthropologist Gail A. Fondahl (1998) spent months conducting fieldwork among the Evenki of southeastern Siberia, she relied on the kindness of a family to help her get over her homesickness. The Evenkis were generous with their hospitality and advice, and helped with arrangements. Students on international exchanges have found that if they make friends, and develop a social support network, they experience a more satisfying and academically productive life. These networks serve to facilitate students in becoming accustomed to their new environment and the behavioural norms, as well as providing social outlets to relieve homesickness and stress.

In 1963, when Richard Lee (2003) was living with the Ju/'hoansi hunting and gathering people of the Kalahari Desert in Africa, tragic news reached him via his transistor radio: President John F. Kennedy had been assassinated. Like all Americans, Lee was in shock, but unlike his compatriots, he had no one with whom to share his grief. His hosts, the Dobe Ju/'hoansi, had never heard of President Kennedy or the United States. Culture shock usually shows itself during these times, even in an experienced ethnographer like Richard Lee.

Although it would be foolish to suggest that people who move to a new country completely assume a new **CULTURAL IDENTITY**, over time they may take on many of the characteristics of an adopted culture. A form of **BICULTURALISM** develops, where they identify with and become a part of two cultures. At times, this comes about through developing a rapport with members of the host community. Richard Lee was adopted into the family of N!eishi and //Gumi. With this acceptance, his position changed from that of an outsider to that of a full member of a Dobe Ju/'hoansi family, and he was expected to learn the role of a Ju/'hoansi son.

Bouts of culture shock experienced by professional anthropologists are rites of passage that forever change them, professionally and personally. The same can be said for other individuals living in foreign countries, who have worked their way through culture shock. The following narrative tells the story of a young man from Canada who moved to Shanghai, China, to teach English.

I have lived in China for two and a half years. Before moving here I traveled often, though mostly in Europe and North America. I also spent five months studying in Hong Kong and six weeks traveling through mainland China in 2002. So I came to Shanghai in the fall of 2003 pretty much knowing what I was getting into—or so I thought.

I teach English at a language training center. Most of my friends are foreigners, most of my life is lived in a Western style, and most of the time I use English, my native language, to communicate. Fortunately, I also enjoy the company of several good local friends, and a girlfriend who is Shanghainese.

Living in Shanghai is not quite like living in the rest of China. Thousands of foreigners make Shanghai their home (20,000–30,000 in a city with 12 million in the metropolitan area). They come here because it is a middle ground—the East and West meet here. There are pubs when I need them, ATMs where I can withdraw directly from bank accounts back home, and good Western food if I want to pay Western prices. Thus, the shock experienced in Shanghai, while significant, is probably quite tempered compared with life in a small Chinese town in the countryside.

My first eight to twelve weeks in Shanghai were fairly positive, mostly because I was so busy settling into a new job, apartment, and meeting new people. Like other new expats, I wondered at everything, and relished the differences in art, technology, food, and lifestyle. I only noticed the positive side of Shanghai culture and social life, and given the amount of information I had to absorb, I really did not have time to make judgments, positive or negative. After all, change was the reason I chose to live abroad, to experience something different. There was a great deal to look at, from the neon signs, to the women with tremendous fashion sense, to the markets and bazaars with unfamiliar products. My initial reaction was wonder and even a bit of awe. I have found that foreigners who are only staying for the short term (less than one year) seem to stick to this stage and not move too deeply into the later stages of culture shock. The fact that they are leaving in a short time leads them to view many problems with a sense of humor, rather than as a life crisis.

Then came stage two, which after two years, I am still experiencing. This was the period when I started noticing the cultural differences more clearly, usually in a negative light. I found myself getting angry and frustrated over little things that can make a day go smoothly or not, and mood swings were frequent. Some of the more unpleasant aspects of Shanghai became more noticeable, like the monstrous traffic problems, inconsiderate people, the awful working conditions most workers suffer, and low-quality workmanship on products. I constantly resisted the urge to educate my hosts and change their ways to something more similar to my own. "Why do you do it this way?" is perhaps the most common question I ask, and usually the answer fails to convince me that the Chinese way is better than my way. I know this is due to my different viewpoint from the locals, who are used to their customs and are relatively indifferent to other options. I continue to struggle with the conflict between accepting my hosts' habits and customs and attempting to change them.

In the third stage of culture shock, a foreigner has lived in their adopted country (perhaps one to five years) and has come to grips with the immense but subtle cultural differences and deals with them with more ease. They understand more of the historical and cultural background, and experience fewer surprises. I have only witnessed stage three in others. I know there are continuing waves of culture shock and corresponding frustration, stress, and anxiety, but they are shorter in duration and less severe than in stage two. At this point, the foreigner is fairly adapted to the local culture (though not necessarily assimilated into it).

One of the problems I continually encounter is what I, with my Western upbringing, consider bad manners or habits. Many Chinese spit, whenever and wherever they please. The Shanghainese claim they do not spit in the streets; it is the millions of migrants that have come to the city. The migrant workers are generally less-educated and very poor. However, to a Westerner, this detail is of little relevance—they live in Shanghai, they are Shanghainese. Hygiene is a problem here, and considering all the deadly diseases developing in this part of the world, is of serious concern. I find it difficult to get used to some of the typical street behaviour, such as the constant pushing to get on the buses, subways, and elevators. Other behaviour is less annoying, and at times even humorous. Elderly men, in particular, have a habit of wearing pajamas out on the street, to do errands in the morning, and sometimes all day. The Shanghainese also throw their garbage everywhere; the logic being that someone has a job to clean it up.

The odd thing is the Shanghainese tend not to say much to change the bad habits of those around them. Since no one speaks up, no one changes, and the spitting continues (even though there are signs forbidding spitting in the streets for hygienic reasons). Part of this attitude comes from the importance of face. One shouldn't lose face, or cause others to lose face, and yelling at someone who has spit on the sidewalk makes both parties lose face. Another reason is probably the Cultural Revolution, when those who displayed good manners and courtesy were accused of being bourgeois lackeys. Thus, middle-aged men and women are the worst offenders, while younger people are generally a little more pleasant to be around.

Obviously, one way that I try to cope with cultural differences is to rationalize them, but it does not always work. Culture, to be sure, is hardly rational at times. I should note, however, that until writing this piece, I never gave much thought to coping techniques, and I would argue that most people don't, they are merely aware that they are 'coping' on a subliminal level. Foreigners do know, however, that certain activities make them feel better.

As you can see, I am not over some things and still mired in stage two of culture shock. Most of the time I ignore the little things—they are merely background noise. I do not want China to become Western, but I still impose some of my Western ideals and values on my vision of what China should and could be. There are often two or more ways of doing things, but the trap I often fall into is selecting one as better or superior, and one as inferior.

The Shanghainese are fairly used to foreigners, but their counterparts across China, in general, are not. Many of them migrate into Shanghai looking for work or to celebrate holidays. Westerners are a curiosity, and in particular white Westerners with blonde or red hair and blue, grey, or green eyes. Many have never seen us before except on television. Luckily, the Chinese tend to have an honest desire to look, smile, wave, and say 'hello' to foreigners. I have had people stare at me with their mouths wide open, and even walk into walls or trip because they were watching me and my friends. How do I respond? I usually ignore it, sometimes I say hello to them, which often provokes laughter and chattering among several locals, as if I was a parrot or even a monkey chirping back at them. It does get annoying at times. Anyone insecure with their looks or body will have a hard time in China. However, some people enjoy being treated as different and interesting. Indeed, I am not an Average Joe in China; I have been transformed into a mini-celebrity because of my skin colour and background

Eating can be a challenge in China, and I don't mean chopsticks, which I mastered in Hong Kong. There are countless other issues involved. Chinese socializing revolves around food. First, the style of food and ordering: Chinese food is meant for several people to eat together and share the dishes. A foreigner eating alone is forced to eat four dishes themselves or order 'something, something on rice.' This, combined with language difficulties, ensures most foreigners have about four or five dishes to choose from for every meal. There is Western food, but not much, and it is expensive, except for places like KFC and McDonald's. Ordering food with unfamiliar idiom-type names is also a problem. Sometimes I think I will never learn it all. Sometimes I just want a hot meal, but I mistakenly order cold dishes. Sometimes I like to experiment, and it can turn out great or ruin the meal. Second, what they do to the food is too different for me. Bone shards in meat are a problem. The locals like their food cooked 'close to the bone.' Once the meat is cooked, it is chopped up, bone and all, resulting in shards of bone, often with blood and marrow seeping out. The Chinese habit of spitting out the bone shards onto the table also disturbs me.

The many positive aspects of Chinese culture include the honest curiosity about foreigners, the love of family, the variety and flavours of the food, and spending hours on end just sitting and talking over meals or drinks. They are a social people, and sensitive, uptight, privacy-loving Westerners find it difficult to fit in. The Chinese do often treat strangers on the street (locals and foreigners) as something insignificant or as an inconvenience, but once within their circle of friends they are the most generous, loyal, and warm-hearted people. I have had the honour of being welcomed into a Chinese family and found that the differences in manner and thought with Westerners are huge, but the love and goals in life are the same.

In sum, to me, culture shock is knowing that someone is talking about me, but not understanding if what they are saying is derogatory or complimentary. It is also the frustration I feel when trying to communicate in some important way—whether telling someone I love them or speaking my mind—but not being able to do it effectively. Getting over culture shock, or at least dealing with it, requires patience, persistence, and time. Shrugging my shoulders is often the best I can do. The best remedy, by far, is frequent gatherings with other foreigners. We get together informally, at a pub, at work, or just on the street, and vent our frustrations. We love the country, we want to stay, but we need to perform this ritual exercise at least weekly to maintain our equilibrium. Feeling validated and more relaxed, we go back to our daily lives in Shanghai.

Conclusion

Culture shock is a common experience among people who spend an extended time in foreign environments. Once they learn the customs, beliefs, and patterns of behaviour in their new culture, the sense of insecurity recedes. This is not to say that culture shock is a fleeting experience. Indeed, foreigners often experience repeated bouts, whenever they encounter unfamiliar situations, or have experiences that they find unacceptable. Nonetheless, culture shock is manageable, and in many ways is a valuable experience that teaches us about ourselves and helps us grow as individuals.

The nature of ethnographic fieldwork means that anthropologists immerse themselves in a culture, interacting on a social level with community members, eating the same food, and participating in various daily activities. As we have seen, this fieldwork generally leads to cultural isolation, feelings of insecurity, and culture shock, but it also leads to insights about human behaviour not possible in a less involved experience. Comparing culture shock to a rite of passage seems apt; it is a period of personal growth and reflects on our ability to learn and accept new and unfamiliar ways of living.

Questions for Consideration

1. Imagine yourself in a strange place, with no friends or family, language difficulties, only unfamiliar foods to eat ... you get the picture. How would you cope with this new life? Draft an action plan for dealing with culture shock in your adopted country, including coping strategies that you would employ.

2. Examine the phenomenon of reverse culture shock. What problems would you anticipate when returning to your home culture? How would you deal with these problems?

3. Research biculturalism. What advantages can you identify from having a bicultural perspective? What disadvantages?

4. If possible, discuss culture shock with someone who has immigrated to your country. What problems did they encounter when they first arrived and what symptoms of culture shock did they experience?

5. If you moved to another country, would you try to hold on to your cultural practices and values or would you adopt (assimilate) your new country's culture? Depending on your answer to this question, how can you expect any more from people immigrating to your country?

6. Do you think it is possible to completely give up a natal culture and completely immerse oneself in a new culture? Why or why not?

7. Based on the young man from Canada's story, would you say he has passed through all the stages of culture shock? If not, where do you see him in the process of overcoming culture shock? Do you think he will experience reverse culture shock when he returns to North America?

NOTES

1   Nolan (1990) calls this phase the re-entry crisis.
2   Temporary residents who anticipate returning to their home countries.

References

BAKER, V.J. (1998). *A Sinhalese village in Sri Lanka. Coping with uncertainty.* Fort Worth: Harcourt Brace College Publishers.

FEDORAK, S. (2006). *Windows on the world: Case studies in anthropology.* Toronto: Thomson Nelson Learning.

FONDAHL, G.A. (1998). *Gaining ground? Evenkis, land, and reform in southeastern Siberia.* Boston: Allyn & Bacon.

GUANIPA, C. (1998). *Culture shock.* Retrieved August 22, 2005, from the World Wide Web at http://edweb.sdsu.edu/people/CGuanipa/cultshokhtm.

HAVILAND, W.A., FEDORAK, S.A., CRAWFORD, G., & LEE, R.B. (2005). *Cultural anthropology* (2nd Can. ed.). Toronto: Thomson Nelson Learning.

HOLMES, E. (1992). Culture shock in paradise. In P.R. DeVita (Ed.), *The naked anthropologist* (pp. 26–34). Belmont, CA: Wadsworth Publishing Co.

LEE, R.B. (2003). *The Dobe Ju/'hoansi* (3rd ed.). Toronto: Thomson Nelson Learning.

NOLAN, R.W. (1990). Culture shock and cross-cultural adaptation: Or I was okay until I got here. *Practicing Anthropology, 12*(4), 2, 20.

OBERG, K. (1960). Culture shock: Adjustments to new cultural environments. *Practicing Anthropology, 7,* 177–182.

TONKINSON, R. (1991). *The Mardu Aborigines: Living the dream in Australia's desert* (2nd ed.). Toronto: Holt, Rinehart & Winston.

WARD, C., BOCHNER, S., & FURNHAM, A. (2001). *The psychology of culture shock* (2nd ed.). Philadelphia, PA: Taylor & Francis, Inc.

WORLDATLAS.COM. (n.d.). *Australia*. Retrieved March 17, 2006, from the World Wide Web at http://worldatlas.com/webimage/countrys/oceania/aussnewld.htm.

YOUNG, W.C. (1996). *The Rashaayda Bedouin: Arab pastoralists of Eastern Sudan*. Toronto: Harcourt Brace College Publishers.

Suggested Readings

BAKER, V.J. (1998). *A Sinhalese village in Sri Lanka: Coping with uncertainty*. Fort Worth: Harcourt Brace College Publishers.

In this well-written ethnography, readers will not only learn a great deal about the lifestyles of the villagers of Suduwatura Ara, but also about the challenges Baker experienced as a lone anthropologist in a very isolated environment.

DEVITA, P.R. (Ed.). (1992). *The naked anthropologist: Tales from around the world*. Belmont, CA: Wadsworth Publishing Co.

DeVita has put together a collection of stories that recount sometimes embarrassing, sometimes startling experiences of anthropologists in the field. Readers should gain an understanding of the challenges faced by anthropologists as they deal with their insecurities, ignorance, isolation, missteps, and happenstance.

YOUNG, W. (1996). *The Rashaayda Bedouin: Arab pastoralists of Eastern Sudan*. Toronto: Harcourt Brace College Publishers.

This book is suggested reading for several reasons: it is one of the very few resources available on the Bedouin; it provides a glimpse into the extraordinary lives of the Rashaayda; and it tells the story of a young anthropologist coming of age.

CHAPTER THREE

Of What Use is Anthropology to the Business World? The Anthropology of Shopping

Introduction

Imagine a marketplace where shoppers casually stroll by an array of shops filled with all manner of merchandise. A group of young people, dressed in sloppy clothes, stand in the centre of the market, joking and teasing each other. Nearby, serious-looking musicians play a catchy melody and a troupe of young entertainers dance in time to the music. A juggler ambles by, his face twisted in concentration as he tosses four colourful balls into the air. Children follow him, laughing in delight each time he drops a ball. A clock chimes, signalling the noon hour, and delicious smells waft through the air from a nearby food stall,

KEY TERMS: diffusion, economic anthropology, corporate anthropology, retail anthropology, class, stratification making shoppers' mouths water. Then an angry shriek fills the air as a harried-looking mother drags her two tired and crying children to the nearest exit—the shopping day is over for them.

The above scenario may sound like a traditional *souk* or bazaar in an exotic locale such as Cairo, Egypt, but in fact describes a typical day in one of the many suburban malls found in North American cities. The mall is not a new concept; it is merely the most recent manifestation of a place for people to congregate and participate in commerce and trade. Indeed, malls are the marketplaces of wealthy industrialized societies (Plattner 1989b). Since the 1950s, this phenomenon has **DIFFUSED** to all corners of the world, and today's malls have become a mainstay of urban life. Paco Underhill (2004: 4) calls them the "dominant arena of American shopping" and "an economic force the likes of which the world has never known."

Anthropologists are often asked, "Of what use is anthropology in the business world?" In this chapter we will explore this question using retail anthropology and the anthropological study of shopping malls. We spend a great deal of time shopping beyond what is necessary to provide for our households, therefore shopping must hold some meaning beyond simply acquiring goods. We will investigate the economic and social functions of malls, the shopping experience and what it means to shoppers, and the use of public space to enhance this experience.

Anthropologist Paco Underhill has been applying his anthropological skills and knowledge to the study of shopping for more than 20 years. We will take a brief glimpse into the world of the suburban mall through his eyes. More specifically we will be addressing questions such as: Why do people shop? Who does most of the shopping, and what enhances the shopping experience? What do shoppers hope to gain from the experience? How does shopping affect relationships between family members, friends, and acquaintances? Retail and corporate anthropology are part of the larger field of economic anthropology; thus we will briefly consider economic anthropology's applications in the world of business.

Anthropologists and the Business World

Not all anthropologists work in academia; indeed, more anthropologists are now employed in international development, government, education, health, and environmental issues than are teaching in university settings. One area where these anthropologists have made great strides is in the applied field of economic anthropology. **ECONOMIC ANTHROPOLOGY** can be defined as "the study of economic institutions and behaviour done in anthropological places and in ethnographic style" (Plattner 1989a: 1).

Economic anthropologists are interested in all things economic—from the social significance of the Ju/'hoansi *hxaro* exchange system to the gendered division of labour among Yanomami horticulturalists, from the annual migrations of Basseri pastoralists in search of new pasture lands to the productive strategies of Mayan peasant farmers. Obviously, the field of economic anthropology is broad in scope, yet in recent years the interests of anthropologists have expanded even further. Anthropologists have shifted their focus from the economic systems of indigenous populations to new fields of study, such as industry, technology, and commerce (Suchman 2003).

In the 1990s, what Suchman (2003) calls **CORPORATE ANTHROPOLOGY** developed into a significant specialization in applied economic anthropology. Corporate leaders and business people recognized the value of understanding their consumers, and began taking note of the methods and expertise of anthropologists. Anthropologists are now employed at major corporations, actively engaged in corporate ethnography for research and development, marketing, and public relations. Indeed, Suchman (2003) suggests that anthropology itself has become a consumable product or commodity.

How has anthropology become relevant to the corporate world? One obvious application is the anthropologist's ability to gain access to consumers as they conduct their everyday shopping exercises. Anthropological research, then, turns a seemingly mundane activity like shopping into an exotic and mysterious experience.

Applied economic anthropologists work in many areas of business, marketing, and so on, using anthropological methods and a holistic perspective to understand the issues that impact commerce. Economic anthropology has influenced market research by pointing out that, to be successful, marketers must understand people—what they do and how they live (Squires 1997). For example, Steve Barnett, who holds a PhD in anthropology, is senior vice president of market strategy at ICM Breakpoint (GBN Global Business Network 2005). He has pioneered the use of anthropological research methods to analyze consumer behaviour. Barnett has also studied long-term global and cultural trends in patterns of consumption (Haviland et al. 2005).

Corporate anthropologists have developed in-depth analyses of Generation Y consumers for Eastman Kodak (NAPA 2005). This study examined how consumers purchase and use cameras. Anthropologists interviewed consumers to get their perspective on the shopping experience, and identified themes and patterns of behaviour that led to changes in Kodak's packaging and displays. In another example, anthropologists on staff at Intel conducted ethnographic research on physicians at work. Their goal was to assess emerging technologies that would work well with the professional routines of physicians. Both these examples of ethnographic research assist product developers in developing products that meet the needs and desires of consumers.

> Factory floors, corporate offices and "middle class" homes, assumed to be so transparently familiar as to not warrant anthropological attention, are turned into sites as mysterious as the colonies once were by the mere fact of the anthropologist's presence. (SUCHMAN 2003: 3)

RETAIL ANTHROPOLOGY, which is the study of people who shop, is a good example of contemporary anthropological research. Retail anthropology merges anthropological interests with those of marketers and the corporate world. Applied retail anthropologists, such as Paco Underhill, work as consultants and researchers for merchants, restaurateurs, marketers, and bankers, investigating the interaction between people and merchandise, and the way people react to the organization of public spaces. For example, why do the teenagers mentioned earlier choose to congregate at a mall? Who does most of the shopping, and why? For what purpose have retailers chosen to supply shoppers with entertainment? Other retail anthropologists, such as Daniel Miller (2001), are interested in the shopping experience and the way these experiences influence social relationships. Miller has studied the everyday lives of people shopping for necessary material goods to explore the meaning of shopping, and how this experience informs us about social relationships and consumer culture. For example, how does taking children on shopping expeditions affect the parent-child relationship? What social relationships are formed when teenagers gather to shop, visit, and enjoy the entertainment?

Retail anthropologists conduct their research in much the same way as other ethnographers—through participant observation—living (or extensively visiting, in the case of shopping malls) in the community they are studying and becoming involved in the daily activities of the people in order to understand their point of view (Plattner 1989b). The practice of participant observation or immersing oneself into someone else's life is a constructive way of understanding what consumers need and want—this is particularly valuable today, when consumers are far more sophisticated, demanding, and indifferent to the products being offered. By observing consumers in a shopping environment, anthropologists offer the corporate world a more accurate and detailed assessment of consumer product needs and desires.

John Seely Brown, former director of Xerox PARC, suggests "anthropologists let you view behaviour through a new set of eyeglasses" (Deutsch 1991). Underhill (2004) and his associates visit shopping malls, armed with video equipment, maps, and customer-profile sheets, to make detailed observations of consumer behaviour. Underhill (2004) often relies on key informants to help him understand shoppers. For example, he bravely spent an afternoon shopping with three teenaged girls in an American suburban mall. By doing so, he gained some insight into the shopping habits of these young women and the retail tribalism their choice of wardrobe symbolized. Underhill (2004) discovered that clothing styles among teenagers signal group (tribal) affiliations, such as punk, surfer, rap, preps, skaters, and skas. This trend continues into adulthood, when individuals, especially women, signal their **CLASS**, ideology, and lifestyle by the type of clothing they wear. By giving voice to these young women,

"Ethnographic study can be a useful and complementary tool, giving us what the individual may be unable to or unwilling to vocalize to other researchers…. If you can observe the subject or consumer in action, you gain a better understanding of possible ways to enrich the consumer's experience, and also better understand the responses obtained from interviews and surveys."

AJAY KOHLI, PROFESSOR OF MARKETING AT THE EMORY'S GOIZUETA BUSINESS SCHOOL (NAPA 2005)

Underhill expanded his analysis of their activities with their interpretations of the meaning of the shopping experience. According to Atkinson (2004) this methodology makes anthropology relevant to the corporate world.

ETHICS IN RETAIL ANTHROPOLOGY

Participant observation, key informants, trained observation, and analysis of the data from an anthropological perspective offers corporations and marketers a deeper understanding of retail dynamics (Atkinson 2004). However, the ethics of such work must be considered as anthropologists become more involved in the corporate world. Have corporate anthropologists traded in their scientific objectivity for personal and professional security (i.e., jobs), and is their research always used for positive applications? As anthropologists uncover new and meaningful ways to entice consumers to purchase more merchandise, is this a disservice to the integrity of anthropology? Klein (1999) believes that anthropologists must provide services to consumers as well, and on a larger scale, the global economy, by aligning with activists who are struggling to hold corporations accountable for their actions. Klein (1999) cites several instances where anthropologists have or could be of service: anthropologists might join forces with activists in an effort to stop Shell Oil's actions in Nigeria,[1] point out environmental hazards caused by corporations, or block the marketing of harmful products.

In a similar vein, Daniel Miller (1998: 9) cautions against anthropologists becoming too involved in analyzing consumable products lest "we find ourselves contributing to, rather than refiguring, dominant forms of commodity fetishism." Rather, Miller suggests that anthropologists remain true to their anthropological goals; in this case, attempting to understand consumer behaviour. To this end, Miller (2001) examined the everyday activities associated with providing for households in North London. He viewed shopping and the material goods acquired on these shopping expeditions as a means of creating and maintaining social relationships between family members and other kin, as well as pets (Carter 2001). Thus, the anthropological study of shopping may provide some insights into the meaning of shopping and consumer behaviour.

A Discussion of Shopping Malls and Consumer Behaviour

Perhaps better than any other public spaces, malls showcase the people of a community in their natural state: how people dress in their everyday lives; the food they will eat when they think no one is watching; and how they interact with their parents and children, friends and

If you really want to observe entire middle-class multi-generational American families, you have to go to the mall.

ANTHROPOLOGIST PACO UNDERHILL (2004: 9)

spouses. The anthropological study of shopping may seem, at first glance, a frivolous choice for research, but in reality can inform us about everyday life in a wealthy industrialized state society. For this reason the following section will focus on shopping in malls, based primarily on Paco Underhill's research.

From the outside, most malls are an eyesore—what Underhill (2004: 33) calls "a big air-conditioned vanilla box with all the action on the inside."[2] Malls are not designed to be pretty; they are designed to hold pretty stores, with even prettier merchandise. Developers show little interest in enticing people into the mall with grand architecture or imposing entrances.[3] Nonetheless, shoppers flock to these behemoths and, through their spending, impact significantly on the economy. The unappealing exterior of malls is not the case in all regions of the world. As an example, the Vasco da Gama Center in Lisbon, Portugal, is a stunning architectural masterpiece—a modern art rendition of a sailing ship (Underhill 2004).

The organization of public space follows a similar pattern in most malls: vast parking lots; small entrances in side wings; several corridors, each with more than one level of stores and restaurants; centre aisle kiosks; strategically situated washrooms; food courts, and elevators and escalators. Some of the larger malls also have vast amusement parks with swimming pools and waterslides, rock climbing walls, ice rinks, aquatic displays, rides resembling a smaller version of Disneyland, video arcades, and so on. These "sideshows" are designed to make the shopping experience more enjoyable, especially for children, which in turn may encourage shoppers to stay longer and shop more. Malls become one-stop entertainment facilities, and as Underhill (2004) notes, non-retail components give a mall its character and reputation.

The consumer experience is central to any shopping mall; if the consumer is unhappy, frustrated, inconvenienced, or unable to easily locate appropriate merchandise, then the shopping experience becomes negative, which translates into limited economic growth for the retailers.[4]

Finding an accessible parking spot is part of the initial customer experience, and can set the tone for the shopping experience (i.e., driving around searching for a stall can put even the most ardent shopper into a dark mood, not conducive to spending money). Being able to find the car after shopping is also a consideration—ask anyone who has wandered aimlessly around a vast parking lot searching for their lost car. Once inside the mall the whole world changes. The mall becomes an insular cocoon, far away from the world outside.

Bright lights, soft music, periodic announcements, the deep rumble of conversations, dancing water fountains, fast food aromas, and colourful window displays—all these sights, sounds, and smells inundate shoppers as they stroll down the nearest corridor. The corridor itself is often so busy with ongoing fashion shows, kiosks for charity events, and exhibits of exotic fish in aquariums, that the retail stores

Shopping malls have also become centres of family entertainment as this "Fantasyland" at the West Edmonton Mall demonstrates.

seem almost secondary. Nonetheless, the mall is a place of commerce, and many of the people in the mall are there to shop. Where they will shop and the quality of their shopping experience will be determined by several factors: type and availability of merchandise, attractiveness of displays, comfort level (e.g., space for shopping, number of fitting rooms, lengths of lineups, soothing music), degree of crowdedness, and helpfulness of the clerks.

The sheer size of many malls creates confusion and wastes the shopper's time, which makes signage and maps indispensable. If a shopper cannot find the stores he or she is looking for, exasperation may set in and the shopper may leave. This behaviour appears to be gender-determined—male "hunters" spend very little time in the mall if lost, while female "gatherers" exhibit more patience and may even ask for help in locating a store (Underhill 2004).

Organization of public space in malls reflects consumer behaviour. Not only is the entrance to the mall nondescript, but the shops just inside the entrance tend to be banks, or other services visited only on a need-to basis, such as post offices and hair salons. Underhill (2004: 47) calls this area the decompression zone. These "entrance" stores are unimpressive because shoppers are looking ahead, into the heart of the mall, not to the side. Most malls have anchor stores on either end of the mall—large department stores that bring in the crowds. Other stores in the mall enjoy the trickle effect from these flagship stores. In large malls, stores are often clustered by category—women's apparel stores, for example, may all be in one wing. This clustering allows shoppers to check out all the fashions conveniently.

Free-standing kiosks or "pushcarts" in mall corridors sell all sorts of merchandise, from the newest kitchen gadgets to candles, cell phones, and strange carved wooden pictures. These kiosks spring up in alarming numbers over the holiday season, making already crowded mall corridors nearly impossible to navigate. However, these pushcarts serve several purposes beyond economics. Pushcarts hearken back to an earlier day of travelling peddlers, and the displays and demonstrations liven up the mall, and add a little entertainment. They are particularly effective at catching the eye of men and keeping them entertained for a short period while women dash into stores and make their purchases.

Charitable organizations often set up booths or tables in the corridors to sell tickets for cars, bikes, campers, and so forth. The Kiwanis sell crisp apples in autumn to benefit children's hospitals, and the Knights of Columbus and other organizations raffle off vehicles to support their charities. Mall owners encourage these charitable activities to draw customers into the mall, and to give the appearance of community service and outreach.

Virtually every mall has a food court—a large circle of food outlets offering ethnic and North American fast food. The main purpose of the food court is to feed shoppers, and then send them out for more shopping. The food court is sometimes the major draw, especially for elderly people looking for a place to have a cup of coffee and socialize with friends. For others (e.g., children, adult men), taking a break at the food court may be a welcome reprieve from the rigours of shopping, a chance for family members to spend time together, and even a bribe and/or reward for reluctant shoppers.

THE PSYCHOLOGY OF SHOPPING

As we have seen, malls, like traditional markets, are places to meet friends, hear the latest gossip and news, find a date or even a spouse, and enjoy the local entertainment. They are also gathering places for charitable organizations, school groups, artists, and the elderly. As an example, mall walking for senior citizens began soon after the first enclosed malls opened and has been gaining popularity ever since, especially in cold climates (Underhill 2004).

Teenaged girls love malls for numerous reasons, most of which have something to do with socialization. They like Internet cafés to hang out with friends. They enjoy movie theatres for the same reason. Although teenage girls will shop until they drop, non-retail activities are what really draw them to the mall. These include all manner of games—video, bowling, miniature golf, rock climbing, and so on. Amusement parks are also a draw, preferably ones with loud techno music, and plenty of food and rides. Surprisingly, even though teenaged girls spend an enormous amount of time in malls, they have the lowest conversion rate—of the percentage of people who buy something, they are the lowest of all demographic groups visiting malls (Underhill 2004). Nonetheless, teenaged

As popular gathering places, food courts in shopping malls such as the Alexandria Mall in Alexandria, Louisiana, provide opportunities for socializing.

girls represent a powerhouse of spending and shopping, and are future major consumers of material goods.

STRATIFICATION of shoppers is readily evident in malls. For example, mall "rats" and mall "junkies" are two identifiable micro-groups outside the mainstream teenage mall population. Mall junkies are always at the mall; they do not shop so much as hang out. Mall rats visit the mall quite often and are more likely to purchase merchandise or participate in some of the activities while there. Consequently, store owners are constantly challenged to renew merchandise for these shoppers (Underhill 2004).

Shopping habits based on gender influence product placement, displays, and general set-up in a store. For example, Underhill (2004) discovered that putting a women's shoe department and cosmetics department side by side makes perfect sense, since a woman waiting for the clerk to bring shoes in her size can occupy her time looking over the cosmetics. This placement recognizes that women do not like to wait with nothing to do, as boredom sets in and takes the fun out of power shopping.

Men do not like malls. Why? With the exception of computer components or tools, men do not like shopping. Underwear is an enlightening example. Underhill (2004) calls the men's underwear section in any department store the "dead zone." There is a reason for this: men don't buy underwear. Their wives or girlfriends buy them underwear, but only at Christmas or perhaps on their birthdays. Malls do not encourage male shoppers, either. Most stores are over-whelmingly geared to women. The few stores that might appeal to a man—bookstores, stereo and television stores, and sporting goods, are fast disappearing from malls. Some men do enjoy the social oppor-tunities in mall shopping—watching people, browsing but not buying, going to the food court, and any non-retail activities offered by the mall. Yet, the dearth of male shoppers in malls is now changing. Men are remaining single longer, and they are learning to shop. When they marry, they are expected to continue performing at least some of the shopping duties because their wives are working longer hours at more demanding careers (Underhill 1999). Those merchants that recognize the potential in this untapped market will reap economic rewards.

Women also like the social aspects of the mall, but social opportunities are secondary to shopping. Indeed, women have always been the targeted consumers. Women have historically shopped to provide for their households while men earned wages. Today, as major wage earners they have more disposable income for making purchases and more independence to make these purchases on their own. However, none of this explains why women *like* to shop more than men.

The organization of floor space in any store can have implications for the shoppers' experience, and perhaps the economic success of the store. Most shoppers have had negative experiences in certain stores—the "remind me never to shop there again" experience. Analyzing the reasons for negative experiences is difficult because they can vary even from one visit to another. Is the store too crowded? Is it difficult to find the products needed? Are the aisles too narrow, the shelves too high or not stocked? Are the clerks helpful or annoying, suspicious or friendly?

If asked, most women complain about poor merchandising—ignoring the needs of consumers. Complaints range from discontinuing favourite clothing items to a poor selection of sizes and colours, and repeated offerings of unwanted apparel—how many times can manufacturers push corduroy pants? I have often heard (and uttered) the comment that "the stores are full of merchandise I don't want or need, yet I can't find a pair of black cotton pants." Merchandisers are particularly hard on larger sized women who often struggle to find quality clothing in up-to-date styles at affordable prices. Women also protest not being able to find selections that are "just right" (Miller 2001).

Miller (2001) found that shopping and purchasing is determined to an extent by the consumers' ethnic, political, and ethical identity. For example, consumers may refuse to purchase products known to be manufactured in so-called sweatshops. Taste or choice in purchases may also be determined by various identities, such as class, age, gender, and ethnicity, although Miller (2001) found that choices are often influenced by our familial relationships, for example, the choices our parents have made in the past, or that our children are making now.

There is little doubt that mall operators like to encourage certain types of customers (e.g., middle-class families, professionals, teenagers with credit cards), and discourage others, (e.g., gang members, vagrants, or the poor). Some malls have experienced waves of crime, but, again, unsavoury characters or those of questionable behaviour are not encouraged to visit the malls. Instead, malls are filled with people of similar class, drawn together in a community of shoppers. Yet, even this seeming homogeneity is an illusion; a cross-section of diverse ethnic groups, age categories, and even socio-economic status are evident in most malls, perhaps even more so than in neighbourhood shopping centres that cater to distinct classes of similar age and economic situations. Aesthetics send messages regarding the expected clientele. Malls with marble flooring, glass and chrome elevators, bright lights and soothing music, and stores like Versace, Victoria's Secret, or Saks are catering to the middle and upper class, while malls with Wal-Mart and Dollar Stores are frequented by people looking for lower cost merchandise. In Shanghai, China, modern shopping malls are beautiful, enticing buildings. These malls are for the rich—those who wish to spend money. This is in sharp contrast to small stalls in local markets where many Shanghainese people and tourists search for low-cost merchandise.

THE FUTURE OF THE MALL

According to Underhill (2004) the mall era is in decline—it is no longer the defining concept of retail activity. In their heyday, malls transformed North American retail culture, but in the early years of the twenty-first century, they have lost some of their lustre. There are several reasons for the stagnation and even pending demise of the mall. First, mall developers were never savvy merchants, and they have been living on the laurels of earlier successes when water parks and Disney stores were a novelty. Since then, they have failed to develop new incentives to draw in potential customers. Some innovators (not mall owners or developers) have created ethnic specialty centres, such as the Crystal Mall in Burnaby, British Columbia, which caters to Chinese Canadians, or Koreatown Mall in Los Angeles, but these are few and far between.

Amazon.com, eBay, and other Internet shopping sites have also impacted on mall shopping. Why would anyone fight traffic, struggle to find a parking spot and the right merchandise in stores that increasingly seem not to understand consumer needs, when, with the click of a mouse, shoppers can order exactly what they need and have it delivered (often free) within a few days. Online shopping will likely continue as consumer demand increases, expanding into smaller establishments with worldwide customers.

Many people are too busy to shop, and when they must, the local strip mall or stand-alone shop is more convenient. Grocery stores have recognized this trend and are devoting half their floor space to hardware, kitchen/bath, and clothing items to create a one-stop shopping experience. Coffee shops, Internet cafés, and other similar venues can provide the same socializing outlets as malls.

A new factor at play in the demise of huge shopping malls is high fuel costs. Since Hurricanes Katrina and Rita in September of 2005, gasoline prices have skyrocketed in North America. CNN reports that consumers seem unwilling to drive to suburban malls, preferring to utilize strip malls and stand-alone stores in their neighbourhoods. Consequently, daily visits to and purchases at malls have declined significantly (CNN Headline News 2005). One way that mall owners can counter this decline is to consider further anthropological research into the meaning of shopping, and the ways they can ensure that shoppers find the experience of mall shopping worthwhile.

Conclusion

Economic anthropology and its sub-fields of corporate and retail anthropology are a growing method of research in the corporate world. These ethnographers have a great deal to offer corporations and retailers as they endeavour to understand consumers better. One area of particular interest is shopping, which is an important and meaningful human activity. Regardless of how we choose to perform this activity, the impact on the ever-evolving consumer culture and the economic well-being of our society should not be discounted. Retail anthropology, as an applied tool, has a significant role to play in improving the quality of our shopping experiences, and the economic viability of commercial districts. Underhill's work is a reflection of this new attitude in the corporate world.

Malls serve to fulfill the needs of shoppers. Many people consider shopping an enjoyable pastime, a form of relaxation and stress relief. The mall is a place of entertainment and leisure, a gathering place for friends and family to socialize and, of course, a place to shop. The role of malls has grown over the last 50 years, and has usurped other outlets, such as drive-in theatres and car-hop restaurants, as a place to socialize and be entertained.

Although on the surface malls appear fairly straightforward, further examination through the eyes of an anthropologist suggest that malls are complex socio-economic systems that perform many roles in contemporary society and, despite their waning popularity, will continue to do so for years to come.

Questions for Consideration

1.   When you enter a shopping mall, what factors influence your shopping patterns? Do you head to the shops with the best bargains, the nicest displays, the most selection, or are you selectively searching for a particular store to buy an already identified product?

2.   Does the availability of other entertainment besides shopping entice you to certain malls? What factors create a positive shopping experience for you, and what factors create a negative experience?

3. This chapter identified several functions of malls. Discuss other functions that were not mentioned.

4. Do you use the mall as a social outlet? Why or why not?

5. Create a chart identifying some uses of anthropological skills and knowledge in the business world.

6. Analyze your patronage of shopping malls. How have your patterns of behaviour when shopping changed since you were quite young? Do you access malls to the same extent as when you were younger or have you changed your preferences? Identify the reasons for your changing shopping patterns.

7. Develop a retail anthropology research project. Choose a store in a mall and describe the layout and use of floor space. Observe customers entering and leaving the store; describe their shopping behaviour. Is the store well organized and the merchandise easily accessible? Are the window displays appealing or distracting? Analyze the success (or failure) of this store in meeting the expectations and needs of its consumers.

NOTES

1 For further discussion of the problems with Nigeria Shell, see *Shell in Nigeria: What are the Issues?* on the World Wide Web at http://www.essentialaction.org/shell/issues.html or *Shell Nigeria Boycott* at http://www.thirdworldtraveler.com/Boycotts/ShellNigeria_boycott.html.

2 There are exceptions, such as Boston's Faneuil Hall and Fashion Show in Las Vegas (Underhill 2004).

3 A case in point, the (not so) Grand Mall in Maadi, Cairo, Egypt, which is repeatedly called an eyesore yet entices people, especially foreigners, to its stores full of inexpensive North American merchandise.

4 This is one area where modern malls have an economic and psychological edge over traditional *souks*, where a shopper is continually barraged with exhortations to "look for free" until the shopper is so annoyed and frustrated, he or she leaves without purchasing any goods.

References

ATKINSON, M. (2004, January). What has Margaret Mead got to do with shopping? *Thinking Retail*. J.C. Williams Group. Retrieved March 29, 2006, from the World Wide Web at http://www.jcwg.com/speeches.htm.

CARTER, A.T. (2001). Foreword. In D. Miller, *The dialectics of shopping* (pp. ix–xii). Chicago: The University of Chicago Press.

CNN HEADLINE NEWS (2005, October 6). Newscast.

DEUTSCH, C. (1991, February 24). Coping with cultural polyglots. *New York Times*.

GBN GLOBAL BUSINESS NETWORK. (2005). *GBN: Book Club Books*. Retrieved October 3, 2005, from the World Wide Web at http://www.gbn.com/BookClubNewsletterDisplayServlet.srv?dt=0101.

HAVILAND, W.A., FEDORAK, S., CRAWFORD, G., & LEE, R. (2005). *Cultural anthropology* (2nd Cdn. ed.). Toronto: Thomson Nelson Learning.

KLEIN, N. (1999). *No logo: Taking aim at the brand bullies*. Toronto: Alfred A. Knopf Canada.

MILLER, D. (1998). *A theory of shopping*. Cambridge, UK: Polity Press.

MILLER, D. (2001). *The dialectics of shopping*. Chicago: The University of Chicago Press.

NAPA. (2005). *Excavating consumer habits: Big business for anthropologists*. Retrieved March 29, 2006, from the World Wide Web at http://www.practicinganthropology.org/?newsid=42.

PLATTNER, S. (1989a). Preface. *Economic anthropology*. Stanford, CA: Stanford University Press.

PLATTNER, S. (1989b). Markets and marketplaces. In S. Plattner (Ed.), *Economic anthropology*. Stanford, CA: Stanford University Press.

SQUIRES, S. (1997). The market research and product industry discovers anthropology. *Anthropology Newsletter, 38*(4), 31.

SUCHMAN, L. (2003). *Anthropology as "brand": Reflections on corporate anthropology*. Centre for Science Studies, Lancaster University. Retrieved March 28, 2006, from the World Wide Web at http://www.lancs.ac.uk/fss/sociology/papers/suchman-anthropology-as-brand.pdf.

UNDERHILL, P. (1999). *Why we buy: The science of shopping*. New York: Simon & Schuster.

UNDERHILL, P. (2004). *Call of the mall*. New York: Simon & Schuster.

Suggested Readings

MILLER, D. (2001). *The dialectics of shopping*. Chicago: The University of Chicago Press.

This is an interesting examination of the dynamics of shopping. Although the writing is fairly academic in tone and directed toward fellow economic anthropologists, there is still much of interest to students curious about the meaning of shopping.

UNDERHILL, P. (2004). *Call of the mall*. New York: Simon & Schuster.

Underhill provides an entertaining and enlightening discussion of the significance of mall shopping, with a minimum of academic jargon. He also provides many examples to highlight his points about use of public space and consumer behaviour.

PART TWO

Why Does Anthropology Matter?

Anthropology is descriptive, explanatory, and issue-based, which has enabled anthropologists to view culture from a broad scope. In this section, we will examine several important issues that affect people and their cultural systems, and how anthropologists play or could play a role in understanding these issues.

The nine chapters in Part Two focus on four general topics: the human condition in body image and aging; the political nature of humans in ethnic conflict and immigration; equality issues in missionism, the practice of purdah, female circumcision, and same-sex marriage; and diffusion through media. Each of these chapters offers a holistic examination of the cultural group and the question at issue and provides a cross-cultural comparison. Cultural relativism, as a founding principle of anthropology, is evidenced in all of these discussions, and you will also note the presence of its antithesis, cultural imperialism, running through these chapters.

Culture is integrated; thus, systems of culture, such as internal and external political organization, can drastically impact on the rest of a culture. This becomes evident in Chapter 4, "What are the Underlying Reasons Behind Ethnic Conflict, and the Consequences of these Conflicts?" and Chapter 5, "What Challenges Do Immigrants in Canada Face?" The political nature of human interaction and the impact politics can have on the social, economic, and religious dynamics of a cultural group are emphasized here.

In the next three chapters, humans as social beings are examined from several directions. First, our desire to project a certain image in order to gain status, position, and security is investigated. In Chapter 6, "How Has the Push for the Perfect Body Impacted on the Self-Image, Health, and Comfort of Women?" we examine perceptions of beauty in the West, and the diffusion of these perceptions to other parts of the world. In Chapter 7, "Is Female Circumcision a Violation of Human Rights or a Cherished Cultural Tradition?" the ancient custom of altering female genitalia to become more desirable and attractive, and thereby gain a higher position within society, is examined. Western opposition to this practice and the cultural imperialism evident in this attitude is examined in some detail. In Chapter 8, "What Does it Mean to Grow Old?" the coping strategies people use to deal with their changing status as they age is examined from a cross-cultural perspective.

The reoccurring theme of cultural imperialism arises once again in Chapter 9, "What Impact Has Missionism Had on Indigenous Cultures?" and Chapter 10, "Is the Practice of Purdah and Wearing the Hijab Oppressive to Women or an Expression of Their Identity?" The influence of religious beliefs on our lifestyle and behaviour is considered from a cross-cultural perspective. In Chapter 11, "How Do Anthropologists View Same-Sex Marriages and Changing Family Structure? How Do We Define Marriage?" the interrelatedness of social norms, religious tenets, economic realities, and political manipulation regarding this contentious issue are all addressed from a cross-cultural perspective. In our final chapter, Chapter 12, "Has the Medium of Television Changed Human Behaviour and World Views?" the powerful influence of the media on our perceptions of the world around us, the diffusion of Western ideals to other parts of the world, and the impact this diffusion is having on culture change is addressed.

Each of these chapters offers a discussion of the issue and the work of anthropologists in this area. As you will see, the relevance of anthropology becomes particularly evident when trying to understand such difficult topics, although in several instances, such as the study of ethnic conflict and homosexuality, it is obvious that anthropologists have some work ahead before becoming significant contributors to the dialogue. Part Two is designed to show readers how anthropology matters in today's world, and how anthropology's role in understanding, mitigating, and sustaining cultural diversity will only increase in the coming years.

CHAPTER FOUR

What are the Underlying Reasons Behind Ethnic Conflict, and the Consequences of these Conflicts?

Introduction

The above question is difficult to answer given the many reasons behind what is euphemistically called **ETHNIC CONFLICT**. Those of us who have not had first-hand experience in a conflict situation cannot understand what it means to harbour memories of wrongdoings passed down through generations, or to deal with daily discrimination and exploitation based on ethnicity. These age-old resentments and a history of conflict and persecution can define a people, and influence their perceptions of the world around them.[1]

KEY TERMS: ethnic conflict, nationhood, discrimination, refugees, ethnic intolerance, cultural diversity, ethno-historical, advocacy and policy development, emic approach, ethnicity, ethnic groups, ethnic identity, ethnic boundary markers, nation, race, ethnic stratification, pluralism, genocide, ethnic cleansing, assimilation, acculturation, relocation, accommodation

Yet, this question is also misleading because it suggests that most conflict is due to ethnic differences, when in fact power struggles over territory, resources, and political dominance are far more likely to cause conflict. Indeed, many ethnic groups are seeking **NATION-HOOD** or increased autonomy within a state, and this can result in prolonged conflict. However, to suggest that historical grievances, ethnicity, and religion do not play a part in these conflicts is also an oversimplification of the situation. A case in point is the removal of Jewish inhabitants from the Gaza Strip on August 15, 2005. This relocation met with strong resistance in some settlements because the people believed that God had given them the land and they had an obligation to resist in His name.

Hatred of a group of people because of their ethnicity or "difference" has also resulted in persecution. The most notorious example of this is Hitler's extermination of Jews, Roma, Slavs, and homosexuals during World War II. More recently, the Rwandan massacre horrified the world with its carnage and senseless loss of life. The ongoing Darfur conflict in western Sudan is genocide in its most obvious form: government-supported Arab paramilitia, known as the Janjaweed, are terrorizing non-Arab peoples living in the region. In North America, Aboriginal peoples have a long history of conflict with Europeans who dispossessed them of their land and freedom, and in the United States, African Americans have experienced generations of **DISCRIMINATION**, exploitation, and hardship. Although all of these examples are predicated on economic and political factors, there is also a powerful element of social, religious, and ethnic prejudice against these ethnic groups.[2]

One of the consequences of ethnic conflict is displaced persons, also known as **REFUGEES**. Refugees are people who have been forced to flee their homes because they are not deemed to "belong." Anthropologists define refugees as "people who have undergone a violent 'rite' of separation" (Harrell-Bond & Voutira 1992: 6). Unless refugees are repatriated or find a permanent (non-refugee camp) home in their host country, they remain in a transient state that dramatically affects their legal, psychological, economic, and social status.

In this chapter we will examine the meaning of ethnicity, and the underlying conditions, such as **ETHNIC INTOLERANCE** and stratification that lead to ethnic conflict. The victims of these conflicts, refugees, and their adaptation to changing social and political conditions are also addressed. Although numerous cultural groups will be featured in an attempt to examine the issues surrounding ethnic conflict, the Kurds' struggle for autonomy in Iraq and the genocidal conflicts in the former Yugoslavia will be investigated in more detail. Ethnic conflict is considered from an anthropological perspective; however, historical and political data also contributes to the discussion in this chapter.

Anthropologists and Ethnic Conflict

Because of their proximity to cultural groups, anthropologists are uniquely qualified to address the question of ethnic conflict. Indeed, one of the major goals of anthropology has been to study **CULTURAL DIVERSITY**, and anthropologists have played a pivotal role in the preservation of ethnicity by documenting the traditions and customs of many of the world's ethnic groups. Anthropologists have also worked as advocates for the rights of indigenous peoples the world over, and they have studied violence, conflict, and warfare among pre-state societies. Where anthropological interpretation is somewhat lacking is in the study of ethnic conflict in state societies (Hinton 2002).

The reasons for anthropology's neglect of ethnic conflict are ambiguous. To study such a complex issue would require a multidisciplinary approach, one that many researchers might not wish to undertake, despite the lip service paid to its value (Harrell-Bond & Voutira 1992 from Baker 1983). As well, the study of ethnic conflict sits outside the parameters of "comfortable" anthropology, where anthropologists typically study well-established cultural systems in small-scale cultures. Displaced persons have always been perceived (erroneously) to live outside of these cultural systems, and they do not fit into a neat model of social change that "makes sense"—war does not make sense (Bringa 1995). Conflict, displacement, and suffering have all been considered temporary aberrations in an otherwise stable community, making these situations less enticing as research projects.[3]

Theoretical bias may also play a role in this negligence: there is a tendency to downplay violence and unhappiness because anthropologists want to promote the stability and efficacy of non-Western cultures (Harrell-Bond & Voutira 1992 from Colson 1989). To study victims of systematic violence, such as mass rape, has been outside the experience and training of most anthropologists.

Although anthropology has been strangely silent on the issue of ethnic conflict, in recent years the anthropology of genocide (Hinton 2002) and the anthropology of suffering (Davis 1992) have addressed at least some of the issues attached to ethnic conflict. Hinton (2002) argues that anthropology is uniquely positioned to determine why genocide occurs (a theoretical stance), and develop policies for preventing future genocides (an applied stance). An anthropological perspective could assist in understanding the **ETHNOHISTORICAL** causes of genocide, as well as consider the ways that genocide affects victims.

Davis (1992) criticizes most anthropologists for expending too much effort on studying orderly, harmonized social organizations, and neglecting disruption and despair—what Davis calls emergency anthropology. He believes that academic and applied anthropology can connect in the study of suffering, especially in the case of **ADVOCACY AND POLICY**

Anthropologist Tone Bringa, who conducted a study in a Bosnian village just prior to the war, reflects on the inadequacy of her preparation for an unstable situation: "My anthropological training had not prepared me to deal with the very rapid and total disintegration of the community I was studying." (BRINGA 1995: XVIII)

DEVELOPMENT, while Hinton (2002) suggests that understanding and mitigating genocide, the most extreme form of ethnic conflict, may be the twenty-first-century challenge for anthropologists.

One area where anthropologists have a great deal to contribute is in the study of refugees (Harrell-Bond & Voutira 1992). Anthropologists can investigate the implications of forced migration, and the events that create refugees. This is a significant research endeavour since an estimated 140 million people were uprooted in the twentieth century (Baker 1983). Anthropologists who document and interpret cultural diversity through ethnographic fieldwork are ideally situated to study the cultural changes that are inherent in displacement and the adaptations refugees must make to survive. Harrell-Bond and Voutira (1992: 7) found that "crossing a state border sharply affects power relations between members of the same ethnic group." They also examined the strategies that people employ to resist entering refugee camps.

Anthropologists can contribute to the understanding of social meanings attached to refugee status, and the consequences of being strangers or aliens in an unfamiliar environment. One area where anthropologists have already contributed is in investigating humanitarian work. Harrell-Bond (1986) found that despite the goodwill and largesse attached to providing aid, refugees are often treated as villains and the aid workers as figures of authority, meaning the refugees have little power or control over their own welfare (Harrell-Bond & Voutira 1992). Aid workers also tend to homogenize refugees, with little consideration for differing values, norms, and social organization among ethnic groups.

According to Waldron (1988), anthropologists are urgently needed to serve as cultural brokers—speaking on behalf of refugees (Harrell-Bond & Voutira 1992).[4] In this way, anthropology becomes relevant in the study of ethnic conflict. An example of anthropology's relevance is Gadi Ben-Ezer's (1990) work among Ethiopian Jews in Israel. Ben-Ezer applied an anthropological approach to his study of the Ethiopian refugees and their problems with authorities. He determined that the clashes were due to differing social norms, and the way the Ethiopians perceived proper interaction between people of differing status: "When children who had stopped eating were referred to him, he was able to identify their 'abnormal' behaviour (eating disorders ... arrests), caused by their experiences of uprooting and the tensions experienced in the process of adapting. He learned that the Ethiopians identified the abdomen as a 'container' of emotions. When it became 'too full' of only troubles and sorrows, the children were unable to eat" (Harrell-Bond & Voutira 1992: 8).

Anthropology brings its own unique perspective and methodology to the study of ethnicity and ethnic conflict. First, anthropologists attempt to take a holistic approach, examining ethnicity and ethnic conflict from an historical, economic, social, political, and religious perspective. As all of these systems play a pivotal role in ethnic conflict, they should not be ignored. Anthropologists also place the concept of culture in the forefront of their study of ethnicity and ethnic conflict. And finally, anthropologists take an **EMIC APPROACH**—listening to the people, and asking questions regarding the meaning of their ethnicity, the reasons behind the conflict, and so on, rather than imposing foreign interpretations on the issues. This is the most difficult task of all—keeping outsider views from the study. This emic approach has become increasingly important as ethnic groups have grown more insistent that their voices be heard and their true histories recounted.

Do anthropologists have the solutions to ethnic conflict? No. What they do have is the ability to understand the conflicts from a broad and holistic perspective using the comparative methods of anthropology. As anthropologists become increasingly involved in the study of ethnic conflict, they will become mediators between ethnic groups, and between refugees and authoritarian institutions.

A Discussion of Ethnicity and Ethnic Conflict

Any discussion of ethnic conflict would be remiss if the basic concepts of ethnicity, ethnic group, and ethnic identity, as well as nation, nationality, and race were not discussed. Indeed, these terms are often used interchangeably, and while there is a certain degree of overlap, we do need to address the differences as well.

ETHNICITY refers to a sense of identity based on cultural traits that have been passed down through the generations. Fenton (2003) suggests ethnicity is about the social construction of descent and culture that has meaning to the people. **ETHNIC GROUPS**, such as the Plains Cree of Canada, the Yoruba of Nigeria, or the Palestinians of Israel, each share a common identity, history, and territory of origin. Members of an ethnic group speak the same language, observe the same customs (e.g., dress, diet, entertainment), and/or hold relatively the same beliefs and values. An ethnic group shares a memory of its cultural past and a sense of continuity with the present and future. Most important, its members see themselves as distinct and separate from other groups. Although people have always shared a sense of group identity, the concept of **ETHNIC IDENTITY** is relatively new and primarily the product of modern politics, involving state building, colonization, and globalization (Bowen 1996; Crawford 1998). Today there are approximately 5,000 ethnic groups in the world (Eller 1999), many of whom are seeking recognition as distinct nations.

The **ETHNIC BOUNDARY MARKERS** of ethnic identity vary from one group to another, and can be quite elusive (De Vos 1995). Religion is one marker that can provide ethnic identity and a sense of who they are; for example, the Sikhs of India take their identity from their religious beliefs, which separate them from other Indians. Religious heritage may also serve to mobilize members of a group and strengthen their resolve in gaining recognition. The mythology or origin myths[5] of an ethnic group often preserve the memories of traditions, beliefs, and even an historical homeland. The Jews carried the mythology of a promised land (Israel) in their hearts for thousands of years. They realized their dream with the formation of the state of Israel in 1948. Other ethnic groups cherish the memory of an ancient place of origin; this is particularly true of groups who have immigrated to another country. For example, Ukrainian Canadian identity originates in several regions in the Ukraine (e.g., Karpatu) from which their ancestors immigrated. This is quite different from the Roma (Gypsies of Europe) who are nomadic and do not claim a homeland, yet possess an ethnic identity based on their lifestyle (De Vos 1995).

Language represents one of the most powerful markers of ethnic identity as is evident among the Québécois of Canada. Indeed, F.O. Call (1926: 41) recognized the importance of the French language 80 years ago when he travelled the territory of the original *Québécois de souche*:[6] "The soul of Canada is a dual personality and must remain only half revealed to those who know only one language." The Acadians of maritime Canada are another example: their language is an integral component of their ethnic identity, although they separate their culture from that of other French-speaking Canadians based on a distinctive history and heritage. Language serves as an ethnic marker even if the members no longer speak the language, but still share the heritage of this language. Jews in North America are a prime example of a group that does not exhibit the common characteristics of an ethnic group. Many Jews no longer attend synagogue, speak Yiddish or Hebrew, nor follow Jewish customs, yet they still consider themselves Jews. Their identity as a Jew fulfills the human need for historical continuity and a sense of belonging.

Physical appearance can also serve as an ethnic boundary marker, such as the distinctive features of Han Chinese.[7] Distinctive clothing and food such as Sikh turbans (*dastar*) and Hamitic Bedouin *jalabiyya*,[8] or Ukrainian perogies and Mexican tacos are symbols that make ethnic groups easily recognizable to outsiders. Regardless of the type of marker, they serve to distinguish one group from another and make them distinct from the larger society.

Despite the importance of ethnic boundary markers, they do not always denote an ethnic group. For example, Serbs and Croats speak the same language, Serbo-Croatian, yet they are distinct ethnic groups. The same can be said for religion—many groups of people the world over follow Islam, yet they are from diverse ethnic groups. For example, the Samals of the Philippines, the Moors of Sri Lanka, and the Pashtun of Afghanistan are all Muslim. Obviously, it can be quite difficult to determine whether a group of people constitute a true ethnic group.[9]

Although ethnic groups tend to share a common set of cultural features, they are seldom homogenous. Take, for example, the Kurds, who possess a strong ethnic identity yet exhibit linguistic variation, hold differing religious beliefs, and lack a coherent homeland (Eller 1999 from Izady 1992). The degree to which ethnic identity is important to a group also varies. In some groups, such as the Palestinians, ethnic identity has considerable importance, whereas in others, it is trivial and hardly acknowledged. This is most evident in countries such as Canada, where the descendants of nineteenth- and early twentieth-century immigrants may seldom consider their ancestry.[10]

New ethnic groups may also arise. For example, Mexican, Peruvian, Chilean, and Guatemalan ethnic groups evolved out of the Spanish who immigrated to North America and mated with indigenous peoples already living in North and South America. Thus, the merging of two or more ethnic groups may create new ethnic groups. When French and Scottish voyageurs married First Nations women in Canada during the fur trade era, their offspring became known as the Métis. African Americans have recently been redefining themselves in terms of ethnicity by searching for their pan-African heritage (De Vos 1995). They are discovering their territorial origins in Africa, and revitalizing traditional customs, artistic expressions, and religious practices. Thus, ethnic identity is a constantly evolving concept.

Quite similar to the concept of ethnicity and ethnic groups, is the idea of **NATION** or nationhood. Haviland et al. (2005: 326) define nation as "communities of people who see themselves as 'one people' on the basis of common ancestry, history, society, institutions, ideology, language, territory, and often religion." How, then, is nationality different from ethnicity? Strictly speaking they are the same; however, nationality can encompass several ethnic groups that are politically unified (De Vos 1995). Eller (1999: 144) believes a nation must fulfill certain requirements to be called a nation: "a common culture, a consciousness of shared identity, and political organization toward a national goal." The Kurds of Iran and the many First Nations of Canada consider themselves nations that as yet do not possess autonomy, although they continue to work toward that goal.

RACE is a difficult term to define, partly because it is based on erroneous facts. Usually race refers to a group of people who have been categorized based on biological and behavioural traits. However, people cannot be definitively categorized into specific "racial" groups based on any type of rigorous scientific data. This means the concept of race is culturally constructed according to economic, political, and social agendas, rather than a biological reality. Even in the 1920s, Franz Boas debunked the concept of race, stating that "(1) a race is not an objective or demonstrable descent group; (2) there is as much physical variation within a race as between races; (3) there are no clear-cut geographical and biological lines between the races; and (4) there is no correlation between race on the one hand and either mental or cultural characteristics on the other" (Eller 1999: 57 from Boas 1932).

Boas' contentions remain true today. For example, a Northern European may be genetically more similar to a San from southern Africa than with someone from Italy. These determinants are based on numerous genetically based characteristics. Skin colour is often used as a criteria for separating people into "races." However, skin pigmentation is merely an adaptive response to ultraviolet radiation and varies considerably even within the same population. The only clear biological difference between populations is blood type, but blood types do not correspond with the so-called racial categories. As well, human populations have always interbred, thereby mixing genetic traits. Despite these challenges, the term "race" continues to be used as a primary identity marker, just as some people continue to categorize themselves and others into racially defined groups that they rank according to traits deemed superior or inferior.

Before moving on to the major focus of this chapter, ethnic conflict, it is important to understand the concept and process of **ETHNIC STRATIFICATION**, which in many cases is the precursor to ethnic conflict, and at the very least is a less overt form of conflict between ethnic groups. Stratification means placing groups in a hierarchy of superior versus inferior. Ethnic stratification limits access of identified groups to reasonable wealth, power, and prestige—three important components to the well-being of an ethnic group. In a stratified society, people are ranked relative to other ethnic groups and face varying degrees of inequality.

In Canada numerous ethnic groups have been viewed as inferior and undesirable—although the group(s) pinpointed as inferior change from one time to another. As evident in the sidebar, when Ukrainians began immigrating to Canada at the end of the nineteenth century, Canadians of French and English descent were less than enthusiastic.

Discrimination, exploitation, and inequality breeds resentment and hostile relationships between ethnic groups, which given the right circumstances and incentives leads to ethnic conflict.

ETHNIC CONFLICT

Ter-Gabrielian (1999: 1) defines ethnic conflict as "a conflict between two or more ethnic groups, one of which possesses the actual state power."[11] According to Hammel (1997) during the Neolithic period kinship groups grew in size and eventually became ethnic groups. Some of these ethnic groups gained dominance over the other ethnic groups and a form of imperialism eventually developed. Herein lies the root of many present-day ethnic conflicts. This imperial domination can take several forms. One dominant group may control several other ethnic groups, with some solidarity developing between the dominated ethnic groups. In some cases, the subordinate (dominated) groups may also be in competition with each other for limited resources, which creates discord. There may also be several dominant ethnic groups in

An article appeared in the Winnipeg Telegram on May 13, 1901, expressing this aversion: That there are few people who will affirm that Slavonic immigrants are desirable settlers, or that they are welcomed by the white people of Western Canada…. Those whose ignorance is impenetrable, whose customs are repulsive, whose civilization is primitive, and whose character and morals are justly condemned, are surely not the class of immigrants which the country's paid immigration agents should seek to attract. Better by far to keep our land for the children, children's children, of Canadians than to fill up the country with the scum of Europe. (CHENEY 2000) competition for resources and power over other subordinate ethnic groups.

Much of the ethnic conflict today can be traced to European colonialism in the nineteenth century, when political boundaries were created with little consideration for ethnicity or historic homelands. When European colonial powers began granting independence to these colonies in the twentieth century, dominant ethnic groups quickly seized power to the detriment of other ethnic groups—this is what happened in Rwanda. The Belgians took control of Rwanda in 1912, and began a policy of favouring the Tutsi, whom they believed were the elite, with education and jobs, while excluding the seemingly lower-class and impoverished Hutus. When the Belgians left Rwanda, Hutu extremists seized power and, spurred on by media spewing hatred against the Tutsis and other political manoeuvers by local and national leaders, massacred a million Tutsis (Bowen 1996). Some have questioned whether the Hutu and Tutsi are actually separate ethnic groups.[12] However, for the purpose of this discussion, we will take the stance that one identified ethnic group perpetuated genocidal violence against another.

Ethnic conflict is rampant around the world: the Irish Republican Army versus the British government; the Serbs' ethnic cleansing of Bosniaks[13] in the former Yugoslavia; Palestinian and Israeli violence in Israel; Kurdish separatist movements in Iraq and Turkey; Rwandan genocide; Mohawk First Nations protests at Oka, Quebec, and ethno-nationalist conflicts on the periphery of Russia. Although by no means a comprehensive list, the prevalence of ethnic conflicts worldwide is a sobering reality—what Brubaker (2004: 88) calls the "new world disorder."

Most modern states are pluralistic, which means more than one ethnic group exists within its borders. The **PLURALISM** in Western states is fairly obvious, but even in smaller states ethnic diversity is pronounced. For example, in Tanzania 120 ethnic groups coexist, many of whom are experiencing an ethnic resurgence (Omari 1987).[14] Although some pluralistic states, such as Switzerland and Belgium, have managed to maintain peace and harmony, pluralism often results in discord that can spill over into ethnic conflict. Yet, this conflict is not *ethnic* in nature; rather, it is most likely due to economic, religious, or political factors (often all three), such as claims to territory and resources—what Ter-Gabrielian (1999) terms "conflict of secession."

In conflict of secession, an ethnic group, or several as the case may be, wishes to separate from the home state and create its own state. This form of ethnic conflict often escalates into open warfare. Of considerable note is the continuous ethnic conflict between the Palestinians and Israelis. In 1948 the state of Israel was established in former Palestine. Conflict between the Palestinians and Israelis escalated over the next 60 years. As previously mentioned, the underlying reason for this conflict is a claim to the same homeland. Palestinians claim an historic occupation of the region, while Israelis claim the same region on the basis of religious beliefs that the land is rightfully theirs (De Vos 1995).

Oftentimes one ethnic group attempts to gain more autonomy and freedom, or conversely, a group seeks political power or dominance over other ethnic groups within the state—what Ter-Gabrielson (1999) terms "conflict of replacement." In conflict of replacement, one ethnic group wants to replace another at the centre of power. In this case, genocide is a very real possibility. The genocide in Rwanda is a good example of replacement conflict. The Hutus attempted to exterminate the Tutsis in revenge for past humiliations. Both of these directions lead to ethnic conflict, suppression, and even genocidal violence (Binder 1999).

The deliberate extermination of an ethnic group is known as **GENOCIDE**, or as has become popular in the media, **ETHNIC CLEANSING**. Genocide almost always has an economic or political motivation. For example, the attempted extermination of the Yanomami in Venezuela is predicated on Western mining companies wanting the minerals beneath the Yanomami land. The gold rush in the mid-1980s brought thousands of illegal miners onto Yanomami territory. Since then the Yanomami have suffered numerous repercussions from this intrusion: noise from supply planes has frightened away game animals, and the river banks have been eroded by high-pressure hose mining. Mercury, which is used to separate the gold from rock, has poisoned the rivers, causing serious problems in the ecosystem and creating neurotoxins in the Yanomami food supply that threatens child development. With little curtailment from politicians or the business elite, miners continued their assaults on the Yanomami. In July 1993, a group of miners attempted to exterminate the entire village of Haximu, and killed 16 Yanomami (Survival International 2006). The Brazilian Attorney General Aristides Junqueira aptly called this action genocide.

The culture clash experienced by the Yanomami reaches beyond the homicidal acts of a few miners and has been ongoing for nearly a half century. Indeed, by the late 1950s, missionaries had reached the Yanomami and set about converting them to Christianity, Brazilians looked to them for cheap labour, the governments of Venezuela and Brazil sought to control them, and anthropologists such as Napoleon Chagnon studied them (Peters 1998). Today the Yanomami are facing increasing pressure on their territory as governments and large commercial mining corporations want access to their mineral-rich land (Albert 1999).

REFUGEES

As mentioned earlier, populations of displaced persons, known as refugees, are one of the consequences of ethnic conflict. Seventy-eight per cent of the world's refugees come from 10 countries: Afghanistan, Angola, Burma, Burundi, Congo-Kinshasa, Eritrea, Iraq, Palestine, Somalia, and Sudan (Human Rights Watch 2004). In the twentieth century, the preponderance of refugees created a vast network of permanent international welfare and institutionalized assistance composed of government agencies, UNHCR (United Nations High Commissioner on Refugees), and NGOs (non-government organizations) (Harrell-Bond & Voutira 1992). The most obvious form of aid is the establishment of refugee camps in "trouble spots" to accommodate displaced people. Conditions in these camps vary greatly, but most anthropologists agree that refugee camps are part of the problem, not the solution.

One of the problems with refugee camps is the culture of dependency created through the humanitarian aid. The food, clothing, shelter, always in short supply, nonetheless lead to dependency and disempowerment of the refugees. In essence the administrators of refugee camps control the refugees' well-being and future survival. As in similar situations, it is the women and children who suffer the most.

Despite this perceived disempowerment, when Makkli (1990) conducted an ethnographic study of a refugee camp in Tanzania, she found that refugee camps provided people with an opportunity to create a collective narrative of their experiences. Close assembly of people of the same ethnicity in the camps created a sense of cohesiveness not found among refugees settled in urban centres (Harrell-Bond & Voutira 1992).

For anthropologists, the study of refugees offers a chance to record and interpret the processes of culture change that reach far beyond systems of transition found within a small-scale society. They have the opportunity to witness the cultural adaptations of refugees to survive the upheaval they are faced with in a new social, economic, and physical

"I want to send my message, this message, to our friends, the other indigenous peoples, and to our white friends too, those who stand by our side, who support us. I want to communicate my news and my message, my feelings and my needs. My full name is Davi Kopenaua Yanomami. The village I live in is called Watoriketheri. It is in the Mountains of the Wind.

"My Yanomami people know, they see what is happening to our community, and they see what is happening to our relatives in other communities. They are terrified of the miners, by the [polluted] rivers.

"The miners invaded our reserve and came to our communities feigning friendship; they lied to us, they tricked us Indians, and we were taken in. Then their numbers grew; many more arrived, and they began bringing in machinery that polluted the river. The pollution killed the fish and the shrimp, everything that lived in our rivers."

YANOMAMI ELDER DAVI KOPENAWA (AMERICAN ANTHROPOLOGICAL ASSOCIATION 2006)

A displaced family on the outskirts of Bucaramanga, Columbia.

environment (Harrell-Bond & Voutira 1992).

THE BOSNIAN CONFLICT

Although the Serbs, Croats, and Bosniaks are considered distinct ethnic groups, they are in many ways very similar. They speak the same language, have lived similar lives, and enjoyed relative peace for many centuries. It is religion that separates these three ethnic groups: the Croats are Roman Catholic, the Serbs, Orthodox Christian, and the Bosniaks, Muslim. However, each of these groups includes members that follow the other two religions, and rising rates of intermarriage would have eventually blurred these religious and ethnic distinctions (Bowen 1996).[15] Indeed, Hammel (1997: 8) calls intermarriage "the ultimate blurring of ethnic boundaries."

The 1990s Serbian extermination of Bosniaks and Croats in the former Yugoslavia was based on political motivation, although the reasons for this ugly page in Eastern European history are complex. Bringa (1995: 3) discounts both the "age-old hatred" model of ethnic conflict and the "peaceful co-existence" approach. In the village where she lived, neither model fit: "there was both co-existence and conflict, tolerance and prejudice, suspicion and friendship." In this case, we witnessed ethnicity becoming nationalism along with aspirations for a monopoly on land, resources, and power (Bowen 1996). Nationalism grew in each region as leaders, such as Marshal Tito, gave the Serbs power in Croatia, and Croats power in Belgrade after World War II. By the 1980s, Yugoslavia was in a state of economic crisis and suffered from a weak central government that created fear in the people. Serbian president Slobodan Milosevic tapped into Serbian nationalism and their desire to expand their territory, while Croatia's president Franjo Tudjman played on Croatian exclusionary nationalism to build a following. Both leaders manipulated history for their own purposes, but also had to dispel the Yugoslavian civil identity and replace it with "ethnic identities"—a divide and conquer strategy. Thus, political manipulation created an atmosphere of distrust and fear in Yugoslavia in the early 1990s: Milosevic persuaded Serbs that all Croats were crypto-Nazi Ustashe—an underground militant organization historically linked to Nazism, and Tudjman convinced the Croats that Serbs were Chetnik assassins bent on controlling the Balkans. Both leaders convinced their people that Bosnian Muslims were the front wave of an Islamic threat.[16] The media also played an influential role in inciting Serbian hatred that harkened back to Serb massacres perpetuated by the Croats during World War II (Bowen 1996).

When Croatia, Bosnia, Slovenia, and Macedonia declared their independence from Yugoslavia in 1991, leaving only Serbia and Montenegro in Yugoslavia, the Serbs in Croatia and Bosnia rebelled, and a bloody war ensued (Brubaker 2004). By 1995, 200,000 people had

ANTHROPOLOGY MATTERS!

died, half the population of Bosnia had become refugees, and the Serb population in Croatia was forced to flee (Crawford 1998).

Anthropologist Tone Bringa spent 18 months living in a mainly Muslim community in Bosnia just before war broke out, and returned in 1993 during the hostilities. She found that what shocked and hurt the people of her village the most was when neighbour turned on neighbour in what had always been a fairly peaceful coexistence between

Serbia

> "Women are often alone, because they lost their family or because the family split after displacement … [b]ut they are courageous and, no matter what, they stick to their children. What is awful is when it is their children who become victims of the violence. I feel very helpless when that happens to my friends."
>
> OLGA LUCIA RODRIQUEZ, A REFUGEE IN COLOMBIA (UNHCR, THE UN REFUGEE AGENCY 2001–06)

Catholic and Muslim residents. During the conflict, the person next door became "a depersonalized alien, a member of the enemy ranks" (Bringa 1995: xvi). When the conflict was over, some Muslims[17] returned to their villages, but the wounds from inter-communal violence take a long time to heal, and people remain socially distant.

Out of Bringa's fieldwork came a book, *Being Muslim the Bosnian Way* (1995), which recounts the story of a community and its people before war destroyed their lives. In many ways, this book epitomizes anthropological fieldwork—it is a description of real lives and real people that has been preserved for future generations. In the case of Bosnian Muslims, Bringa's work preserves a way of life that has been all but lost.

KURDISH SEPARATIST MOVEMENTS

The Kurds are a vast ethnic group that lives in the mountainous regions of Iraq, Turkey, Syria, and Iran in their self-proclaimed state of Kurdistan.[18] This segmentation was created after World War I, when the Ottoman Empire was carved up and the Kurds found themselves widely dispersed. The fierce independence and nomadic pastoralism they had always enjoyed was then curtailed.

The majority of Kurds are Sunni Muslims in Turkey and Iraq, while 6–7 per cent are Shi'ites in Iran.[19] Kurds speak several dialects of the "Kurdish language." The vast majority speak Kurmanji in Turkey, Syria, and the former Soviet Union. In Iran and Iraq, the Kurds speak Sorani, while Kurdi is spoken by Kurds in southern Iran and Iraq, Zaza in Turkey and northern Iraq, and a Persian dialect in southeastern Kurdistan (Eller 1999).

The Kurds came to the attention of the world during the 1991 Persian Gulf War (Eller 1999) when they demanded an autonomous state, Kurdistan; however, Kurdish struggles to gain autonomy and freedom date back to at least the early nineteenth century. The Iraqi government quickly put down the 1991 uprising, and two million Kurds fled to Turkey and Iran. Saddam Hussein also punished the Kurds of Iraq for supporting Iran in the 1980–88 war by destroying their villages and attacking them with chemical weapons. Following the Gulf War, the United Nations established a no-fly zone in northern Iraq to protect the Kurds from Saddam Hussein.

Besides ruthless repression from national governments and sporadic international support, the Kurds face several internal challenges to their quest for nationhood. They are not a harmonious, cohesive group; tribal divisions and rivalries between leaders hamper any nationalistic movements and prevent them from developing a unified Kurdish identity. Two Iraqi Kurdish factions—the Kurdistan Democratic Party, led by Massoud Barzani, and the Patriotic Union of Kurdistan are constantly involved in shifting alliances, petty feuds, competition, and treachery as they vie for land, wealth, power, and prestige (The Washington Post 1999). These Kurdish factions are opportunistic and in a constant state of flux.

Despite their dispersal and lack of an officially recognized homeland, the Kurds identify themselves as an ethnic group, and possess a deep sense of ethnic consciousness that makes them an ethnic group. Whether they will be able to establish their homeland of Kurdistan and gain international recognition of their ethnic identity remains to be seen.

RESOLUTION OF ETHNIC CONFLICT

Attempts to resolve various forms of ethnic conflict have taken several directions: assimilation, acculturation, relocation, genocide, and accommodation.

ASSIMILATION involves the absorption of an ethnic group into a more dominant group, resulting in their disappearance. The dominant group is favoured; their language becomes the official language, and

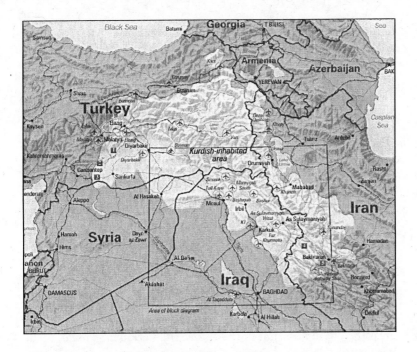

Region inhabited by Kurds

the education and other institutions of culture are designed to nurture the dominant ethnic group while marginalizing other ethnic groups. During the colonial period, assimilation was the official ideology for "civilizing" indigenous ethnic groups. Assimilationist policies may offer incentives, such as economic opportunities and political representation to make assimilation more attractive.

ACCULTURATION is a more vigorous form of assimilation, often involving coercion or use of force. For example, in Franco's Spain, the Basques were banned and the Eskedun language was prohibited in public (Ter-Gabrielian 1999). In the New World, the Spanish forcefully converted the Aztecs and other Meso-American peoples to Christianity through coercion, force, and even death.

RELOCATION or forced migration results in the removal of groups of people from their territory. One million Turks were forced to leave Bulgaria and settle in Turkey in 1987, and 74,000 Asinias were removed from Uganda in 1972 (Ter-Gabrielian 1999). During the nineteenth century, First Nations peoples in Canada and the United States were removed from their lands and placed on desolate reservations that until recently were little more than undeveloped prisons.[20]

As previously discussed, the most violent "solution" to ethnic conflict is genocide. Historic examples of genocide are numerous: in 1915, 1.8 million Armenians were murdered in the Ottoman Empire and the Caucasus; in the Soviet Union, Chechens, Tatars, and others were exterminated after World War II because of alleged collaboration with the Nazis; during Stalin's rule, 40 to 60 million Russians were murdered; in 1971, 1.2–3 million Bengalis were killed by the Pakistani army (resulting in the secession of Bangladesh); and in 1972 the Tutsis murdered 200,000 Hutus (Ter-Gabrielian 1999).

These solutions seldom work; ethnic groups are tenacious and have long memories of wrongdoings that fester until sooner or later their nationalism resurfaces, and often erupts in violence against the perpetrators of their past suffering. The Serbs justified their genocidal acts against the Croats on the basis of massacres perpetuated by the Croats during World War II. Ethnic groups may bide their time until circumstances allow them to reassert their nationhood. Such is the case in the former USSR, where ethnic conflict was ruthlessly extinguished after the Bolshevik Revolution, only to resurface in regions such as Chechnya after the collapse of the Soviet Union (Ter-Gabrielian 1999).

Accommodating the needs of an ethnic group may build more peaceful relations. An example of this type of **ACCOMMODATION** is found in Canada, where French- and English-speaking nationalities are an example of a working (albeit constantly challenged) model of ethnic co-operation. Despite periodic separatist rumblings and even the possibility that in the future the nation may break up, it has been a relatively peaceful association.[21] This early accommodation has paved the way for other ethnic groups to peacefully coexist in Canada.

Accommodation is rare because it counters the one nation-one state ideology so firmly entrenched in state societies as the most effective way to govern. There is a fear that power sharing will eventually result in a splintering of the state. Indeed, this happened in Czechoslovakia when Slovakia seceded only one year after the Czech and Slovak federal republics were formed. Nevertheless, this was a peaceful separation, called the Velvet Divorce (Slovakia.org n.d.). Ter-Gabrielian (1999) points out that where conflict was resolved through compromise, as in South Tyrol,[22] conflict disappeared because of accommodation. The August 2005 departure of Israelis from the Gaza Strip, although a heart-wrenching and emotional process, illustrates the potential for peace if compromise and accommodation are employed. If this first step succeeds in bringing peace to the people of Israel, then it may serve as a model for other states embroiled in seemingly insurmountable ethnic conflict.[23]

These four methods of resolving conflict are not mutually exclusive of each other. Indeed, the treatment of First Nations peoples in Canada is a classic example of employing all of these methods. In western Canada, Euro-Canadians attempted to assimilate First Nations—removing children from their communities and families to live at residential schools where they would learn the "white man's way." As the number of European settlers grew and they pushed westward, First Nations groups were relocated to reservations to free up the land for farming. Although some would argue that acculturation was not an official policy, removing children from their homes and forcing bands to settle on reserves contained a strong element of acculturation. Examples of genocide were more common to the south, but nonetheless, the Beothuk of Newfoundland are an example of a First Nations group in Canada that was exterminated by Euro-Canadians. Today, socio-political relations with First Nations peoples have become much more accommodating: First Nations are more in control of their own well-being, including education, justice, and social welfare.

Conflict resolution has proven elusive in most regions of the world. There are several reasons why this is so. States often fail or refuse to recognize that there is a problem until violence erupts, and even then they seldom take the necessary steps to diffuse tensions. Rather than listening and attempting to accommodate the needs of ethnic groups, states choose confrontational methods to put down an uprising, leading to escalation of the conflict (Ter-Gabrielian 1999). The international community is also slow to intervene, often waiting until many innocent people have been murdered and the situation has deteriorated past redemption, as in the case of Darfur, Sudan, where thousands of people have been displaced or murdered with little more than lip service from other countries. Peacemaking is seldom the goal of states or international organizations. Rather, they seek to contain the situation, which only exacerbates the conflict. The international community is also slow to recognize the legitimate claims and status of ethnic groups.

Conclusion

Ethnic conflict is a complex issue wrapped up in political, social, religious, and economic factors. As should be obvious by now, the term "ethnic conflict" is somewhat of a misnomer. Although ethnic groups are at the centre of these conflicts, the underlying reasons have little to do with ethnicity, and everything to do with power. Nonetheless, the incidence of this so-called ethnic conflict appears to be on the rise.

The pressing issue of millions of displaced persons living out their lives in horrendous conditions makes it imperative that anthropologists work to understand the phenomenon of ethnic conflict. The future of anthropology and the study of ethnic conflict lies in the people themselves, rather than larger nationalistic processes. This is evident in recent endeavours, such as the anthropology of suffering that embodies a shift in anthropological attention. According to Harrell-Bond & Voutira (1992), recognizing that survival, loss, and suffering are part of the permanent human condition will make anthropology politically relevant and remove the aura of detachment still prevalent in academic anthropology.

Questions for Consideration

1.   The question is often asked whether conflict can be reduced if ethnic minority groups are encouraged to assimilate into mainstream society (whatever that means). Do you agree or disagree with a policy of assimilation? Explain your stand. What would we gain if everyone identified with one homogenous "ethnic" group? What would we lose?

2.   In this question, focus on the individual. We have all heard a great deal about the harmful effects of racism and ethnic prejudice on the victims. But have you ever thought about the perpetrators—the people who hold these views, and how these attitudes affect their lives? In other words, have you ever met a happy bigot? Create a list of the ways racists limit their lives because of their views.

3.   Choose a nation and research the history of ethnic conflict. What are the underlying causes of this conflict? What level has this conflict reached, and have any of the issues been resolved?

4.   What does ethnicity mean to you? Do you identify with an ethnic group? Why or why not?

5.   Research the term "race." What criteria have been used to categorize people into different races? Examine the weaknesses with these criteria. Why have these criteria failed to work for every group?

6.   Locate a refugee camp (e.g., Darfur) and research the economic, social, political, and religious organization found within this camp. How do these systems of culture enable the refugees to survive camp life? Are these systems as well-developed as in cultures outside a camp environment?

NOTES

1   Davis (1992) has suggested that war is embedded in the social experience of many cultures, including Americans. For these populations, war, loss, and suffering is a part of their world view and their culture.

2   Ethnic group will be used here because as you will see later in this chapter, the validity of the term "race" is questionable.

3   Since refugee camps have been in existence for several decades, and many people spend their entire lives living in a camp, the attitude that they are temporary must change.

4   Preferably, anthropologists will find ways for the refugees to speak for themselves.

5   The terms "myth" and "mythology" are not meant to suggest falsehoods.

6   For a detailed discussion of the *Québécois de souche*, see Fedorak, S. (2006). *Windows on the world*. Toronto: Thomson Nelson Learning.

7   China officially has 56 distinct ethnic groups within its borders.

8   A long, hooded robe.

9   I would suggest that if a group of people self-define as an ethnic group, then they are an ethnic group, regardless of what categories outsiders may employ.

10   Many of my students, most of whom are third-generation Canadians, have "lost" the ethnic identity of their great-grandparents, and only consider themselves Canadian.

11   State power refers to the group that controls the economic, political, and religious systems of a nation; in other words, a group that dominates and controls the society.

12   See Bowen (1996).

13   Formerly known as Muslims.

14   The original inhabitants of Tasmania were exterminated by colonialists in the 1800s—a classic case of genocide.

15   During hostilities some people were forced at gunpoint to declare their ethnic and religious allegiance since intermarriage made it unclear.

16   In the former Yugoslavia, the term "Muslim" referred to their religion, but also represented a nation within Yugoslavia that set them apart from Serbs and Croats (Bringa 1995).

17   Mostly the elderly, while young people had found new homes in urban centres where they were employed.

18   Although the Kurds recognize the state of Kurdistan, the international community has not acknowledged the state or the Kurd claim to the region.

19   There are two main branches of Islam: the Sunnis and Shi'ites. The Sunni branch recognizes heirs of the four caliphs (Muhammad's successors) as the leaders of Muslims, while the Shi'ites only recognize the heirs of the fourth caliph, Ali. Sunnis comprise 85–90 per cent of Muslims today. Shi'ite Muslims empower their clergy to serve as mediators between God and humans, whereas the Sunni interact with God directly, and their clergy act only as advisors. Shi'ites believe that the imams are descendants of Ali.

20   People were not allowed to leave the reservations unless they had the permission of the Indian Agent.

21   An exception to this statement is the bombings, robberies, and murders perpetuated by the *Front de libération du Québec* (FLQ) in the 1970s, which forced Prime Minister Trudeau to implement the *War Measures Act*.

22   A province of Italy that gained its autonomy after World War II. The largely German-speaking population now enjoys close relations with Austria and a degree of self-rule within Italy.

23   The resurgence of violence in the Gaza Strip in the summer of 2006 and the bombardment of Lebanon calls this statement into question.

References

ALBERT, B. (1999). *Yanomami*. Retrieved March 6, 2005, from the World Wide Web at http://www.socioambiental.org/pib/epienglish/yanomami/yanomami.shtm.

AMERICAN ANTHROPOLOGICAL ASSOCIATION. (2006). *Interview with Davi Kopenawa Yanomami*. Retrieved March 6, 2006, from the World Wide Web at http://www.aaanet.org/committees/cfhr/rptyano5.htm.

BAKER, R. (1983). *The psychosocial problems of refugees*. British Refugee Council and European Consultation on Refugees and Exiles. Luton: L and T Press.

BEN-EZER, G. (1990). Anorexia nervosa or an Ethiopian coping style? *Mind and Human Interaction, 2* (October).

BINDER, L. (1999). Introduction. The international dimensions of ethnic conflict in the Middle East. In L. Binder (Ed.), *Ethnic conflict and international politics in the Middle East* (pp. 1–40). Gainesville: University Press of Florida.

BOAS, F. (1932). *Anthropology and modern life*. New York: W.W. Norton.

BOWEN, J.R. (1996). The myth of global ethnic conflict. *Journal of Democracy, 7*(4), 3–14.

BRINGA, T. (1995). *Being Muslim the Bosnian way*. Princeton, NJ: Princeton University Press.

BRUBAKER, R. (2004). *Ethnicity without groups*. Cambridge, MA: Harvard University Press.

CALL, F.O. (1926). *The spell of French Canada*. Boston, MA: L.C. Page & Co.

CHENEY, B. (2000, October 28). *Ukrainian immigration*. Retrieved March 13, 2001, from the World Wide Web at http://www.mbnet.mb.ca/~rfmorris/Featuring/Immigration/Ukrainian.Immigration.html.

COLSON, E. (1989). Overview. *Annual Review of Anthropology, 18*, 1–16.

CRAWFORD, B. (1998). The causes of cultural conflict: An institutional approach. In B. Crawford & R.D. Lipschut (Eds.), *The myth of "ethnic conflict": Politics, economics, and "cultural" violence* (pp. 3–43). Berkeley: University of California Press.

DAVIS, J. (1992). The anthropology of suffering. *Journal of Refugee Studies, 5*(2), 149–161.

DE VOS, G.A. (1995). Concepts of ethnic identity. In L. Romanucci-Ross & G.A. De Vos (Eds.), *Ethnic identity, creation, conflict, and accommodation* (3rd ed., pp. 15–47). Walnut Creek: Altamira Press.

ELLER, J.D. (1999). *From culture to ethnicity to conflict: An anthropological perspective on international ethnic conflict*. Ann Arbor: The University of Michigan Press.

FEDORAK, S. (2006). *Windows on the world: Case studies in anthropology*. Toronto: Thomson Nelson Learning.

FENTON, S. (2003). *Ethnicity*. Cambridge, UK: Polity Press.

HAMMEL, E.A. (1997). Ethnicity and politics. Yugoslav lessons for home. *Anthropology Today, 13*(3), 5–9.

HARRELL-BOND, B.E. (1986). *Imposing aid: Emergency assistance to refugees*. Oxford: Oxford University Press.

HARRELL-BOND, B.E. (2000). Are refugee camps good for children? New Issues in Refugee Research. Working Paper No. 29. *The Journal of Humanitarian Assistance*. Retrieved March 8, 2006, from the World Wide Web at http://www.jha.ac/articles/u029.htm.

HARRELL-BOND, B.E., & VOUTIRA, E. (1992). Anthropology and the study of refugees. *Anthropology Today*, 8(4), 6–10.

HAVILAND, W.A., FEDORAK, S.A., CRAWFORD, G., & LEE, R.B. (2005). *Cultural anthropology* (2nd Cdn. ed.). Toronto: Thomson Nelson Learning.

HINTON, A.L. (2002). *Annihilating difference: The anthropology of genocide.* Berkeley: University of California Press.

HUMAN RIGHTS WATCH. (2004). *Refugees and Displaced Persons*. Retrieved March 8, 2006, from the World Wide Web at http://www.hrw.org/doc/?t=refugees&document_limit=0,2.

IZADY, M.R. (1992). The Kurdish conflict in Turkey: Obstacles and chances. In *The Kurds: A concise handbook* (pp. 23–49). Washington: Taylor and Francis International Publishers.

LONELY PLANET. (n.d.). Yugoslavia map. Retrieved March 11, 2006, from the World Wide Web at http://www.lonelyplanet.com/mapshells/europe/yugoslavia/yugoslavia.htm.

MAKKLI, L. (1990). Context and consciousness: Local conditions for the production of historical and national thought among Hutu refugees in Tanzania. In R.G. Fox (Ed.), *National ideologies and the production of national cultures*. American Ethnological Society Monograph series, No. 2.

OMARI, C.K. (1987). Ethnicity, politics and development in Tanzania. *African Study Monographs*, 7, 65–80.

PETERS, J.F. (1998). *Life among the Yanomami: The story of change among the Xilixana on the Mucajai River on Brazil*. Peterborough, ON: Broadview Press.

SLOVAKIA.ORG. (n.d.). *The guide to the Slovak republic*. Retrieved March 8, 2006, from the World Wide Web at http://www.slovakia.org/history-summary.htm.

SURVIVAL INTERNATIONAL. (2006). *Yanomami genocide: Goldminers attack Yanomami community, leaving 16 dead*. Retrieved August 16, 2006, from the World Wide Web at http://www.survival-international.org/related_material.php?id=29.

TER-GABRIELIAN, G. (1999). Strategies in "ethnic" conflict. *The Fourth World Journal*. Retrieved August 20, 2005, from the World Wide Web at http://www.cwis.org/fwj/41ethnic.html.

UNHCR, THE UN REFUGEE AGENCY. (2001–2006). *UNHCR to move refugees further away from Chad/Sudan border*. Retrieved March 11, 2006, from the World Wide Web at http://www.unhcr.org/cgi-bin/texis/vtx/home.

VALDIVIESO, G. (2006). *Forced displacement in Colombia: A woman's story*. UNHCR, The Refugee Agency. Retrieved March 8, 2006, from the World Wide Web at http://www.unhcr.org/cgi-bin/texis/vtx/news/opendoc.htm?tbl=NEWS&id=440f04774/.

WALDRON, S. (1988). Working in the dark: Why social anthropological research is essential in refugee administration. *Journal of Refugee Studies* (1), 2.

THE WASHINGTON POST COMPANY. (1999). *Who are the Kurds?* Retrieved August 1, 2005, from the World Wide Web at http://washingtonpost.com/wp-srv/inatl/daily/feb99/kurdprofile.htm.

Suggested Readings

BRINGA, T. (1995). *Being Muslim the Bosnian way*. Princeton, NJ: Princeton University Press.

This book is an ethnographic account of Bosnian Muslims living in a rural village near Sarajevo. Bringa focuses on religion as a boundary marker for ethnic identity, and the role of individual households in creating this identity. The issues of ethnicity and nationality are explored as Bringa recounts the struggles of a small community trying to deal with the horrors of conflict and war.

ELLER, J.D. (1999). *From culture to ethnicity to conflict: An anthropological perspective on ethnic conflict*. Ann Arbor: University of Michigan Press.

A comprehensive collection of essays on ethnic conflict from an anthropological perspective. The concept of ethnicity is discussed as are several cases of ethnic conflict: Sri Lanka, the Kurds, Bosnia, and Rwanda and Burundi.

KECMANOVIC, D. (2001). *Ethnic times: Exploring ethnonationalism in the former Yugoslavia*. Westport, CT: Praeger Publishers.

An insider's examination of ethno-nationalism in the former Yugoslavia. An opportunity to gain some insight into the three major players in the war: Serbs, Croats, and Bosniaks/Muslims.

CHAPTER FIVE

What Challenges Do Immigrants in Canada Face?

Introduction

Canada is a nation of immigrants. They have come to this country from virtually every corner of the world, beginning some 400 years ago.[1] That first trickle of intrepid pioneers set in motion the European settlement of what would later become Canada. By the beginning of the twentieth century, immigrants were spreading across the country. This flow of people continues today, although most immigrants now originate from Asia, Southeast Asia, and Africa.

KEY TERMS: immigration, globalization, immigrants, multiculturalism, pluralistic, ethno-nationalists, systemic racism, language retention

Canada's multicultural image is the envy of the world, and draws new immigrants to the country every year. But is this image accurate? Is the history of Canadian immigration a story of open arms, or have there been darker periods when Canadians were less than welcoming? To examine these questions, we will consider Canadian immigration through the historical and contemporary experiences of Chinese and Sikh immigrants. Every wave of immigrants has faced daunting challenges in leaving their familiar homes and beginning a new life in a strange environment. Some of these challenges are addressed in this chapter.

Anthropologists and Immigration

Large-scale **IMMIGRATION**, although not a new phenomenon, is considered one of the processes of globalization. **GLOBALIZATION**, including migrations of populations, has had a dramatic impact on the anthropological study of human cultures. Attention has shifted away from studying specific cultures living in clearly defined areas to the flow of people from one area to another and the corresponding disruptions in cultural systems. Today, anthropologists analyze population movements, the mixing of populations, and the discontinuity of cultural behaviour in these migrating groups (Eriksen 2003). Indeed, the study of change and disruption on a global scale has become a major focal point of recent anthropological research.

One of the results of immigration is increasing ethnic diversity in state societies around the world. Anthropologists are particularly interested in the interrelationships between new immigrants and other members of their adopted countries, in social disparities that immigrants must deal with, and in the relationships between immigrant communities and the outside world (Eriksen 2003). For example, Karen Fog Olwig studied the sense of community among Caribbean immigrants in North America. To do this type of research, Eriksen (2003) suggests that some changes in methodology and conceptual frameworks must be made, such as viewing culture not as a thing but a process.

Although participant observation is still a major field research method, other sources, such as historical literature, formal interviews, and questionnaire surveys are also employed more frequently than in the study of a single, stationary population. The close relationships with key informants created while conducting fieldwork in one region is not possible with this type of research, where the anthropologist seldom remains in one place for long.

Immigration is a multidisciplinary subject; hence, the anthropological information presented in this chapter is complemented by research from other disciplines, such as sociology, political science, history, cultural studies, and human geography.

A Discussion of Immigration

IMMIGRANTS are people who move from one country or locality to another, usually on a permanent basis. They can be loosely categorized as political or economic immigrants, refugees, sojourners (temporary residents, such as students), and family-sponsored immigrants. Immigrants are often seen as economically and socially disadvantaged or marginalized people who display a distinct ethnicity based on their "culture, race, religion, language and/or national identity with roots elsewhere" (Neuwirth 1999: 57).

There are numerous reasons why people immigrate. Many are seeking a politically stable and safe environment for their families. Others leave their homelands in search of new economic opportunities. Joining family members already ensconced in the host country is also a key reason for immigration. Canada has become a destination of choice because of its relative political stability, low crime rate, economic opportunities, and a global reputation for embracing **MULTICULTURALISM**. In Canada's case, soon after its "discovery," immigrants from Europe were encouraged to settle here in order to generate economic enterprise and wealth. The fur trade and fisheries were the initial enterprises. Later, the federal government encouraged immigrants to settle on the Canadian prairies and begin farming the land.

Today, the situation is slightly different. Virtually all Western countries, including Canada, are experiencing declining birth rates. One of the main reasons for encouraging immigration is population replenishment and, more specifically, to replenish an aging workforce (Halli & Driedger 1999).[2] Humanitarian reasons also play a role, albeit not a central one; Canada has been inundated with requests to accommodate refugees and asylum seekers.[3] The need for foreign investment also determines government immigration targets. For example, during the 1980s and 1990s, Hong Kong entrepreneurs and investors were encouraged to immigrate to Canada. In turn, they created economic boons for major urban centres such as Vancouver and Toronto.

A 1992 Angus Reid poll found that three-quarters of Canadians feel people should not dwell on how different they are, but rather on all the things they have in common (Frideres 1999). Moreover, most Canadians in the twenty-first century proudly tout the cultural mosaic that characterizes Canada, and there appears to be a strong public commitment to continued immigration and multiculturalism (Kymlicka 2003). However, as you will see later in this chapter, multiculturalism is by no means universally accepted in Canada, and the day-to-day reality is quite different from idealistic rhetoric.

Canada's immigration policy has changed throughout the years, based largely on demographic and economic needs that to a certain extent mirror those of other Western countries. Since the 1960s, Canada has used a points system similar to that used by Australia for selecting immigrants. Both countries have experienced massive waves of immigration in the past, first from England, and then from other parts of Northern Europe. Early immigration policies were highly ethnocentric and could even be labelled racist (Simmons 1999). The goal was to entice desperate people who were willing to work for low wages, keep them on the margins of society (e.g., limit their economic opportunities and social acceptance), and ensure a continuous supply of labourers.

In the 1960s, Canada changed its policies and began admitting qualified immigrants from all parts of the world. Immigrants from Asia, Southeast Asia, Africa, and Latin America, who were historically refused entry, now made up the bulk of new immigrants to Canada. Refugees and asylum seekers were also regularly accepted. Both of these policies reflected an easing of restrictions against visible minorities and recognition of the need to expand Canada's population and economy.

In the 1980s and 1990s, immigrant entrepreneurs, investors, and professionals were most often accepted (Simmons 1999). At the time of this writing, Canadian immigration policy is once again changing from the previous selection criteria based on financial standing to an emphasis on encouraging educated and skilled foreigners to choose Canada as their new home, and thereby reduce the country's looming skilled labour shortage. Indeed, the Canadian government is encouraging immigrants with trade skills, such as pipe fitters and truck drivers, and graduate students already here, to choose Canada as their permanent home (United Press International 2005). The federal government is also examining ways to encourage immigrants to live outside major urban centres where labour shortages are already having an impact on the economy.

In the United States, immigration from developing countries began much earlier than in Canada, and many immigrants originated in the Caribbean and Central and South America, as well as Europe (Simmons 1999). Rather than a points system, family sponsorship appears to have played a larger role in the United States than in Canada. Recently American immigration policy has focused on curtailing illegal immigration from Mexico, as well as Central America and the Caribbean. Since Canada does not border on any developing countries, the problem of illegal immigration is much less pronounced.

For several centuries Europe was the main source of immigration for the New World, yet today most European countries maintain tough restrictions over immigration. Some EU countries view foreigners as solutions to short-term labour shortages, rather than permanent residents—in the 1950s and 1960s many immigrants were only allowed temporary work visas (Simmons 1999). Indeed, today some European countries are trying to drastically curtail or even eliminate immigration from non-European countries. In September 2005, EU ministers from Spain, Germany, Italy, and Belgium met to discuss "the immigration problem" (de Francisco 2005). Spain proposed a plan to develop a joint European-Mediterranean police and judicial network to stop illegal immigration, drug smuggling, and terrorism. On a more positive note, the United Kingdom has accepted many non-European immigrants and supports a multicultural policy similar to that of Canada (Simmons 1999).

IMMIGRATION CHALLENGES AND ISSUES

The dynamics of immigration present some interesting challenges for the Canadian government as well as immigrants themselves: 1) national identity; 2) cultural diversity and integration; 3) ethnic relations and racial conflict; 4) language preservation and acquisition; and 5) economic implications of immigration.

Most Western countries are **PLURALISTIC**; they contain numerous ethnic subcultures that to a certain extent remain culturally distinct, and thereby create a multicultural atmosphere. Multiculturalism is a mechanism designed to peacefully manage a nation founded on ethnic diversity. However, the degree to which this multiculturalism is welcomed and facilitated varies from one society to another. In Canada, multiculturalism is officially acknowledged and on the surface, at least, is embraced. Ethnic and cultural diversity is recognized, promoted, and incorporated into the country's global image.

One of the issues faced by a multicultural nation is its sense of national identity. The question of Canada's national identity is often raised, especially by **ETHNO-NATIONALISTS** who champion a homogenous, unilingual, and unicultural nation. They complain that everyone in Canada seems to be a hyphenated Canadian (e.g., Chinese-Canadians), and that giving ethnic diversity priority has created a heterogeneous rather than a homogeneous nation. Ethno-nationalists claim that multiculturalism dilutes nationalism, and that Canada needs to create a common culture (Frideres 1999 from Jusdanis 1996). On the other hand, multiculturalists believe that ethnic, cultural, religious, and social diversity enhances the quality and variety of life in Canada (Frideres 1999). My students have time and again extolled the value and "interest quotient" of their multicultural society. While older generations may be uncertain of Canada's multiculturalism, these young people clearly see the beauty and richness of their culturally diverse nation.

When immigrants arrive in a new country, they face a period of adjustment as they struggle to become accustomed to their new home while also clinging tenaciously to their traditional, and comfortably familiar, cultural practices. New immigrants must decide whether to fully assimilate into the society, remain isolated from mainstream society to preserve their traditional culture, or assimilate some Canadian social and cultural features while also protecting their cultural traditions and values (Frideres 1999). Those who consciously choose to assimilate into the social and cultural milieu of Canadian society appear quite willing to adopt new ideals and behaviours. Other groups, such as the Hutterites and Hasidic Jews, choose to remain isolated in a concerted effort to maintain their cultural traditions and values, and, most important, their religious beliefs.

Most immigrants choose the third route; they attempt to fit into Canadian society while also preserving parts of their culture. For example, Chinese Canadians have a cultural identity that is neither Canadian nor Chinese, but Chinese Canadian (Chow 1996). This dual identity enables them to maintain their Chinese cultural heritage while adopting Canadian cultural elements. Multiculturalism has aided in preserving and celebrating Chinese heritage while encouraging the Chinese to adapt to Canadian society (Ng 1999). This is a trend in many nations with large immigrant populations. Even in the United States, which has always touted a melting pot philosophy, immigrants have maintained their ethnic identity, and in reality the United States is as pluralistic as Canada (Soria 2005).

Regardless of how willing immigrants are to integrate into Canadian society, they will undoubtedly suffer from culture shock, which causes considerable distress and may slow the process of integration into Canadian society.[4] Immigrants naturally gravitate to those who are similar to them; hence, new immigrants often settle in urban centres where there are well-established populations of the same ancestry or point of origin. This practice reduces culture shock and helps new arrivals ease into their environment and learn how to function.

Balakrishnan and Hou (1999) found that residential segregation helps maintain cultural identity, but also prolongs the sense of separateness from mainstream society. In other words, living in ethnic enclaves may help immigrants feel more comfortable and maintain their traditional culture, but it also slows their integration into Canadian society. This argument has been used against multiculturalism—that it slows immigrant incorporation into mainstream society (Frideres 1999). To cope with the difficulties they encountered during the early years, many Chinese immigrants retreated into enclaves known as Chinatowns. Hidden away in these enclaves, they were able to preserve their culture, maintain their identity, avoid racial attacks, and enjoy a sense of belonging (Li 1988). As a consequence, many Chinese immigrants, especially the elderly, never became fully participating members of Canadian society because they remained inside Chinatown.

Neuwirth (1999) argues that integration is a two-way process of commitment. Immigrants, for their part, must learn one of the official languages, obey the laws of the land, seek employment, and become involved in the community. The host country must ensure meaningful employment is available, and share the basic values, ideology, and traditions of the country with new immigrants. Above all, immigrants need to be viewed as an asset, not a liability (Soria 2005). Protests that immigrants take jobs away from citizens and increase the crime rate do nothing to help immigrants feel secure. Hence, the attitudes of citizens toward immigrants will determine how successfully they integrate into Canadian society.

Economic and social integration appear to be at the root of cultural integration. Immigrants must become economically independent, which means finding employment, and assist in social integration, which means participating in social institutions (e.g., education, health care, political agencies). If immigrants are excluded from economic and social institutions, they will not adopt the host country's practices and norms, and will, out of a sense of preservation, try to maintain their traditional culture. The quandary here is, while anthropologists champion the rights of people to keep their cultural traditions, immigrants must adopt some elements of Canadian society to become comfortable in their new country. It would be naive to think that assimilation does not occur, especially among young children and the next generation.

The federal government and other agencies have endeavoured to accommodate the needs of a diverse population. The Canadian philosophy has been to build a national identity of unity through ethnic diversity. Canada offers immigrants peace and security, and cultural autonomy that enables immigrants to retain as much of their traditional culture as they choose while also integrating into Canadian society. Yet, some wonder at what point accommodation goes too far—such as the recent debacle with Shariah[5] law in Ontario, which incited outrage among many Canadians, including Canadians of Islamic heritage (Keith 2005). Many women fear that Shariah law in Canada would threaten the equality of Muslim women—since Muslim women only count as half a man under Shariah law. Although public reaction led the Ontario government to ban Shariah law, it also meant other tribunals used by Jews and Christians for years were outlawed as well. This is a contentious point, one that thoughtful Canadians will have to resolve in the near future.

Global transportation enables family members separated by thousands of miles to see each other far more often than the early settlers that came to Canada—many of whom never returned to their home country, or saw their relatives again. Modern communication systems also enable immigrants to stay in close touch. The Internet and ensuing e-mail and instant messaging provide a daily means of communicating with loved ones. Our global transportation and communication systems also provide a means of maintaining close cultural ties, creating an ability to live multi-locally and maintain multiple ethnic identities.

Canada's history of immigration is rife with episodes of discrimination, such as that experienced by Ukrainians who were exploited as low-paid labourers, then declared enemy aliens during World War I (Gruske 1989). Nearly 6,000 Ukrainian immigrants had their land

> Proponents say it [Shariah law] is the only way Muslims can live true to their faith. Critics see it as an unsettling expansion of a system that stones women and hangs apostates in the street.
>
> SUSAN BOURETTE (2004)

confiscated and were interned during the war. Yet, today people of Ukrainian heritage are successful members of the Canadian cultural mosaic. An episode such as this leads us to ask how this and the later internment of Japanese Canadians could happen in Canada. The fact is, very few ethnic groups have come to Canada and not suffered some form of prejudice—contrary to official doctrine, Canada has not accepted people with open arms. However, like the Ukrainians, most groups prevail and take their place in Canadian society, and another ethnic group becomes the target of those who fear ethnic diversity.

Today, visible minorities in Canada still experience barriers that prevent them from accessing economic opportunities—what Li (1988) calls **SYSTEMIC RACISM**—much more commonly than "white" immigrants (Frideres 1999). Because of physical and behavioural differences (e.g., darker skin, religious beliefs), they have been kept on the margins of Canadian society. Refugees are particularly vulnerable because of the political turmoil and hardships they have escaped, and the likelihood they fled with few employable skills or economic resources. They are most likely to experience economic stress in the form of unemployment or underemployment, and various forms of discrimination. This is not only true of Canada. In France, illegal immigrants from Mali live in squalor and are widely viewed as taking jobs away from French citizens, as well as increasing the crime rate (Kamber & Lacey 2005). French citizens have reacted negatively to non-European immigrants, such as banning headscarves, which are a symbol of Muslim religious beliefs, from French schools. The riots in France at the time of this writing are partly due to the racist policies (e.g., marginalization and exploitation) against Muslims, even those who are native-born French citizens.

In Canada, there are fears in some quarters that cultural diversity may soon destroy national symbols and icons and replace them with "foreign" cultural components. An example is the controversy over Christmas as a Christian celebration. In an effort to avoid offending or making people of different faiths or no religious faith uncomfortable, Christmas as a religious symbol has all but disappeared from school celebrations. This trend has angered Canadians who value the religious aspects of Christmas. Developing a compromise that is sensitive and balances the needs of all Canadians will be an interesting challenge.

Since 9/11, fears of terrorist attacks have targeted visible minorities from certain areas of the world—the Middle East in particular—as potential terrorists and made life even more difficult for immigrants, especially in the United States and Europe. The spectre of immigration restrictions directed at certain groups is becoming a reality in the United States where immigration policies have shifted to security control (Spencer 2003). In Canada a 2005 survey taken by Innovative Research Group, *The World in Canada: Demographics and Diversity in Canadian Foreign Policy*, suggested that two-thirds of Canadians fear that immigrant groups will bring their ethnic conflicts[6] to Canada with them. They call for tough screening of potential immigrants to weed out terrorists. On a more positive note, 63 per cent of Canadians polled worry that concerns over terrorism could lead to a decline in civil rights for Canadians from Arabic or Islamic countries (Butler 2005).

Learning a new language, as anyone who has tried can attest, is a long and difficult task, but one that immigrants must tackle as soon as they arrive in Canada. At least half of all immigrants coming to Canada do not speak English or French when they arrive (de Vries 1999), creating a barrier to communication. Language proficiency impacts on an immigrant's ability to find higher paying jobs; indeed, most immigrants with poor language skills are trapped in low-paying, menial jobs (Boyd 1999), and have difficulty adapting to their new life. The Canadian model for citizenry includes a language proficiency test; therefore, to eventually become a permanent citizen of Canada, immigrants must learn one of the two official languages (Kymlicka 2003).

Preservation of traditional languages is also an issue with which immigrants must deal. Chinese Canadians have managed to preserve their traditional languages by opening language schools. However, the present generation of Chinese Canadians does not appear to hold their traditional language, whether Mandarin or Cantonese dialects, in much regard. Young Chinese Canadians prefer to speak English, although this limits their ability to find employment in Chinatown. On the other hand, those Chinese who do not speak English or French find it difficult to live or work outside of Chinatown.

Once immigrants arrive in Canada, one of their primary goals is to secure employment. However, many immigrants cannot find jobs in their field. Anecdotal stories of engineers, for example, who are forced to drive cabs because their degrees are not recognized, or foreign-trained doctors who must undergo time-consuming and rigorous challenges to achieve accreditation—even though Canada is experiencing a shortage of practising medical doctors—are common. Many immigrants possess post-secondary education and only require some vocational training or upgrading (Neuwirth 1999). Yet, very few have received this training and consequently end up taking low-paying "dead-end" jobs that create further marginalization. Visible minorities often have a more difficult time finding higher paying jobs, regardless of their education and training (Piché, Renaud, & Gingras 1999). In Canada, this seems particularly true of sub-Saharan African immigrants.

The common misconception that immigrants take jobs away from native-born citizens is refuted by economists. In the United States, those states that have a high immigration rate have lower unemployment rates and enjoy job creation because of increasing demands for goods and services (Soria 2005). A second misconception is that immigrants put pressure on an economy. However, immigrants "pay taxes, pay into Social Security and boost the economy with their added consumption" (Soria 2005: 301). The same holds true for Canada where

"I couldn't order anything off the menu in a restaurant because I couldn't read the language, nor could I ask for help because I couldn't speak the language. The grocery store was the same—often I came home with weird food."

A RECENT IMMIGRANT TO
A FOREIGN COUNTRY

immigration results in a net increase in jobs (Kymlicka 2003: 205). Although originally created to protect Chinese immigrants from xeno-phobic attacks, Chinatowns have since become economic boons both to Chinese Canadians and to the surrounding urban centres. They have become tourist destinations—Vancouver's Chinatown was designated a provincial historic area in 1971 (Yee 1988), and today the Chinatown Revitalization Committee, along with other agencies, is developing a long-term plan to ensure the cultural and economic viability of Van-couver's Chinatown. The tendency to accuse immigrants of hurting the economy becomes particularly evident during times of economic recession when immigrants are made scapegoats for the economic woes of native-born Canadians. As well, immigrants are often blamed for increasing welfare costs (Spencer 2003).

CHINESE CANADIANS

The history of immigration in Canada begins with the French colonists in New France and *Acadie*. These colonists and later arrivals, also from Northern Europe, made up the foundations of early Canada. How-ever, Canadian immigration has always been dynamic, and today most immigrants come from Asia and Southeast Asia,[7] further enhancing the ethnic and cultural diversity of the Canadian landscape. Chinese Canadians have been both the benefactors and victims of Canadian immigration since the nineteenth century. Much of their early history in Canada tells the story of systemic discrimination and overt racism.[8] Interestingly, the history of Chinese immigration also reflects the his-tory of changing attitudes among Canadians toward immigrants.

The earliest Chinese immigrants to Canada[9] were considered sojourners—here to work on the construction of the Canadian Pacific Railroad, then leave. From the beginning, Chinese immigrants faced serious challenges. These men were extremely poor, and desperate to flee the social, economic, and political instability in China (Li 1992). The life of Chinese labourers while building the railroad through the Rocky Mountains was unbearable; they endured harsh weather, and suffered malnutrition and disease. Many starved or froze to death in inadequate housing. Others died from the gruelling and dangerous work—digging tunnels, hauling tons of rock by hand, building bridges, and transport-ing explosives. They were viewed as little more than workhorses to be easily discarded or replaced. Following the completion of the railroad, these men were no longer wanted in Canada, but most lacked the funds to buy passage back to China. Then a recession hit British Columbia, and the Chinese became scapegoats for the province's economic prob-lems. Chinese men were accused of taking employment away from other Canadians, and an anti-Chinese movement began (Li 1988).

Various forms of legislation were passed to marginalize the Chi-nese and prevent more Chinese from immigrating to Canada. Of note,

Early Chinese immigrants working on the Canadian railway endured squalid conditions.

in 1885, a $50 head tax was introduced for each Chinese person immigrating to Canada,[10] thus preventing the men from bringing over their families (Li 1988). In 1923, the *Chinese Exclusion Act* was passed, in effect shutting down Chinese immigration and preventing any Chinese in Canada from becoming naturalized citizens. Hoe (1989) calls this period in Canadian immigration history the "dark age."

Besides immigration restrictions, the Chinese faced other forms of discrimination. For example, in Saskatchewan a law was passed in 1912–1915 forbidding Chinese restaurant owners from hiring white females (Dawson 1991). Measures like this are a reflection of the racial prejudice rife in Canadian society at the time. Chinese immigrants became the scapegoats for socio-economic difficulties—from epidemics and depressed wages to overcrowded cities. The Chinese were stereotyped as corrupt opium-smokers and prostitutes. The 1887 and 1907 anti-Chinese riots in Vancouver exemplify the hostility of some Canadians toward Chinese immigrants. Canadians protested in the streets, carrying banners reading "A white Canada and no cheap Asiatic labour," and "White Canada—patronize your own race and Canada" (Li 1988: 32). Even native-born Chinese Canadians were considered second class citizens: they faced considerable social, economic, and residential separation from mainstream Canadian society. Indeed, the professionally educated children of Chinese immigrants could not open or own their own law or medical practices.

The *Chinese Exclusion Act* was repealed in 1947,[11] and Chinese immigrants were able to become Canadian citizens, vote in federal elections, and sponsor their families to join them in Canada (Li 1988). In the 1960s, with the advent of the points system, many Chinese came to Canada in search of new economic opportunities, beginning a trend that continued into the 1990s when Chinese immigrants with money or marketable skills were preferred immigrants (Star 1997). Indeed, immigrants from Hong Kong brought with them enormous financial resources, skilled labour, and an entrepreneurial spirit that helped revitalize major Canadian cities.

The *Charter of Rights and Freedoms* and the 1988 *Canadian Multiculturalism Act* helped increase cultural awareness and sensitivity among Canadians, and visible minorities such as Chinese Canadians began to gain equality. Today Chinese Canadians enjoy the same civil rights as other Canadians (Li 1988; 1992). As their populations have increased and economic standing has improved, Chinese Canadians have demanded social equality. Yet, the struggle continues. Linguistic abilities have limited the opportunities of some Chinese Canadians, while others have not had their credentials recognized in Canada. In Vancouver, the financial power of Hong Kong Chinese is resented, and although their investments have revitalized the city, they are also accused of increasing property prices and building tacky "monster houses." When Chinese stowaways were discovered in cargo containers in Vancouver, the Canadian public demanded their deportation (CBC News 2004). This open hostility calls into question the public's compassion for people desperate enough to risk their lives in search of a better life (Fedorak 2006).

Despite this hostile incident, social activism and education have increased cultural awareness and sensitivity among Canadians, and today, Chinese Canadians have found a place in Canadian society. Many of the cultural elements of the Chinese have diffused into mainstream Canadian society, and many Canadians have embraced Chinese culture, especially the foods, festivals, and philosophies. Chinese Canadians have introduced medicines and medical practices, martial arts, cultural activities, and Chinese cuisine (albeit much altered) to Canadians, and, in turn, contributed to local economies by drawing in visitors to annual festivals and celebrations.

CANADIAN SIKHS

The story of Sikh[12] immigration to Canada is similar to that of the Chinese. They too were exploited and forced to take menial jobs in sawmills and on the railway. The first Sikh men from Punjab began arriving in Canada in 1903 (Singh 1994), fleeing the political and economic instability of India. Most settled in the lower British Columbia mainland (Statistics Canada 2004). Although Canada has been good to

As a result of discrimination, in the early twentieth century Chinese Canadians often lost their jobs to white workers, and it was increasingly difficult for them to make a living. Here a group of Chinese squatters pose with a visiting Reverend outside their makeshift cookhouse.

the Sikhs in many ways, they have also faced challenges in adapting to their new country. Prejudice and discrimination, especially concerning their religious customs, have dogged them through the years.

Like the Chinese, Sikhs were accused of taking jobs away from Euro-Canadians (Minhas 1994). The public demanded action and, in 1908, the federal government placed restrictions on immigration, effectively shutting down Sikh immigration (Singh 1994). The most tragic consequence of this policy was the separation of family members. Sikhs were also denied the basic rights of Canadian citizens—they could not vote provincially or federally, they could not work as professionals, purchase land in many parts of Vancouver, or serve on juries. Indeed, the Asiatic Exclusion League, formed in 1907, issued a statement of exclusion: "Canada is best left in the hands of the Anglo-Saxon race.... [I]t shall remain white and our doors shall be closed to the Asians" (Singh 1994: 34).

Challenges aside, Sikhs found employment at sawmills and shingle mills, on the railways, in construction, forestry, dairy, fruit packing, and on cattle farms (Singh 1994). They endured spartan, crowded living conditions, sending most of their wages back to their families in Punjab. Organizations such as the Khalsa Diwan Society, a religious, social, and political organization formed in 1907, tried to overturn the immigration ban and fought against the rampant discrimination of the day.

Immigration rules were relaxed in 1919, and many Sikhs were finally able to bring their families to Canada (Minhas 1994). However, it was not until 1947 that Sikhs gained the right to vote (Singh 1994). The points system of the 1960s allowed more Sikhs to come to Canada. Many settled outside urban British Columbia, some even heading to the prairies where there was a shortage of professionals, such as teachers and doctors (Minhas 1994). Others headed to Ontario to work in the manufacturing sector, or to open businesses.

Pragmatically, Canada needs immigrants, to respond to demographic factors such as our low birthrate, but also to provide stimulus to the Canadian economy. In twenty years time, there will be three retired persons for every young, working person. Our immigration target of 200,000 per annum could not be met last year. In the recent bill, the goal has been increased to 300,000, and the parameters for acceptance have been changed in order to meet this increase.

SENATOR POY (2000: 2)

An incident that calls into question the existence of true multiculturalism occurred in 1985. Balteij Singh Dhillon wanted to join the RCMP, and formally requested permission to wear his turban while on duty (Minhas 1994). It is important for readers to understand that the turban is a symbol of a Sikh man's faith and religious obedience, and is required of all baptized Sikh men. In other words, it means a great deal to them. Commissioner Inkster granted Baltej Singh Dhillon permission to wear his turban in 1990.

A vocal minority of Canadians, most in Alberta, protested this accommodation. Some protesters believed altering the traditional RCMP uniform detracted from the force's international image. They ignored the fact that the RCMP uniform has changed several times during its history, without dire consequences. In a desperate attempt to lend credibility to their xenophobic attacks, some protesters suggested worker safety would be threatened: wearing a turban, ceremonial dagger, and beard while on duty could pose a danger for both Sikh and other officers.[13] Others protested the special status given to Sikhs and their religious customs. In Calgary some people wore pins that featured a Sikh wearing a turban and a RCMP uniform with a line drawn through it, and the words "Keep the RCMP Canadian." These actions by a vocal minority led other Canadians to wonder if religious and cultural freedom is truly a reality in Canada, and if racism is really as buried as most Canadians would like to believe (Fedorak 2006).[14]

Petitions from groups such as the Defenders of RCMP Tradition and the RCMP Veterans' Association in Charlottetown were dismissed (Pelot 1993). The courts ruled that the *Charter of Rights and Freedoms* was not being violated (The Sikh Coalition 2004), and that discrimination based on religion was forbidden in Canada. To prohibit Sikhs from wearing their turbans would prevent them from entering the RCMP, meaning they were being discriminated against. Balteij Singh Dhillon's request was not precedent setting—Sikhs have been wearing turbans and other Sikh symbols in police forces around the world, including in the United Kingdom, Singapore, Thailand, India, and the United Nations Peacekeeping force (Singh 1994).

Twenty years have passed and the RCMP as a venerated institution has not collapsed, nor have any of the other dire predictions come true. Balteij Singh Dhillon, who continues to serve as an RCMP officer, recently received recognition for his outstanding work in solving a forgery case (Minhas 1994). Oddly, the turban controversy refuses to die, rearing its ugly head once again in 2006 when a young Sikh soccer player was barred from playing while wearing his turban (Canadian Press 2005).

Despite the challenges they have faced, Sikhs have made Canada their home, and contributed a great deal to their adopted country, enhancing the Canadian experience by their very presence. While doing so, they have also managed to maintain important elements of their traditional cultural and religious values. This is the true nature of Canadian multiculturalism.

To be effective in its role and to continue to be a national institution, in a true sense, it [the RCMP] must reflect the changing realities of Canadian society.... Sikh turbans pose absolutely no threat to the traditions, functional effectiveness, respect, esteem, and goodwill of the RCMP. (SINGH 1994: 138)

Despite embarrassing incidents, such as the turban controversy, discriminatory and economic barriers have been torn down, and today Canadian Sikhs enjoy the full range of opportunities Canada has to offer.

WHAT IT MEANS TO BE AN IMMIGRANT

Over the years I have had the pleasure of teaching many students who have immigrated to Canada. They have taught me a great deal about what it means to be an immigrant. In the following section some of these insights are presented.[15] The challenges they face in their daily lives can be divided into several categories: parental disputes, gender relations, language competency, and climate shock.

A common difficulty young immigrants face is disagreement with their parents regarding social relationships—what I have labelled generational culture clash. Parents may wish to hold onto their traditional family values in matters such as dress code, association with peers, dating, marriage, and future goals. Two sisters of East Indian heritage recounted how they reached a compromise with their parents regarding dating and marriage: the parents would choose appropriate partners for their daughters to date, with the goal of marriage, but the young women had veto power if they did not like the men their parents chose. In this way, customarily arranged marriages were modified to meet Canadian norms, while also satisfying the desire of parents to choose their daughters' spouses. Another student told me she has not been so

Revisiting the turban controversy.

lucky; her parents are insisting she discontinue her university education at age 25, and get married. She continues to resist.

Gender relationships and power structures within the family may also be strained. For example, when Hispanic families, who are traditionally patriarchal, move to Canada, where families tend to be more egalitarian, how do they reconcile their ideals of family life and gender roles with the social norms in Canadian society?

LANGUAGE RETENTION is another challenge. Older generations often complain that second- and especially third-generation offspring show little interest in learning their traditional language. Some of my students have suggested that a reasonable compromise is to learn their heritage language and use it at home when speaking with their parents and grandparents, but when out in public (e.g., work, school, shopping), to speak English.

Climate shock was mentioned by several of my students. One young man recounted how he could not believe the cold when he stepped out of the Saskatoon airport one January and his nostrils stuck together. Indeed, when culture shock overcame him, it was mainly due to the frigid weather. He began to wonder why he had ever left the sun and warmth of South Africa for the land of ice and snow.

The consensus among my students is that meeting new people and making friends is the best way to overcome culture shock. They also recommended joining a sports team for something fun to do, and to meet new people.

Conclusion

I often ask my students to put themselves in the shoes of new immigrants. They must outline the challenges they will face in a new country and how they will deal with these challenges—and there are many. Immigrants must become enculturated in order to predict behavioural norms. Until they do so, they will experience a sense of insecurity and alienation. Realistically, it is impossible to step into a new environment and immediately absorb the social customs and norms of behaviour, nor will immigrants likely want to give up their familiar and comforting culture. Yet to function in day-to-day life, they must learn a new language, find employment, and deal with the challenges of integrating into their new society. Obviously, people who come from cultural backgrounds that differ greatly from what they find in their host country will have the most difficult time adjusting.

Although most of the misconceptions and ignorance at the root of discrimination have given way to a growing social maturity and acceptance among Canadian citizens, we would be naive to assume that intolerance and bigotry have disappeared from Canada. Certainly the experiences of Chinese Canadians and Canadian Sikhs suggest that the "open door" policy of Canadian immigration is not as straightforward or long-standing as Canadians might like to believe.

Although immigrants to Canada now enjoy the same civil rights (e.g., freedom of speech), social benefits (e.g., public health care), and legal protection from anti-discriminatory laws as other Canadians (Kymlicka 2003), we still have some distance to go concerning attitudes toward immigrants. As an example, many Chinese Canadians today are fifth- or sixth-generation Canadians—far more attached to Canadian soil than most second- or third-generation "white" Canadians, yet their "differences" supersede this fact. Despite obvious deficiencies, in the twenty-first century there appears to be an increasing recognition of the needs and rights of immigrants, and a growing acceptance of cultural diversity among the vast majority of Canadians. Canadians, for the most part, have embraced multiculturalism as a positive characteristic of Canadian society, and this is relevant regarding our national identity. As former Prime Minister Jean Chrétien succinctly stated when asked to define Canada's national identity: "It's multicultural: that's the essence" (Lloyd 2003: 96).

Questions for Consideration

1.   Put yourself in the shoes of a new immigrant. You are in a strange country, unable to speak the language, with only a limited supply of money, and you must quickly find a place to live, a job, and living necessities, such as food and water. Outline your strategy. What assistance would you welcome from the locals?

2.   Here's a second scenario. You are in a strange country. The people stop and stare at you because you look so different, they make fun and laugh at you, and when you approach someone for help, they walk away with an impatient shrug at your feeble attempt to speak their language. Analyze why they are responding to you this way. How would these responses make you feel?

3.   In Chapter 2 we discussed culture shock and the coping strategies for integrating into another country. Do these coping strategies apply to immigrants moving to Canada? Identify those most useful to immigrants and explain your choices.

4.   Sikhs wearing their turbans in the RCMP force created considerable controversy. Why do you think some people reacted so negatively? Was the decision to allow Sikhs to wear their turbans the right one? Explain your reasoning. Research the issue in more detail. Have there been any problems resulting from allowing Sikhs to wear turbans in the RCMP?

5.   Based on the two case studies in this chapter, do you think Canada offers immigrants cultural freedom? Why or why not? What can we, as individuals, do to improve the experiences of new immigrants to Canada?

6.   The story of Chinese immigration to Canada is rife with difficulties, discrimination, and marginalization. Why do you think Canadians reacted so negatively to the Chinese? Are there cultural groups in Canada today who are experiencing similar discrimination?

7.   Identify how Canadian immigration policies have restricted the ability of immigrants to settle comfortably into Canadian society. Choose an immigrant group and discuss how they have coped with the limitations placed on them.

8.   Examine Canadian immigration policies today. Identify some of the strengths and weaknesses in this policy. For example, is it still difficult for a Chinese citizen to immigrate to Canada? Why or why not?

9. Define multiculturalism and discuss the positive and negative aspects of this policy. Is Canada a better place to live in because of multiculturalism? Explain your reasoning.

NOTES

1   The author recognizes that ancestors of contemporary First Nations, Métis, and Inuit peoples were the original immigrants, coming to North America thousands of years ago.

2   According to Foreign Affairs Minister Pierre Pettigrew, we need 40 million people in Canada just to offset the aging baby boomers heading for retirement (Macleans.ca 2005).

3   Five to 10 per cent of the approximately 300,000 immigrants allowed entry into Canada each year are refugees or asylum seekers (Lloyd 2003).

4   See Chapter 2 for a detailed discussion of culture shock.

5   Shariah law follows the teachings of the Koran, and is considered a faith-based arbitration to settle Muslim family disputes, such as divorce and child custody.

6   For a detailed discussion of ethnic conflict, see Chapter 4.

7   By 1993, seven of the top ten countries of origin for Canadian immigrants were in Asia (Halli & Driedger 1999).

8   The term "racism" is problematic. Although used to describe bigotry and discrimination against visible minorities, it is impossible to scientifically categorize people into "racial" groups. The concept of race is a social construct based on economic, political, and social agendas, not a biological reality (Fedorak 2006).

9   The first Chinese arrived in Canada in 1858 to search for gold in the Fraser River Valley (Hoe 1989).

10 By 1903, this head tax had risen to $500 (Li 2000).

11 Discriminating against citizens of an Allied country became an embarrassment to the federal government.

12 Sikhs are disciples who follow the beliefs and practices of Sikhism, and maintain a close and loving relationship with God (Singh 1994). Sikhs believe in reincarnation but not the hierarchical Hindu caste system.

13 To justify this rather ludicrous suggestion, they asked whether Sikhs who wore a turban would be able to wear a gas mask or helmet in an emergency situation.

14 To put this in perspective, these protests were happening in 1989, not the early 1900s.

15 Based on casual conversations over a period of 15 years.

References

BALAKRISHNAN, T.R., & HOU, F. (1999). Residential patterns in cities. In S.S. Halli & L. Driedger (Eds.), *Immigrant Canada: Demographic, economic, and social challenges* (pp. 116–147). Toronto: University of Toronto Press.

BOYD, M. (1999). Integrating gender, language, and race. In S.S. Halli & L. Driedger (Eds.), *Immigrant Canada: Demographic, economic, and social challenges* (pp. 282–306). Toronto: University of Toronto Press.

BOURETTE, S. (2004). Can tolerant Canada tolerate *sharia*? *The Christian Science Monitor* (August 10).

BUTLER, D. (2005, October 31). Immigrants threaten Canada's peace: Poll. *The Star Phoenix*, B1.

CANADIAN PRESS. (2005, September 6). B.C. tourney bars Sikh soccer player over turban. *CTV.ca*. Retrieved March 31, 2006, from the World Wide Web at http://www.ctv.ca/servlet/ArticleNews/story/CTVNews/20050906/sikh_soccer_player_050905?s_name=&no_ads=.

CBC NEWS. (2004). *Indepth: China. Chinese Immigration*. Retrieved January 18, 2005, from the World Wide Web at http://www.cbc.ca/news/background/china/chinese_immigration.html.

CHOW, L. (1996). *Sojourners in the north*. Prince George, BC: Caitlin Press Inc.

DAWSON, J.B. (1991). *Moon cakes in gold mountain. From China to the Canadian Plains*. Calgary: Detselig Enterprises, Ltd.

DE FRANCISCO, A.G. (2005, September 9). EU seeks better cooperation on stemming illegal immigration. *EFE World News Service*. Retrieved October 15, 2005, from the World Wide World at http://www.infotrac.galegroup.com.

DE VRIES, J. (1999). Foreign born language acquisition and shift. In S.S. Halli & L. Driedger (Eds.), *Immigrant Canada: Demographic, economic, and social challenges* (pp. 262–281). Toronto: University of Toronto Press.

ERIKSEN, T.E. (Ed.). (2003). *Globalisation: Studies in anthropology*. London: Pluto Press.

GRUSKE, C. (1989, February 3). Ukrainians want acknowledgement of injustice. *The Gazette*. Retrieved October 14, 2005, from the World Wide Web at http://www.infoakes.com/history/internment//booklet02/doc-040.html.

FEDORAK, S. (2006). *Windows on the world: Case studies in anthropology*. Toronto: Thomson Nelson Learning.

FRIDERES, J.S. (1999). Managing immigrant social transformations. In S.S. Halli & L. Driedger (Eds.), *Immigrant Canada: Demographic, economic, and social challenges* (pp. 70–90). Toronto: University of Toronto Press.

HALLI, S.S., & DRIEDGER, L. (1999). The Immigrant Challenge 2000. In S.S. Halli & L. Driedger (Eds.), *Immigrant Canada: Demographic, economic, and social challenges* (pp. 3–7). Toronto: University of Toronto Press.

HOE, B.S. (1989). *Beyond the golden mountain: Chinese cultural traditions in Canada*. Canadian Museum of Civilization.

JUSDANIS, G. (1996). Can multiculturalism disunite America? *A Journal of Critical Theory and Historical Sociology, 44*, 100–110.

KAMBER, M., & LACEY, M. (2005, September 11). For Mali villagers, France is a workplace and lifeline. *The New York Times*, A6. Retrieved October 16, 2005, from the World Wide Web at http://www.infotrac.galegroup.com.

KEITH, L. (2005, September 11). McGuinty rejects Ontario's use of Shariah law and all religious arbitrations. *Canadian Press*. Retrieved October 21, 2006, from the World Wide Web at http://www.nosharia.com.

KYMLICKA, W. (2003). Immigration, citizenship, multiculturalism. In S. Spencer (Ed.), *The politics of migration: Managing opportunity, conflict and change* (pp. 195–208). Malden, MA: Blackwell Publishing.

LI, J.N. (2000). *Canadian steel, Chinese grit: A tribute to the Chinese who worked on Canada's railroads more than a century ago*. Toronto: Paxlink Communications.

LI, P.S. (1988). *The Chinese in Canada*. Toronto: Oxford University Press.

LI, P.S. (1992). Essay: The Chinese minority in Canada, 1858–1992. A quest for equality. In E. Huang (Ed.), *Chinese-Canadians: Voices from the community* (pp. 264–275). Vancouver: Douglas & McIntyre Ltd.

LLOYD, J. (2003). The new populist parties. In S. Spencer (Ed.), *The politics of migration: Managing opportunity, conflict and change* (pp. 88–99). Malden, MA: Blackwell Publishing.

MACLEANS.CA. (2005, October 13). *Pettigrew says more immigrants needed to help augment dwindling labour force*. Retrieved October 23, 2005, from the World Wide Web at http://www.macleans.ca/topstories/politics/news/shownews.jsp?content=n101351A.

MINHAS, M. (1994). *The Sikh Canadians*. Edmonton, AB: Reidmore Books Inc.

NEUWIRTH, G. (1999). Toward a theory of immigrant integration. In S.S. Halli & L. Driedger (Eds.), *Immigrant Canada: Demographic, economic, and social challenges* (pp. 51–69). Toronto: University of Toronto Press.

NG, W.C. (1999). *The Chinese in Vancouver, 1945–80: The pursuit of identity and power*. Vancouver: UBC Press.

PELOT, J.B. (Ed.). (1993). *Diary of a national debate: Mounties in turbans*. Orleans, ON: In-tel-ek Consulting.

PICHÉ, V., RENAUD, J., & GINGRAS, L. (1999). Comparative immigrant economic integration. In S.S. Halli & L. Driedger (Eds.), *Immigrant Canada: Demographic, economic, and social challenges* (pp. 185–211). Toronto: University of Toronto Press.

POY, V. (2000). *Canadian Immigration: A Chinese Perspective*. Speech to Association of Asian-American Studies (AAAS) Annual Conference. Retrieved March 31, 2006, from the World Wide Web at http://www.sen.parl.gc.ca/vpoy/english/Special_Interests/speeches/Speech%20-%20AAAS%20Conf.htm.

THE SIKH COALITION. (2004). *Canadian judicial opinions regarding the Sikh religious identity*. Retrieved October 18, 2004, from the World Wide Web at http://www.sikhcoalition.org/LegalCanada2c.asp.

SIMMONS, A.B. (1999). Immigration policy: Imagined futures. In S.S. Halli & L. Driedger (Eds.), *Immigrant Canada: Demographic, economic, and social challenges* (pp. 21–50). Toronto: University of Toronto Press.

SINGH, G. (2004). *Immigrants claim that Canada conned them. Straight.com*. Retrieved March 31, 2006, from the World Wide Web at http://www.straight.com/content.cfm?id=15526

SINGH, N. (1994). *Canadian Sikhs: History, religion, and culture of Sikhs in North America*. Nepean, ON: Canadian Sikhs' Studies Institute.

SORIA, M. (2005, September 19). Immigration is an asset, not a liability. *Business Record* (Des Moines), 301. Retrieved October 16, 2005, from the World Wide Web at http://www.infotrac.galegroup.com.

SPENCER, S. (2003). Introduction. In S. Spencer (Ed.), *The politics of migration: Managing opportunity, conflict and change* (pp. 1–24). Malden, MA: Blackwell Publishing.

STAR, M. (1997, March). Asian Canada: The economic and cultural energy that Asia immigrants are bringing may turn a green and promising land into the next California. *Transpacific, 68*, 40.

STATISTICS CANADA. (2004, October 14). 2001 Census: Population by selected religions, provinces and territories. *The Daily*. Retrieved October 14, 2004, from the World Wide Web at http://www.statcan.ca/english/Pgdb/demo30a.htm.

UNITED PRESS INTERNATIONAL (2005, September 24). Canada plans to increase immigration. *UPI NewsTrack*. Retrieved October 16, 2005, from the World Wide Web at http://www.infotrac.galegroup.com.

YEE, P. (1988). *Saltwater City: An illustrated history of the Chinese in Vancouver*. Vancouver: Douglas & McIntyre Ltd.

Suggested Readings

CAMERON, E. (Ed.). (2004). *Multiculturalism and immigration in Canada: An introductory reader*. Toronto: Canadian Scholars' Press Inc.

A comprehensive collection of essays on the historical, social, and cultural issues of immigrating to Canada. This book deals with many of the issues presented in this chapter.

LI, P.S. (1988). *The Chinese in Canada*. Toronto: Oxford University Press.

Although a bit dated, this book still offers significant information on the situation of Chinese immigrants to Canada from a social science perspective.

MINHAS, M. (1994). *The Sikh Canadians*. Edmonton, AB: Reidmore Books Inc.

This book offers a significant contribution to the history and struggles of Sikh immigrants to Canada.

CHAPTER SIX

How Has the Push for the Perfect Body Impacted on the Self-Image, Health, and Comfort of Women?

Introduction

The perfect body—what does this mean? Is it a size 2 woman with an impossibly small waist and large breasts, or a woman with an artificially elongated neck? Is it a man with bulging muscles and a flat stomach, or a man covered with intricate scarification? Every culture has its own image of beauty and attractiveness, and men and women are to a certain extent defined by their bodies. In North America the pursuit of the perfect body has taken on a will of its own. Indeed, the Western perception of beauty is diffusing to other regions of the world via the media, resulting in many of the same body image problems as seen in the West. Nevertheless, there are still some cultures that maintain their own concept of beauty.

KEY TERMS: body image, cross-cultural perspective, medical anthropology, body modification, ethnographic research, eating disorders, body adornment

Despite some rather convoluted psychological definitions, quite simply **BODY IMAGE** is the way we think our body looks. It is also how we think our body *should* look—a mental image of beauty as defined in a given culture. In North America, tall, blond, thin women continue to represent the ideal body.[1] This narrow and impossible-to-achieve standard of beauty is perpetuated by the media: film, television, magazines, and cyberspace all glamorize thinness and equate it with beauty and perfection. Women are flooded with advertisements for Botox, cosmetic surgery, diets, and exercise equipment designed to work wonders, as well as "self-help" programs that more often than not focus on ways to "improve" our appearance—what Nichter and Vuckovic (1994) call body work. This cultural emphasis on the perfect body has led many women to feel inadequate and dissatisfied with their bodies, and like a failure if they cannot meet their culture's standards. Most of these women identify the image of beauty perpetuated by the media as a major factor in creating their insecurity.

Not all cultural groups agree with the North American perception of beauty, especially the view that a thin body is ideal; indeed, we will discuss several cultures where the opposite is true. However, it is also evident that other cultures are being increasingly influenced by Western ideals concerning the ideal body image. Although body image is a broad term encompassing many concepts of beauty and many methods of achieving this beauty, in this chapter we will focus on the Western preoccupation with thinness and the diffusion of this ideal to several other cultures, followed by a brief cross-cultural examination of body adornment and modification practices.

Anthropologists and Body Image

The anthropological study of body image is relatively recent and, to date, rather limited in its scope (Sault 1994). For the most part, anthropologists have concentrated on the body, rather than body image. As scientists, anthropologists have witnessed the harm that distorted body images can cause to individuals and entire groups, and they have observed the negative influence Western body ideals are exerting on other cultures.

Anthropologists bring a **CROSS-CULTURAL PERSPECTIVE** to the study of body image and the concept of beauty. They attempt to understand how other cultures give meaning to body image. As you will see in this chapter, beliefs and behaviours regarding body image can vary significantly from one culture to another. Anthropologists are beginning to study how the diffusion of Western body image and ideals to other cultures is distorting traditional perceptions of beauty.

Contemporary anthropologists approach the study of body image from an applied perspective, using their cross-cultural knowledge to enter into the dialogue on body image. This is particularly evident in **MEDICAL ANTHROPOLOGY**, where the cultural meanings and social dynamics of fasting, overeating, and **BODY MODIFICATION** have been considered. For example, Massara (1989) studied the cultural meaning and the social implications of being overweight among older Puerto Rican women. This study was particularly relevant because Massara employed **ETHNOGRAPHIC RESEARCH** methods and, in doing so, provided a model for medical professionals to understand their patients within a cultural context (Mackenzie 1991).

"When I'm out of control of my eating and my weight, I'm out of control of my life!"
(MACKENZIE 1991: 408)

A Discussion of Body Image

In *The Body Image Trap*, Crook (1991) defines the perfect body as tall, blond, and size 10. This is somewhat surprising, since most twenty-first-century North American women preoccupied with thinness would be horrified to reach a size 10. The pursuit of thinness among Western women is highly valued, and even though there are other cultures that value thinness (e.g., Arab cultures), Counihan (1999) has never encountered a culture where it is acceptable to starve in order to attain a thin body, and contends that the self-destructive relationship many Western women have with their bodies is different than that of women in non-Western cultures.

Body image is about power; women seek to exert control over something—in this case their weight, hair, makeup, clothes, and so on (Edut 1998). Brumberg (1989) found that fasting is one of the few forms of protest available to young girls, both today and in the past. In other words, refusing to eat offers a sense of empowerment—a way for young women to gain control and autonomy over their lives (Hesse-Biber 1996). Mackenzie (1991) noted that fasting is also an expression of concern over virtue, feelings of being unlovable, and a desire to improve self-esteem through losing weight.

Massara (1989) found that being overweight offered a certain amount of freedom to Puerto Rican women—they were allowed to leave their homes without fear of being accused of infidelity.[2] Thus they had little incentive to lose weight, despite health risks cited by their physicians. Conversely, overeating was an expression of stress in a culture where women could not openly express their anger.

Hesse-Biber (1996) likens the quest for thinness to a religious cult, with all the requisite characteristics—isolation, obsession, and excessive ritual (dieting, exercise, daily weigh-ins, and calorie counting). The media and entertainment industry provide icons to worship (e.g., Jennifer Aniston) and ceremonies such as beauty pageants to reaffirm the ideal. Diet clubs (e.g., Weight Watchers), sages (e.g., Dr. Atkins), and gurus (e.g., Oprah Winfrey) often take on a quasi-religious connotation. It is difficult to shed the attitude that the perfect body and, in particular, perfect weight are not important when popular shows such as *Entertainment Tonight* regularly feature at least one and sometimes several vignettes on a celebrity's rising or falling weight. Economically, the cosmetic, fitness, and diet industries have burgeoned in North America, as has cosmetic surgery. Women spend enormous sums of money, time, and energy trying to emulate the North American concept of beauty.

The ideal body image is culturally defined (Sault 1994). Chinese foot binding involved bending the toes under the sole, making a pointed front—arching the foot like a small hook (Ping 2000). This practice was popular in tenth-century China and for a thousand years afterward, but eventually faded out when Mao Zedung and the Cultural Revolution transformed China's political and social environment. Most North Americans find foot binding cruel, yet this symbol of traditional Chinese femininity and beauty is remarkably similar to the current Western practice of young women undergoing breast augmentation, or the historical practice of wearing a tightly cinched and extremely damaging corset. Like all ideals, body image is dynamic, changing over time. In the early years of the twenty-first century, the ideal body image in North America has begun to shift slightly to one of fitness and health, although the quest for thinness is still readily evident and continues to cause all manner of physical and emotional trauma.

Ethnicity can play a role in body image (Kawamura 2002). Western media tends to stereotype the features of minority groups, and seldom uses them as role models for exemplifying beauty in mainstream Western society. Discrimination based on physical characteristics can be harmful to self-esteem, leading many young people to dislike their physical features based on ethnicity.

Language use influences body image; for example, the images conjured up by the words "fat" and "plump" are significantly different. Our perception of terms such as "fat-thin," "old-young," "beautiful-ugly," "strong-weak" are all defined within a culture and can differ from one culture to another. Language also reflects cultural attitudes. For example, Nichter and Vuckovic (1994) commonly encountered the phrase "I'm so fat" during their ethnographic research on body image and dieting among adolescent North American girls. This "ritualized talk" signals unhappiness, a call for peer support, apology for bad behaviour, and so on. Whether the body is viewed as the sum of its parts or as a whole entity is also reflected in language choice. In North America, where the body is viewed in parts (e.g., thighs, breasts, head), we would say "my head aches." Among the Wintu of California, where the body is viewed as a whole, they may say "I head ache" (Sault 1994: 13 from Lee 1959: 124).

The desire to look appealing is not a new phenomenon. Indeed, archaeological evidence of decorative jewellery and other forms of body beautification and modification are fairly common, especially in ancient societies such as the Egyptians and Mayans. The Canadian

Plains Cree of the nineteenth century also wore jewellery, such as disc-shaped earrings and necklaces made from bison teeth, elk tusks, and bear claws. At a fairly young age, children's ears were pierced using an awl, then sinew was pulled through the openings (Mandelbaum 1979). Men plucked their facial hair, and both men and women braided their hair. Tattooing was common among both sexes—the men on their arms and chests, and the women on their lips to chins. At large gatherings and ceremonies, men and women painted their cheeks red. These practices likely had more of a symbolic meaning than simply to create an ideal body image. Nonetheless, the concept of beautification was clearly evident.

The first recorded diet began in 1558, when Italian Luigi Coronaro ate sparingly to change his overall health, becoming thin and energetic. His writings on the value of "dieting" convinced others to try losing weight to improve their health (Crook 1991). In the nineteenth and twentieth centuries, the trend was toward increasing slenderness, but the contemporary obsession with a thin body in Western society can be traced to the 1960s when British fashion model Twiggy came on the scene. Before this time, the ideal woman was full figured and healthy looking, signifying her ability to bear children. Then Twiggy appeared, and the desperate quest for thinness began. Barbie, the fashion model doll, first appeared on store shelves in the 1960s. This doll inspired young girls and women to strive for her impossible-to-emulate beauty standard—what Gilman (1998) calls the Barbie doll syndrome.

Psychologically, preoccupation with dieting and idealizing thinness is often linked to low self-esteem and distorted body image (Brewis 1999). Women with bodies outside the ideal often suffer from society's disapproval, and are marginalized. Those individuals deemed unattractive often experience difficulty finding jobs or climbing the corporate ladder. Indeed, some jobs, such as those of flight attendants, have height and weight restrictions; those who fail to adhere are grounded or

You're busted, Babs. You've been found guilty of inspiring fourth-grade girls to diet, of modeling an impossible beauty standard, of clinging to homogeneity in a diverse new world. OPHIRA EDUT (1998: 1)

This extensive collection of Barbie dolls not only symbolizes an impossible to achieve standard of beauty but our obsession with her beauty.

Media portrayal of young, beautiful, "perfect" women has led many women to feel inadequate.

dismissed. They may be labelled "fat" or unattractive, and be considered lazy and lacking in self-discipline and willpower. Hence, we develop a sense of body image (negative or positive) from the way others see us or the way we think others see us. Our attempts to change or improve our bodies are usually a response to the opinions of other people.

Our concept of the ideal body is learned. Enculturation begins early in life, and is learned from our parents, peers, and of course, the media. Indeed, if children grow up in a household where one or more adults is constantly dieting and exercising, they may develop skewed priorities, focusing on the way they look rather than on other achievements. Add to that the daily exposure to "perfect" people in the entertainment industry, and young people grow up with deeply ingrained cultural perceptions of body image. The quest for that perfect body is beginning at a younger age in North America, with children as young as seven aware of whether eating a particular food will make them fat, and judging their worth according to their body size.

Although body image distortion is more prevalent among women, this pattern is not age or gender-restricted—both males and females are concerned with their appearance, and expend enormous time, energy, and money in achieving the perfect body. Hesse-Biber (1996) found that the trend is also toward weight loss among men, thereby opening up a huge market for weight-loss programs, exercise equipment, health spas, and various men's products. The strategy appears to be working because the percentage of body dissatisfaction among men is increasing.

EATING DISORDERS

The all-consuming desire to achieve a perfect body has led to serious psychological, socio-cultural, economic, and health consequences in the West and, increasingly, in other parts of the world. **EATING DISORDERS**, so common in contemporary North American society, are symptomatic of this quest. Anorexia nervosa, the avoidance of food to the point of starvation, and bulimia, binge eating followed by self-induced vomiting, are two of the most common diseases (Holmberg 1998) that have ravished young people, particularly women. Excessive exercising and taking appetite suppressants are also symptoms of this obsession.

CROSS-CULTURAL COMPARISON

Although this discussion has focused predominantly on the North American body image, the following cross-cultural comparison shows that pressures to conform to a certain body size are not the sole domain of Westerners. Southeastern Nigerians identify curvaceous woman as the ideal. They see a plump woman as healthy, her family as prosperous, and her sexuality as alluring (Simmons 1998). To this end, young women undergo an age-old rite of passage. They are isolated in a fattening room, where they are fed excessively to gain weight and instructed in the ways of becoming a proper wife and mother. The age when girls enter the fattening room varies, from as young as seven to just before marriage. The general guideline is the bigger the better, although most families can only afford to support their daughters in the fattening room for a few months rather than the traditional two years. Today, Nigerians, especially urban dwellers, are experiencing relentless pressure from the West to conform to the thin ideal. However, in rural areas the custom persists.

In Florence, Italy, Florentines view the body as a source of pleasure and a reflection of family (Counihan 1999). Both men and women love food (*gola*) and love to eat and nurture their bodies. Though they enjoy eating, Florentines also believe in control—gluttony destroys the pleasure of eating and leads to obesity. Thus, Florentines believe in "enjoying food greatly but consuming it moderately" (Counihan 1999: 182). Unlike North Americans, who may feel guilty after a day of overeating and resort to strenuous exercise and dieting, the Florentines

"Anorexia nervosa (and other eating disorders) is not really about losing weight, eating or not, exercising like a maniac or not, it is about self-esteem, it is about how you feel about yourself."

JUDY, A RECOVERING ANOREXIC (SARGENT N.D.)

do not. A plump body signifies health and fertility, while a thin body may mean physical illness or emotional upset.

Despite their healthy relationship with food and their bodies, Western influence is seeping into Italian consciousness. Florentine women are being bombarded with North American images of thin women as the ideal, which is affecting the way young Florentine women view themselves, despite the contention of men that they prefer plump women. Counihan (1999) also found that eating disorders in Italy, such as anorexia nervosa, were on the upswing in the 1990s.

One startling example of altered body image in Vietnam is the newly infused Westernized perception of the proper height for humans, which lies at the root of a dangerous fad—leg-lengthening surgeries (Cudd 2005). This new body image has even influenced employment opportunities where companies have set height restrictions and will not hire individuals who do not fit within this ideal body height.

Today, some Asian women are having cosmetic surgery to remove their epicanthic folds and create a double eyelid to meet Western standards of beauty; thus, a form of medicalization of so-called racial features is developing. In Korea, China, Japan, and the Philippines, plumpness used to be considered a sign of prosperity, good health, and beauty. However, recent studies have shown that this is no longer the case; the North American quest for thinness has diffused to these regions via the media (Kawamura 2002). The same holds true for Latino cultures. Latinos living in their native countries and those who have immigrated to North America have been exposed to Western ideals of thinness, which has led to a dramatic increase in eating disorders. As an example, girls in private schools in Brazil have adopted Western body ideals, leading to abuse of laxatives and diuretics (Altabe & O'Garo 2002). It appears the more acculturated a group becomes to North American values, the less body satisfaction they experience. Even in relatively isolated indigenous cultures, Western influences are being felt. In Samoa, feeding of the body to make it plump is a sign of social success. However, as Brewis (1999) discovered, those Samoans living in an urban setting in Auckland, New Zealand, (and by association, more exposed to Western ideals) possessed slimmer body ideals than those still living in Samoa.

BODY ADORNMENT

Body image is not entirely tied to physicality; it is also created through cultural practices, such as **BODY ADORNMENT**, modification, and fashion. Contemporary small-scale cultures, such as the Ju/'hoansi foragers of Namibia and Botswana, tattoo geometric designs on their foreheads and cheekbones. The women wear beaded necklaces and armbands, and ostrich shell ornaments in their hair (Lee 2003). Trobrianders of Papua New Guinea dress and decorate their bodies to increase their attractiveness to potential sexual partners. Young Trobrianders enjoy adorning

"We now have damning evidence from Fiji of the impact of Western ideals of beauty where, in a three-year period after the introduction of TV (mainly US programmes), 15 per cent of the teenage girls developed bulimia. The penetration of Western images coupled with an economic onslaught, had destabilised Fijian girls' sense of beauty, infecting them with a virus more lethal than the measles Britain exported to the colonies 100 years ago."

(ORBACH 2001: 1 FROM WYKES & GUNTER 2005: 14)

their bodies: girls wear short, red miniskirts made of woven dried banana leaves, and red shell necklaces that symbolize their availability to the young men in the village. Males appear to have been influenced by outside forces; instead of the white *pandanus* (penis coverings) they used to wear, today they wear cotton shorts or colourful *laplaps* (long pieces of cloth tied at the waist) (Weiner 1992). The men and women commonly tease their dark, thick hair using carved wooden combs, then slip red hibiscus flowers into their hair. Using black and white vegetable dyes, they paint designs on their faces, and rub charmed coconut oil into their skin to make it shine.

Among the Rashaayda Bedouin of eastern Sudan, tattooing is used to communicate identity and symbolize relations with others. Rashiidy women tattoo their bodies in three places: the forearms, the lower half of the face, and the upper legs and thighs (Young 1994). Arm tattoos are merely decorative, while face and leg tattoos are private symbols reserved for the eyes of their loved ones. An unmarried girl may have her thigh tattooed with a man's camel brand to announce her love for him. Among married women, only their husbands will see the tattoos because their faces are covered with veils and their legs with long skirts.

Makeup use in North America is another form of body adornment—one that has invoked harsh criticism and a great deal of misinterpretation. Current feminist thinking is that women wear makeup to please men; that it is a manifestation of female oppression in a patriarchal society. This may be an over-analysis of an extremely common practice. Anthropologists, such as Beausoleil (1994), have moved away from the view of makeup as oppressive and begun listening to what makeup actually means to the women who wear it. Some women wear makeup, not to please men, but to please themselves—to increase their own sense of attractiveness and security. To suggest that women who wear makeup are manipulated, oppressed, and passive victims of a patriarchal society is insulting. Nevertheless, this practice also exemplifies body manipulation in order to enhance attractiveness.

Conclusion

Body image is virtually a universal concept that influences and is influenced by cultural ideals. Our sense of belonging and even identity is determined through body image; thus, women are willing to endure all sorts of inconvenience and difficulty to attain the ideal body, and earn the status and approval of their society. Yet, body manipulation can be empowering as well as restrictive.

In the last half century, Westerners, particularly women, have developed a distorted sense of the ideal body that has created emotional and physical problems. This Western body ideal is also permeating other cultures. Through the media, young people the world over are adopting the Western ideal of beauty, and developing similar body image problems as in the West.

A continuing theme running through this chapter has been the influence of culture and the social relations within that culture on body image. As is obvious, North American society stresses thinness as the ideal body form; therefore, women in particular strive to emulate that ideal. In other cultures, health and childbearing capabilities are the ideal. Body image, the different forms of body modification, and the many meanings of "the perfect body" are extremely complex issues that require more extensive investigation from an anthropological perspective.

Questions for Consideration

1.   How much influence does current fashion have on your choice of clothing and other body adornments? Have you committed any fashion faux pas? Investigate the fashions of your parents' teen years. Are any of those fashions currently being recycled in your generation? How do they view their earlier fashion choices (this might give you some inkling of how you will view your current fashion choices in the future).

2.   Develop a research design for a cross-cultural study of body image.

3.   Diffusion of the Western ideal of beauty to other parts of the world is affecting young women's sense of well-being. Choose a country or cultural group and research the influence Western ideals have had on their perception of beauty and how they have responded to these changes.

4.   How prevalent are eating disorders in your network of friends and family? Identify the symptoms and behaviours of someone with an eating disorder.

5.   Conduct an honest self-analysis of your body image and efforts you expend to improve your appearance. Analyze the reasons for your behaviour.

NOTES

1   Although men certainly have body images, this discussion will focus primarily on female bodies, reflecting the overwhelming emphasis in North America and, indeed, the world over, on female beauty.
2   The attitude being that overweight women will not be sought after by other men.

References

ALTABE, M., & O'GARO, K. (2002). Hispanic body images. In T.F. Cash & T. Pruzinsky (Eds.), *Body image: A handbook of theory, research, and clinical practice* (pp. 250–256). New York: The Guilford Press.

BEAUSOLEIL, N. (1994). Makeup in everyday life. An inquiry into the practices of urban American women of diverse backgrounds. In N. Sault (Ed.), *Many mirrors: Body image and social relations* (pp. 33–57). New Brunswick: Rutgers University Press.

BREWIS, A.A. (1999). The accuracy of attractive-body-size judgment. *Current Anthropology, 40*(4), 548–553.

BRUMBERG, J.J. (1989). *Fasting girls: The surprising history of anorexia nervosa*. New York: New American Library.

COUNIHAN, C.M. (1999). *The anthropology of food and body: Gender, meaning, and power*. New York: Routledge.

CROOK, M. (1991). *The body image trap: Understanding and rejecting body image myths*. International Self-Counsel Press Ltd.

CUDD, A.E. (2005). Missionary positions. *Hypatia*. Retrieved October 23, 2005, from the World Wide Web at http://www.infotrac.galegroup.com.

EDUT, O. (1998). Introduction. In O. Edut (Ed.), *Adios, Barbie: Young women write about body image and identity*. Seattle, WA: Seal Press.

GILMAN, S.J. (1998). Klaus Barbie, and other dolls I'd like to see. In O. Edut (Ed.), *Adios, Barbie: Young women write about body image and identity* (pp. 14–21). Seattle, WA: Seal Press.

HESSE-BIBER, S. (1996). *Am I thin enough yet? The cult of thinness and the commercialization of identity*. New York: Oxford University Press.

HOLMBERG, C.B. (1998). *Sexualities and popular culture*. Thousand Oaks, CA: Sage Publications.

KAWAMURA, K.Y. (2002). Asian American body images. In T.F. Cash & T. Pruzinsky (Eds.), *Body image: A handbook of theory, research, and clinical practice* (pp. 243–249). New York: The Guilford Press.

LEE, D. (1959). *Freedom and culture*. Prospect Heights, IL: Waveland Press, Inc.

LEE, R.B. (2003). *The Dobe Ju/'hoansi* (3rd ed.). Toronto: Thomson Nelson Learning.

MACKENZIE, M. (1991). [Review of the books *Fasting girls: The emergence of anorexia nervosa as a modern disease; Fasting girls: The surprising history of anorexia nervosa; !Que Gordita! A study of weight among women in a Puerto Rican community; Never too thin: Why women are at war with their bodies*]. *Medical Anthropology Quarterly, 5*(4), 406–410.

MANDELBAUM, D.G. (1979). *The Plains Cree: An ethnographic, historical, and comparative study*. Canadian Plains Studies, No 9. Canadian Plains Research Center, University of Regina.

MASSARA, E.B. (1989). *!Que Gordita! A study of weight among women in a Puerto Rican community*. Immigrant Communities and Ethnic Minorities in the United States and Canada, No. 46. New York: AMS Press.

NICHTER, M., & VUCKOVIC, N. (1994). Fat talk: Body image among adolescent girls. In N. Sault (Ed.), *Many mirrors: Body image and social relations* (pp. 109–131). New Brunswick: Rutgers University Press.

ORBACH, S. (2001, June 24). Give us back our bodies. *Observer*. Retrieved October 23, 2005, from the World Wide Web at http://observer.guardian.co.uk/comment/story/0,6903,511730,00.html.

PING, W. (2000). *Aching for beauty: Footbinding in China*. Minneapolis: University of Minnesota Press.

SARGENT, J. (n.d.). *Judy's story*. Retrieved March 24, 2006, from the World Wide Web at http://www.angelfire.com/ms/anorexianervosa/.

SAULT, N. (1994). Introduction: The human mirror. In N. Sault (Ed.), *Many mirrors: Body image and social relations* (pp. 1–28). New Brunswick: Rutgers University Press.

SEID, R.P. (1989). *Never too thin: Why women are at war with their bodies*. New York: Prentice Hall.

SIMMONS, A.M. (1998). Where fat is a mark of beauty. *Los Angeles Times*. Reprinted in E. Angeloni (Ed.). (2005). *Annual Editions Anthropology: 05/06*. Dubuque, IO: McGraw-Hill/Dushkin.

WEINER, A. (1992). *Inalienable possessions: The paradox of keeping-while-giving*. Berkeley: University of California Press.

WYKES, M., & GUNTER, B. (2005). *The media and body image*. London: Sage Publications.

YOUNG, W. (1994). The body tamed: Tying and tattooing among the Rashaayda Bedouin. In N. Sault (Ed.), *Many mirrors: Body image and social relations* (pp. 58–75). New Brunswick: Rutgers University Press.

Suggested Readings

EDUT, O. (Ed.). (1998*). Adios, Barbie: Young women write about body image and identity*. Seattle, WA: Seal Press.

A delightful collection of cross-cultural essays that consider the social impact of the Barbie doll. The young women featured in this book show little interest in resembling a Barbie doll, yet address many of the body image concerns and issues faced by women.

MASSARA, E.B. (1989). *!Que Gordita! A study of weight among women in a Puerto Rican community*. Immigrant Communities and Ethnic Minorities in the United States and Canada, No. 46. New York: AMS Press.

An interpretation of oral histories of Puerto Rican women living in Philadelphia in the 1970s. The book examines the cultural meaning of overweight women and the impact on their social position.

SEID, R.P. (1989). *Never too thin: Why women are at war with their bodies*. New York: Prentice Hall.

An historical examination of America's preoccupation with diet and exercise to achieve an acceptable thinness in the twentieth century. Although an historical account, the book reads like ethnography and uses contemporary magazines as informants.

CHAPTER SEVEN

Is Female Circumcision a Violation of Human Rights or a Cherished Cultural Tradition?

Introduction

Perhaps no other cultural practice has raised the ire of the international community more than **FEMALE CIRCUMCISION**. Feminist and human rights groups, medical practitioners, religious and political organizations, the media, and many others have voiced their opposition to this ancient practice. Yet, many anthropologists believe we must look beyond the "shock" value of female circumcision and try to understand the deeply rooted reasons behind this practice. This does not mean that anthropologists condone female circumcision, nor does it mean we champion the rights of cultural groups to continue the practice. Rather, most anthropologists recognize that we cannot understand the cultural meanings behind this custom without *listening* to the women who value the practice of female circumcision. Only then can we offer an informed opinion.

KEY TERMS: female circumcision, *sunna* circumcision, clitoridectomy, pharaonic circumcision, infibulation, feminist anthropologists, patriarchal society, initiation rite, polygyny, development and modernization approach, female genital mutilation, female genital cutting, medicalization, symbolic circumcision, male circumcision

In this chapter we will enter the ongoing debate surrounding female circumcision, a debate that pits cultural relativism, a fundamental principle of anthropology, against global advocacy for human rights. The goal is to investigate the practice of female circumcision, the perspectives of anthropologists, and the controversy attached to female circumcision. To offer insight into the complexity of this issue, several narratives are presented in margins. Readers should note that while it is easy to find people who hold negative views on female circumcision, giving voice to people who support this practice is much more challenging. The reasons for this one-sided debate are likely many: the researcher, usually of Western origin, may be unconsciously showing his or her bias by seeking out those who will speak against the practice. Those who still practise female circumcision may be less willing to speak out for fear of reprisals from government officials or condemnation from the interviewer, or they may feel no need to justify female circumcision to outsiders. Approximately two million females undergo circumcision each year; therefore, regardless of literature bias, the practice is still highly valued and prevalent.

FEMALE CIRCUMCISION

Female circumcision is the cutting, removal, or altering of the external genitalia. The procedure is most often performed by traditional or government-trained midwives who are older women in the community. There are three major types of female circumcision (Gordon 1991). The simplest and least invasive procedure is **SUNNA CIRCUMCISION**, where only the clitoral prepuce (hood) is removed. The second type of circumcision is known as excision or **CLITORIDECTOMY**, where part or all of the clitoris is removed, as well as part or all of the labia minora.[1] **PHARAONIC CIRCUMCISION**, the third type, involves the complete removal of the clitoris, labia minora, and most or all of the labia majora.[2] In pharaonic circumcision, the cut edges are then stitched together with thorns, leaving only a small opening for urine and menstrual flow. This stitching is known as **INFIBULATION**. A stick is inserted to maintain the opening, and the female's legs are bound together to promote healing. Before intercourse, an infibulated woman may have to be cut open, then re-infibulated after the birth of her child.

The age at which female circumcision is performed varies from one ethnic group to another and depends on the main reason(s) for the practice. The most common times are soon after birth, before puberty (typically between the ages of five and seven), at the onset of puberty, just before marriage, in the seventh month of a woman's first pregnancy, or after the first birth (Mackie 2000).

Anthropologists and Female Circumcision

From an anthropological perspective, female circumcision is a highly valued cultural tradition that is embedded in the systems of a culture. However, this is likely the only point on which anthropologists agree. The practice presents an ethical dilemma in anthropology; anthropologists grapple with the intellectual, emotional, and moral issues attached to female circumcision. Some anthropologists, particularly **FEMINIST ANTHROPOLOGISTS,** view the practice as oppressive and symptomatic of a **PATRIARCHAL SOCIETY**. Indeed, for some feminists, female circumcision has come to symbolize worldwide patriarchal oppression. Anthropologists who adhere to a more culturally relativistic perspective believe that outsiders, including anthropologists, have no business interfering with this ancient cultural practice.

Those anthropologists attempting to maintain a culturally relativistic perspective are often accused of advocacy and overcompensating for Western ethnocentrism. The first part of this accusation misses the point. Anthropologists are not advocates for female circumcision; indeed, it is safe to say virtually all anthropologists are against the practice. What many of us do advocate is the freedom for cultural groups to choose this practice or not, without pressure from outsiders. Since the practice is so common, it would appear the people have already made their decision—the West simply refuses to accept it. However, the issue is not that simple. The word *choice* is a vague term that often fails to recognize that, as individuals, the girls and indeed their families may not have much in the way of a choice between meeting the social expectations of their community or facing ostracism if they refuse to follow group norms. As far as group choice, the issue is even more complicated—who in the group makes the decision? Are the women of the community equal decision makers or is tradition established by the males only? Are opponents to the ruling hierarchy silenced, or do all members have some say in the group decision? There does appear to be some community autonomy, with each community independently making its own decision on whether to continue or stop female circumcision. When I discussed this issue with several male students from Nigeria, they pointed out that their village "no longer practices female circumcision, while the village down the road still does."

The second part of the criticism may have some merit. Certainly, I find myself attempting to explain traditions and beliefs from a culture's point of view, and perhaps overemphasizing the validity of these practices because students have only been exposed to a very limited and ethnocentric Western point of view.

Most anthropologists, although as conflicted as others, recognize that any attempt to end this practice must take into consideration its cultural meaning and context. This is the difference between an

Protecting the rights of "a minority of women who oppose the practice is a legitimate and noble cause ... mounting an international campaign to coerce 80 million African women to give up their tradition is unjustified."

ANTHROPOLOGIST FUAMBAI AHMADU QUOTED IN SHELL-DUNCAN & HERNLUND (2000: 2)

informed and uninformed opinion. Janice Boddy is one anthropologist who has attempted to see beyond her own cultural biases to understand the cultural meanings and value of female circumcision. In northern Sudan, 98 per cent of the women are circumcised. The Sudanese practice pharaonic circumcision, which means the clitoris and labia minora are removed and the labia majora is sewn closed (infibulation), leaving a small opening for urine and menstrual passage. As an anthropologist, Janice Boddy recognized that her responsibility was to the Sudanese women—to tell their story in their own words. Boddy's perspective has drawn the wrath of feminists bent on eradicating the practice, regardless of the value people place on it. Again, it all comes down to respect—enough respect for these women to listen to their point of view and attempt to understand the importance of female circumcision to their physical, spiritual, and cultural identity (Blackburn-Evans 2002).

The question then becomes, what next? After listening to all sides, should anthropologists express their opinion regarding the practice? Can they ethically support or reject a cultural practice such as female circumcision? Some anthropologists feel that they have the obligation to speak their mind, while others feel that supporting or rejecting cultural practices outside of their own home culture is not the role of an anthropologist, unless asked to do so by the community.

A Discussion of Female Circumcision

Female circumcision is an ancient and widespread practice, although in some nations (e.g., Chad) it has been adopted only recently. Some estimates suggest 130 million females living in 28 countries are circumcised at a rate of two million per year (Leonard 2000). It is practised extensively in Africa, and in some regions of Indonesia, Malaysia, and the Arabian peninsula. The practice has also found its way to North America with immigrants from these regions.[3] Toubia and Izette (1998) suggest that 85 per cent of all circumcisions involve *sunna* circumcision or clitoridectomies, while infibulation is practised mainly in Somalia, Sudan, northeastern Kenya, Eritrea, parts of Mali, and a small region in northern Nigeria. In Djibouti, Mali, Eritrea, and Somalia, the practice is nearly universal, while in other countries, such as Tanzania, Senegal, Cameroon, and Niger, less than 20 per cent of the women are circumcised. The practice appears to be declining in some regions, while in others it is spreading, partly because of diffusion, and partly as a backlash to Western meddling. However, statistics on the extent of the practice are unreliable since much of the data is anecdotal.[4]

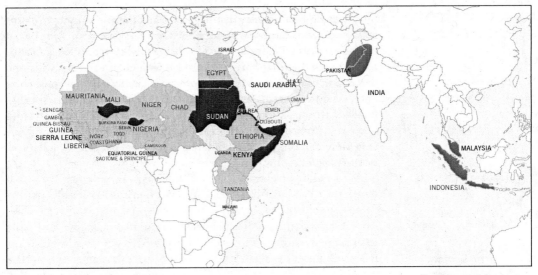

Statistics for Africa Map[5]

COUNTRY	PREVALENCE	TYPE
Benin	50%	Excision
Burkina Faso	70%	Excision
Cameroon	20%	Clitoridectomy and excision
Central African Republic	50%	Clitoridectomy and excision
Chad	60%	Excision and infibulation
Côte d'Ivoire	60%	Excision
Democratic Republic of Congo	5%	Excision
Djibouti	90–98%	Excision and infibulation
Egypt	97%	Clitoridectomy, excision, infibulation
Eritrea	90%	Clitoridectomy, excision, infibulation
Ethiopia	90%	Clitoridectomy and excision
Gambia	60–90%	Excision, infibulation
Ghana	15–30%	Excision
Guinea	70–90%	Clitoridectomy, excision, infibulation
Guinea-Bissau	50% average	Clitoridectomy and excision
Kenya	50%	Clitoridectomy, excision, infibulation
Liberia	50–60%	Excision
Mali	90–94%	Clitoridectomy, excision, infibulation
Mauritania	25% average	Clitoridectomy and excision
Niger	20%	Excision
Nigeria	50%	Clitoridectomy, excision, infibulation
Senegal	20%	Excision
Sierra Leone	80–90%	Excision
Somalia	98%	Infibulation
Sudan	80% n. Sudan	Infibulation, excision
Tanzania	10%	Excision, infibulation
Togo	12%	Excision
Uganda	5%	Clitoridectomy, excision

Countries practicing female circumcision.

■ Area where most women are initiated

Circumcision and excision widespread in some groups

Some cases reported

Circumcision practiced by some Muslim population groups (the shading in Pakistan and India represents Bohra Muslims, not exact locations)

The origin of female circumcision is lost in time, although it is at least 3,000 years old. Mackie (2000) believes female circumcision began in ancient Sudan, where it served to ensure fidelity and paternity assurance. The practice may have developed independently in several regions of sub-Saharan Africa in tandem with male circumcision, beginning as puberty or **INITIATION RITES**. Janice Boddy (1982: 685) points out that knowing this "custom's remote historical origins [does not] contribute to our understanding of its present significance." Nevertheless, for those who believe in this practice, and find themselves continually having to justify it, an ancient origin may be significant.

HEALTH RISKS ASSOCIATED WITH FEMALE CIRCUMCISION

Any discussion of female circumcision would be incomplete without consideration of the health risks and complications that can arise. These health risks are used as a medical justification for stamping out the practice, although much of the information on complications is dated, originating with British colonial medical practitioners in the 1930s and 1940s (Shell-Duncan & Hernlund 2000). These "facts" are often not supported by the experiences of women in the communities. Significantly, most of the problems described are the result of bungled infibulations, not the far more common clitoridectomy or *sunna* circumcision. In other words, we need to view Western propaganda against female circumcision with caution.[6]

As Westerners we may find this procedure appalling, especially since it is often performed without benefit of anaesthetic to dull the pain. However, it should be pointed out that in some cultures, such as the Mandinga of Guinea-Bissau, the ability to bear the pain with courage and fortitude is an important part of the initiation rite and brings honour to the girl and her family (Johnson 2000; Sargent 1991). In areas where medical services are available, anaesthetic may be used, as well as antibiotics to prevent infection, and if infibulation is practised, cat gut or silk sutures are used rather than thorns.

The actual prevalence of complications is difficult to assess; the women[7] are often unwilling to seek medical care, or they may not associate their medical problems with circumcision. Nevertheless, we can identify the more common problems women have encountered. Shortly after the procedure, some women have experienced hemorrhaging, severe pain, local and systemic infections, shock, and in extreme cases, death. Young girls may refuse to urinate for fear of the stinging, which can lead to urinary tract infections. Infections at the wound site are also common. Infibulation may lead to chronic complications, such as lifelong difficulties in passing urine and menstrual flow, renal failure or septicaemia from untreated urinary tract infections, and serious pelvic infections that may cause infertility. The inelasticity of the scar tissue may cause prolonged labour and delivery, risking the life of the infant and the mother. Besides physical harm, female circumcision may also cause psychological injury although the degree of psychological trauma is impossible to assess, but personal accounts reveal feelings of anxiety, fear, and humiliation.

Boddy (1982) looked beyond the medical issues that consume Westerners, and instead examined the social role this practice plays in the lives of Sudanese women. To the Sudanese, this is a time of celebration—gift giving, feasting, and visiting with well-wishers. Since the procedure may reduce sexual pleasure, their role as sexual beings is downplayed and their role as future mothers of men is emphasized. The process of removing the clitoris, which is considered a masculine organ, purifies the girl and enhances her femininity. Lutkekaus and Roscoe (1995) agree; the Sudanese believe circumcision marks a transition from an androgynous[8] childhood into a distinct female gender. Thus, female circumcision is an integral part of Sudanese gender identity.

Decreased sexual pleasure is often cited by opponents as a consequence of circumcision. However, Toubia and Izette (1998) report that up to 90 per cent of infibulated women enjoy sex and experience orgasms. Some respondents have even reported increased pleasure. On the other hand, El Dareer (1982) found that up to 50 per cent of his respondents experienced reduced sexual enjoyment. These conflicting statistics are a reflection of the raging academic debate surrounding female circumcision.

REASONS FOR FEMALE CIRCUMCISION

Given the seriousness of these complications and the agony of the procedure, the question uppermost in readers' minds will be, why? For what reason(s) would parents put their daughters through the ordeal and dangers of this procedure? This is where examining female circumcision becomes complicated because the issue is hampered by deeply embedded Western cultural assumptions, notions of human rights, and a lack of consensus regarding the practice—what it means, why it is done, and the value it holds for the people who practice it.

Westerners hold several misconceptions regarding this practice. First, female circumcision is not an act of cruelty or child abuse. Those who practise it are not cruel; they care about their daughters' well-being as much as any parents do. Women who are circumcised are *not* victims. Whether female circumcision is a violation of human rights or not depends on how we define the concept. As some of my more insightful students have pointed out, taking away a woman's right to be circumcised and enjoy her new status in the community, such as the right to marry and bear sons to ensure her security, is in itself an infringement on her human rights. Feminists often blame female circumcision on men and their need to oppress and control women; although some men are

"It was one morning in September before celebrating the *Nairuz* {Coptic New Year} that a woman came to circumcise me. I can't remember whether or not she was a *daya*. It was common practice to circumcise girls during the time of the Nile flood which was also the season for dates and guavas. I used to hear people around me explain that circumcision at this time of the year was good and helped the girl grow fast and develop. It was also cooler and marked the end of the school holidays.

"On that morning the woman who was to perform the operation stretched out her hands to me and said: 'Come, clever girl, don't be afraid; you won't feel anything.' Meanwhile her assistant caught hold of me in a brutal way. She held my arms tight and twisted them under my legs, which she pulled apart. The woman then disinfected the razor with cotton and alcohol, and cut off the parts. I screamed from pain and fear, but it was soon bandaged and I was carried to bed. The operation took place in the hall of our apartment. My eldest sister stood beside me to ensure that the razor was well cleaned with alcohol. My mother hid in the kitchen.

"Later on I learned that they had cut off all the clitoris and the two leaves {labia minora}. I spent one whole day in bed

purported to prefer circumcised women, this is by no means universal, and the procedure itself is controlled and perpetuated by women. Banning circumcision has not (and likely will not) improved the status of women; indeed, it often has the opposite effect, and there is growing evidence that female circumcision actually empowers women.[9] Furthermore, to suggest that these women are submissive and "brainwashed" into thinking circumcision is a good practice is an insult to the intelligence and strength of all women.

Female circumcision is performed for social, economic, cultural, and religious reasons. The most common reason given for female circumcision is to ensure a young woman remains a virgin until marriage and that any children born of the marriage are the husband's progeny. Among northern Sudanese, circumcised and infibulated young women are considered a preferred marriage choice. A tightly infibulated woman can earn a higher bride price and make a better marriage (Gruenbaum 2000). Although women contribute significantly to the household economy in this patriarchal society, they gain most of their economic security from their husbands (e.g., access to land and livestock), and in old age from their sons. Thus, female circumcision may ensure a good marriage and socio-economic well-being for a woman, which until recently has been a woman's only means to social status, acceptance, and security.

Economic factors are also significant for the practitioner. Women who become circumcisers benefit economically. In Sierra Leone, one of the poorest countries in Africa, girls as young as 10 perform circumcisions to earn income for their families. Their training may begin as early as age 3. For each circumcision they are paid approximately $6, which far exceeds the family income of most people. Thus, in this case, extreme poverty serves to perpetuate the practice (BBC News 2005). To outsiders, especially Westerners with all manner of social and economic opportunities, it may be difficult to grasp the severely limited economic options available to these girls. Performing circumcisions offers them desperately needed income when there are no other avenues of support.

For many groups, maintaining an age-old tradition is the underlying reason. The practice continues because the women do not want to break with an ancient custom that came from their grandmothers (Hernlund 2000). A bond of solidarity is forged between generations of women when grandmothers, mothers, and daughters have all undergone the ritual. However, tradition is a vague euphemism, and should not be taken as the only reason. Most analyses have found that female circumcision is highly symbolic. It is a rite of passage, symbolizing the passing from girlhood to womanhood. A girl's status rises once she is circumcised and she is now considered pure, clean, and womanly, whereas in cultures such as the Samburu of Kenya, uncircumcised girls are considered unclean, promiscuous, and immature (Althaus 1997). Female circumcision also announces and maintains cultural and ethnic identity. Gruenbaum (2000) found that, among the Sudanese,

ANTHROPOLOGY MATTERS!

pharaonic circumcision reinforces class distinctions and is a symbol of northern Sudanese identity that distinguishes them from other Sudanese.

Various beliefs, whether substantiated or not, also influence the prevalence of female circumcision. For example, the Yoruba believe if the clitoris touches the baby's head during birth, it will die; thus, the Yoruba practice female circumcision to ensure the survival of their children (Orubuloye, Caldwell, & Caldwell 2000). The less drastic forms of circumcision, clitoridectomies and *sunna* circumcision, are believed to lower a woman's sexual desire, thus reducing the chance she will become sexually active before marriage or seek extramarital affairs after marriage. Infibulation, for the most part, prevents any sexual intercourse outside of marriage. Infibulation is also alleged to contribute to a man's sexual pleasure. However, Shandall (1967) found that **POLYGYNOUS** Sudanese men preferred their uncircumcised wives for sexual intercourse over their circumcised wives.

Female circumcision is often associated with Islam. Despite pharaonic circumcision predating Islam by hundreds, perhaps thousands of years, the practice has been incorporated into Islamic beliefs (Gruenbaum 1982). This incorporation ignores the fact that Islamic scholars are adamant that the Quran does not promote female circumcision, and that many Islamic groups do not practice female circumcision. Those that do, such as the Mandingas of Guinea-Bissau, see the practice as a cleansing rite that marks the woman as a Muslim and gives her the right to pray (Johnson 2000). Regardless of whether the connection to Islam is legitimate or not, if the people believe that their religion commands it, then it is an important religious practice. Activists, both foreign and local, have tried to persuade Mandinga women that Islam does not advocate circumcision, but they have failed because the people are convinced that it is commanded.

Northern Sudanese women have vehemently resisted attempts to ban pharaonic circumcision. It would seem that ending this practice would improve at least the physical lives of women, yet they refuse to give up the custom. Part of the reason has to do with religion. Sudanese women believe they must be circumcised on religious grounds, although as Boddy (1982) found, they do not separate religion from tradition. Even more significant, female circumcision is deeply embedded in Sudanese gender, economic, marriage, and reproductive systems. The integrative nature of culture means that eliminating female circumcision from Sudanese culture would greatly impact on these other systems.

THE WESTERN VIEW OF FEMALE CIRCUMCISION

When Hilary Rodham Clinton addressed the 1995 United Nations Fourth World Conference on Women in Beijing, she stated unequivocally: "It is a violation of human rights when young girls are brutalized

afraid even to urinate. However, the following morning I was carried to the bathroom and my mother kept reassuring me by saying: 'Don't be afraid. As soon as you urinate you will feel normal again.' She made me sit in a basin of warm water and I was able to urinate in spite of the burning feeling. Then I defecated without any pain.

"I stayed in bed five days. Every morning as soon as I woke up and every evening my mother used to make me sit in warm water with a disinfectant and would clean me up. Three days after the operation a neighbour volunteered to examine the wound and advised that it was clean and that there was no more need for the bandage."

CAMILIA, AN EGYPTIAN WOMAN, QUOTED IN ASSAAD (1980: 11)

by the painful and degrading practice of female genital mutilation" (*San Francisco Examiner*, September 11, 1995). Senator Clinton's forceful statement is extremely ethnocentric, which is understandable given it is coming from a woman living in the West where we have strong opinions about basic human rights, especially the right to health and safety. The problem lies in the fact that this is a Western position, and it does not take into consideration how other cultures perceive female circumcision or how they define human rights. Indeed, the whole issue of human rights, although based on a desire to ensure that everyone, the world over, is free from harm, is a vaguely understood and by no means universally acknowledged concept often used to justify "making people over in the Western image"—what Shell-Duncan & Hernlund (2000: 34) label the **DEVELOPMENT AND MODERNIZATION APPROACH**.

As is obvious from Senator Clinton's statement, the terms we use often provide a barometer for the attitudes we hold. The "politics of names" is particularly evident when it comes to female circumcision. In the West, the practice is called **FEMALE GENITAL MUTILATION** to symbolize our universal disapproval of female circumcision. It was first coined at the International Conference on Population and Development in Cairo in 1994 (Althaus 1997). Even when the term "female circumcision" is used, the word *circumcision* is often placed in quotation marks to distinguish it from male circumcision, which is still practised in North America and considered a legitimate custom.[10] To avoid the judgmental tone of female genital mutilation, but to also separate the practice from male circumcision, some researchers prefer to use the term **FEMALE GENITAL CUTTING**. In cultures where this practice is valued, it is called circumcision. Opponents object to the word *circumcision* because it detracts from the severity of some of the procedures, and prefer the term "mutilation." However, mutilation is a judgment term and does not belong in an intellectual discussion of a time-honoured custom.

Opponents of female circumcision are often accused of Western imperialism, while defenders are accused of ignoring the rights of women. Campaigns against female circumcision, funded by the West and often cocooned in development projects, are well-entrenched in most African communities, although they have met with limited success. These campaigns have failed because the goal has always been to change women's minds about female circumcision with little consideration given to what the practice actually means to them socially, economically, and culturally. As well, the assumption that education and awareness programs will put an end to the practice once people realize the health risks is naive and condescending, and except for isolated cases, most practitioners are fully aware of the dangers.

The main impact of these anti-circumcision movements has been to bring to light the pervasiveness of the practice, which, in turn, has resulted in unwanted international attention (Ginsburg 1991), especially since the 1970s when international organizations such as the World Health Organization and the United Nations took notice. These movements have outraged women, including activists, in the countries where female circumcision is practised. Women, such as anthropologist Soheir Morsy, have expressed indignation over Western interference and condescension. The paternalistic concept of "helping" other people—what Morsy (1991) calls "rescue and civilizational missions," really amounts to an attack on their culture.

Not all opposition to female circumcision comes from Westerners. African women's organizations, such as the Inter-African Committee Against Harmful Traditional Practices, was formed in 1984 and now has national committees in more than 20 countries (Althaus 1997). Their mandate has been to bring the harmful effects of the procedure to the attention of African governments in an attempt to get the procedure banned. Western funding for developing education programs to teach the woman about the harmful effects of female circumcision helps support these indigenous women's groups.

Some activists have promoted criminalization of female circumcision as the only effective way to end the practice. They believe making the practice illegal may counter social pressures to continue it. In 1994 a law was passed in Sudan banning female circumcision. It caused a public furor and a backlash that actually increased the incidence of female circumcision (Shell-Duncan & Hernlund 2000). As an example of how extreme the resistance can become, a ban on clitoridectomies in Kenya's Meru District resulted in adolescent girls excising each other (Thomas 2000). Legislation may also force the practice underground where sanitation and quality of care are even more tenuous, and circumcised women experiencing difficulties may be unwilling to seek medical assistance for fear of prosecution. According to Mackie: "You simply can't outlaw cultural practices.... It is not possible to criminalize the entirety of a population, or the entirety of a discrete and insular minority of the population, without methods of mass terror. People have to decide to stop on their own" (Shell-Duncan & Hernlund 2000: 34 from *The Economist*, February 13, 1999: 45). Although an ineffective way of ending female circumcision, legislation banning the procedure continues to be passed. Some Western countries have even threatened to make international aid conditional to the country's banning of female circumcision. These threats will likely not be successful. Again, governments may yield to Western pressure, but if the ban is not enforceable, then it is irrelevant.

The "medical view" that female circumcision is a pathological practice given the risk of health problems has not resonated with people who practice female circumcision. Gruenbaum (1982) notes that medical complications have little relevance for changing or ending the practice, and although Westerners may believe eradication of female circumcision

"Foreigners from America, from London, who call us bad names, call us primitive and call our circumcision rites genital mutilation, adding: 'It makes us want to do more.'"

KAPCHORWA MAGISTRATE ALBERT LAIGIYA, A UGANDAN ELDER, QUOTED IN MASLAND (1999: 2)

The heads of the WHO, Unicef, and the United Nations Population Fund published a statement last week calling for an international effort to bring about a "major decline" within 10 years in what they termed an "unsafe and unjustifiable traditional practice." The aim is to eliminate female genital mutilation worldwide within three generations. The agencies announced plans to work with governments and political and religious organisations in countries where female genital mutilation is practiced. (HAMILTON 1997)

is a priority, women in developing nations have more serious concerns on their minds—like poverty, childhood diseases and malnutrition, ethnic conflict and war, and a lack of resources due to decades of exploitation by the very Westerners bent on changing their traditions.

Toubia (1988) asserts that female circumcision is not a medical problem. Rather, it is part of their social sphere, where cultural pressures (e.g., peer, parental, societal) and the whole concept of marriageability supersedes any perceived risks, and the suggestion that female circumcision must be eradicated as if it were a disease reeks of medical imperialism.

Both opponents and defenders of female circumcision have raised alarms over efforts to medicalize the procedure. If female circumcision becomes institutionalized—performed in medical institutions by licensed practitioners—opponents fear this would amount to tacit approval of female circumcision that will stymie efforts to eliminate the practice. Others suggest that if **MEDICALIZATION** improves the health and saves the lives of women, then it is worth any risk of seeming to approve of the procedure. Defenders of the traditional practice fear that medicalization will shift control of female circumcision from women in the community to male practitioners in biomedical facilities (Shell-Duncan & Hernlund 2000). Johnson (2000: 230) found that among the Mandinga of Guinea-Bissau the woman refused a hospital circumcision because "the cutting is not the same."

Recent efforts to find alternative rituals, such as **SYMBOLIC CIRCUMCISION**, where the clitoris is only nicked, have met with limited success. Practitioners do not value the symbolic procedure in the same way, and some of the reasons for the practice, for example, ensuring chastity, are not served by this procedure. Western activists have also protested symbolic circumcision, stating that any form of female mutilation is oppressive. Even in North America, where symbolic circumcision would have offered immigrants a safe alternative to more invasive procedures, activists have protested loudly and effectively shut down the programs. As Coleman (1998) points out, these activists fail to appreciate that **MALE CIRCUMCISION** is still performed in North American hospitals and is much more invasive than symbolic circumcision.[11] The activists also appear to ignore the various forms of mutilation accepted in North American society: breast implants, face lifts, piercings, liposuction, gastric bypasses, and so on, all of which are designed to make the female body more attractive and acceptable to men.

Conclusion

From the preceding discussion, it is obviously difficult to step outside our Western bias when examining the practice of female circumcision. Yet, in order to fully comprehend the symbolic complexities of this practice, this is what we must do. As Boddy (1982) points out, we will never eliminate female circumcision if we do not understand why it is so important and why it continues to be practised despite international pressure. Herein lies the challenge: to respect cultural traditions and values, and cultural autonomy while promoting global human rights.

Anthropologists such as Sargent (1991) believe any efforts to change or end this custom must come from within these cultures, and will happen only when women have opportunities for economic security other than marriage and childbearing. Others, such as Leonard (2000), have even found that the practice is spreading in the face of modernization—oftentimes the poorer social classes, for example, in Sudan and Chad, are adopting infibulation in the hopes that their circumcised daughters will make a good marriage, thereby increasing their status. Certainly, Western interference has been met with strong resistance—both from within the cultures that practice female circumcision and others who resent this Western intrusion.

While hopes for eradication remain high, in reality there is little evidence that female circumcision is on the decline, despite community "successes." Young people appear more amenable to ending the practice than the older generations; however, this does not necessarily mean that as they mature this generation will reject the custom—honouring the traditions of forebears is a very powerful force. Legislation appears ineffective and difficult, if not impossible, to enforce, and if the people value the custom, it will continue despite its illegality. Some data suggests that women with higher education levels are less likely to be circumcised. However, in many upper-class urban families, for example, in Egypt, where the women have higher educations and opportunities, the practice is still very common, even to the point of taking their educated, sophisticated daughters back to their traditional villages to have the procedure done. Indeed, in quite a few cases, women of middle and upper classes are more likely to be circumcised than the poorer classes.[12]

Will female circumcision ever be eradicated? The question itself is controversial because it harkens back to the West's desire to eliminate an ancient custom because we consider it wrong. The issue is incredibly complex because it is natural, and even human, to want everyone to enjoy the rights and freedoms we enjoy in the West. Some would argue that in the West we honour human life, individuality, and freedom, and that we want to give other people the same quality of life—a laudable sentiment, but if examined closely, somewhat hollow. To barge in and demand that people change because we consider these acts cruel and barbaric is unethical and immoral to say the least. Shell-Duncan and Hernlund (2000: 25) ask a very valid question: "Who, if anyone, has the moral authority to condemn this practice?"

Over the last decade the West has acted as though they have suddenly discovered a dangerous epidemic which they then sensationalized in international women's forums creating a backlash of over-sensitivity in the concerned communities. They have portrayed it as irrefutable evidence of the barbarism and vulgarity of underdeveloped countries ... [and] the primitiveness of Arabs, Muslims, and Africans all in one blow. (TOUBIA 1988: 101)

Questions for Consideration

1   In your opinion, should Westerners attempt to eradicate the practice of female circumcision? Why or why not? (Support your answer with culturally relativistic reasons.) If yes, what is the best way to go about ending this practice? If no, why do you feel this way?

2.   Immigrants to Western countries (e.g., the United Kingdom, Canada, Australia, and the United States) may wish to continue this practice. How should this issue be addressed in these Western countries? For example, should we stop the practice or make it safer? Should we arrest the practitioners or supply them with medical equipment and supplies?

3.   Is female circumcision illegal in your country? If illegal, find out when the legislation was passed.

4.   In Chapter 6, the issue of body image is addressed. How is the practice of female circumcision connected to body image?

5.   Chinese foot binding was condemned as torture and eradicated in China. Do you think female circumcision will also eventually be eradicated? Why or why not?

6.   Compare female circumcision to male circumcision. How are these procedures alike and how are they different (e.g., the procedure itself, the reasons for practice, etc.)?

7.   In some cultures a woman who is circumcised is considered more attractive. How is this similar to North American cosmetic surgery, such as breast implants, face lifts, or liposuction? How is it different—or is it?

8.   Imagine an anthropologist from another country studying your community and negatively judging some of your traditional customs (e.g., rodeos, compulsory school attendance for girls, ear piercing, junk food, alcohol consumption, wearing revealing clothing, teen dating). How would you and the rest of your community react? Would this condemnation make you stop these practices? Why or why not?

9.   Cultural relativism is an underlying theme in this chapter, yet it is extremely difficult to maintain a culturally relativistic stance when confronted with what we perceive to be a harmful or unnecessary cultural practice. How do we reconcile our ideas of right and wrong with the needs of cultural groups for self-determination?

NOTES

1 Inner lips of the vulva.

2 Outside lips of the vulva.

3 In the early 1900s, female circumcision was practised (although not commonly) in Western countries to cure "illnesses" such as masturbation, hyper-sexuality, frigidity, and so on.

4 For a discussion of the problems with anecdotal data, also see Shell-Duncan and Hernlund (2000). Female "circumcision" in Africa: Dimensions of the practice and debates. In *Female "circumcision" in Africa: Culture, controversy, and change* (pp. 1–40). London: Lynne Rienner Publishers. .

5 Amnesty International. (1997). *Female genital mutilation in Africa: Information by country*. Retrieved March 17, 2006, from the World Wide Web at http://web.amnesty.org/library/index/ENGACT770071997.

6 The proliferation of articles on the "evils" of female circumcision found on the Internet is an example of this one-sided debate.

7 The term "woman" is used here although female circumcision is often performed on infants or young girls.

8 Not clearly distinguishable as either sex.

9 For further discussion of this contested stance, see Ahmadu, F. (2000). Rites and wrongs: An insider/outsider reflects on power and excision. In B. Shell-Duncan & Y. Hernlund (Eds.). (2000). *Female "circumcision" in Africa: Culture, controversy, and change* (pp. 283–312). London: Lynne Rienner Publishers. Anthropologist Fuambai Ahmadu has first-hand experience with this procedure; she was circumcised during initiation into a secret women's society in Sierra Leone.

10 If the term "female genital mutilation" is used, then the same must hold true for male circumcision—it is male genital mutilation. For further discussion of sexual mutilation of boys, see Scheper-Hughes (1991).

11 Male circumcision is performed without anesthesia. See Scheper-Hughes (1991).

12 For more discussion of these findings, see Obermeyer (1999).

References

AHMADU, F. (2000). Rites and wrongs: An insider/outsider reflects on power and excision. In B. Shell-Duncan & Y. Hernlund (Eds.), *Female "circumcision" in Africa: Culture, controversy, and change* (pp. 283–312). London: Lynne Rienner Publishers.

ALTHAUS, F.A. (1997). Special report. Female circumcision: Rite of passage or violation of rights? *Family Planning Perspectives, 23*(3), 1–9. Retrieved May 13, 2005, from the World Wide Web at www.agi-usa.org/pubs/journals/2313097.html.

AMNESTY INTERNATIONAL. (1997). *Female genital mutilation in Africa: Information by country*. Retrieved March 17, 2006, from the World Wide Web at http://web.amnesty.org/library/index/ENGACT770071997.

ASSAAD, M.B. (1980). Female circumcision in Egypt: social implications. Current research and prospects for change. In *Studies in Family Planning, 11*(1): 3–16.

BBC NEWS (2005, July 24). *Poverty prolonging circumcision practice*. Retrieved March 19, 2006, from the World Wide Web: http://news.bbc.co.uk/2/hi/uk_news/4674463.stm.

BLACKBURN-EVANS, A. (2002). Women's rites: Janice Boddy explores a shocking tradition in northern Sudan. *Edge magazine, 3*(2). Retrieved May 2, 2005, from the World Wide Web at http://www.research.utoronto.ca/edge/fall2002/leaders/boddy.html.

BODDY, J. (1982). Womb as oasis: The symbolic content of pharaonic circumcision in rural northern Sudan. *American Ethnologist, 9*, 682–698.

COLEMAN, D.L. (1998). The Seattle compromise: Multicultural sensitivity and Americanization. *Duke Law Journal, 478*, 717–783.

THE ECONOMIST (US). (1999, February 13). 350(8106), 45.

EL DAREER, A. (1982). *Woman, why do you weep? Circumcision and its consequences*. London: Zed Press.

GINSBURG, F. (1991). What do women want? Feminist anthropology confronts clitoridectomy. *Medical Anthropology Quarterly, 5*(1), 17–19.

GORDON, R. (1991). Female circumcision and genital operations in Egypt and the Sudan: A dilemma for medical anthropologists. *Medical Anthropology Quarterly, 5*(1), 3–14.

GRUENBAUM, E. (1982). The movement against clitoridectomy and infibulation in Sudan: Public health policy and the women's movement. *Medical Anthropology Newsletter, 13*(2), 4–12.

GRUENBAUM, E. (2000). Is female "circumcision" a maladaptive cultural pattern? In B. Shell-Duncan & Y. Hernlund (Eds.), *Female "circumcision" in Africa: Culture, controversy, and change* (pp. 41–54). London: Lynne Rienner Publishers.

HAMILTON, J. (1997, April 19). *UN condemns female circumcision*. BMJ.com. Retrieved March 1, 2006, from the World Wide Web at http://bmj.bmjjournals.com/cgi/content/full/314/7088/1145/g.

HERNLUND, Y. (2000). Cutting without ritual and ritual without cutting: Female "circumcision" and the re-ritualization of initiation in the Gambia. In B. Shell-Duncan & Y. Hernlund (Eds.), *Female "circumcision" in Africa: Culture, controversy, and change* (pp. 235–252). London: Lynne Rienner Publishers.

JOHNSON, M.C. (2000). Becoming a Muslim, becoming a person: Female "circumcision," religious identity, and personhood in Guinea-Bissau. In B. Shell-Duncan & Y. Hernlund (Eds.), *Female "circumcision" in Africa: Culture, controversy, and change* (pp. 215–234). London: Lynne Rienner Publishers.

LEONARD, L. (2000). Adopting female "circumcision" in southern Chad: The experience of Myab. In B. Shell-Duncan & Y. Hernlund (Eds.), *Female "circumcision" in Africa: Culture, controversy, and change* (pp. 167–192). London: Lynne Rienner Publishers.

LUTKEKAUS, N.C., & ROSCOE, P.B. (1995). *Gender rituals: Female initiation in Melanesia*. New York: Routledge.

MACKIE, G. (2000). Female genital cutting: The beginning of the end. In B. Shell-Duncan & Y. Hernlund (Eds.), *Female "circumcision" in Africa: Culture, controversy, and change* (pp. 253–282). London: Lynne Rienner Publishers.

MASLAND, T. (1999, July 5). The ritual of pain. In Uganda, tradition overpowers a United Nations drive against female genital mutilation. *Newsweek*, 61.

MORSY, S.A. (1991). Safeguarding women's bodies: The white man's burden medicalized. *Medical Anthropology Quarterly*, 5(1), 19–23.

OBERMEYER, C.M. (1991). Female genital surgeries. *Medical Anthropology Quarterly*, 13, 79–106.

ORUBULOYE, I.O., CALDWELL, P., CALDWELL, J.C. (2000). Female circumcision among the Yoruba of southwestern Yoruba: The beginning of change. In B. Shell-Duncan & Y. Hernlund (Eds.), *Female "circumcision" in Africa. Culture, controversy, and change* (pp. 73–94). London: Lynne Rienner Publishers.

SAN FRANCISCO EXAMINER, SEPT. 11, 1995.

SARGENT, C. (1991). Confronting patriarchy: the potential for advocacy in medical anthropology. *Medical Anthropology Quarterly*, 5(1), 24–25.

SCHEPER-HUGHES, N. (1991). Virgin territory: The male discovery of the clitoris. *Medical Anthropology Quarterly*, 5, 25–28.

SHANDALL, A.A. (1967). Circumcision and infibulation of females. *Sudan Medical Journal*, 5, 178–212.

SHELL-DUNCAN, B., & HERNLUND, Y. (2000). Female "circumcision" in Africa: Dimensions of the practice and debates. In B. Shell-Duncan & Y. Hernlund (Eds.), *Female "circumcision" in Africa. Culture, controversy, and change* (pp. 1–40). London: Lynne Rienner Publishers.

THOMAS, L. (2000). Ngaitana. I will circumcise myself: Lessons from colonial campaigns to ban excision in Meru, Kenya. In B. Shell-Duncan & Y. Hernlund (Eds.), *Female "circumcision" in Africa: Culture, controversy, and change* (pp. 129–150). London: Lynne Rienner Publishers.

TOUBIA, N. (Ed.). (1988). *Women of the Arab world: The coming challenge*. Papers of the Arab Women's Solidarity Association Conference. Atlantic Highlands, NJ: Zed Books.

TOUBIA, N., & IZETTE, S. (1998). *Female genital mutilation: An overview*. Geneva: World Health Organization.

WOMEN@SPINIFEX.COM. (n.d.). *Prevalence of female genital mutilation*. Map. Retrieved March 2, 2006 from the World Wide Web at http://www. spinifexpress.com.au/kadi/kadimap.htm.

Suggested Readings

BARNES, V.L. (1994). *Aman: The story of a Somali girl*—As told to Virginia Lee Barnes and Janice Boddy. London: Bloomsbury Publishing.

This book presents the personal account of a young girl living in Somali. She describes being circumcised at age 8, and married to a much older man at age 13. Her life is hard—a constant struggle to survive. Barely 17, she has already endured rape, two divorces, and giving birth to two children, one of which died. Anthropologists Virginia Barnes and Janice Boddy present a straightforward, objective account of Aman's life and the patriarchal society she lives in.

BROOKS, G. (1994). *Nine parts of desire: The hidden world of Islamic women*. New York: Anchor Books.

Geraldine Brooks travels through the Middle East on a journey of discovery. Her riveting book examines the lives of Muslim women. Brooks' insights are remarkably objective, and serve to dispel many of the misconceptions Westerners hold about Islamic people and the status of women in Islamic countries.

LITTLE, C.M. (2003, Spring). Female genital circumcision: Medical and cultural considerations. *Journal of Cultural Diversity*. Retrieved March 10, 2006, from the World Wide Web at http://www.findarticles.com/p/articles/mi_m0MJU/is_1_10/ai_102025141.

A comprehensive discussion of the medical and cultural implications of female circumcision. Presents a fairly balanced discussion and is easily accessible to students. The site also provides numerous links to related articles.

CHAPTER EIGHT

What Does it Mean to Grow Old?

Introduction

I listened in amazement as a cheerful young radio host announced to the world that she would "do radio until the day I kick it." Did she understand what she was saying—how unrealistic her long-term plans were? No, of course not, because none of us, deep down, ever believe we will grow old or become infirm, even if we do intellectually understand that one day we will die. It is not the destination that we ignore, but the stages of getting there. In Western society we plan to be "forever young," and we have created a culture of youth that rejects the realities of aging. Is this true in all cultures? How do other people perceive aging? The following discussion will explore how four cultures and one sub-cultural group view the process of growing old, and how they deal with the "culture of oldness."

KEY TERMS: age-sets, modernization, aging, subculture, egalitarianism, uxorilocal, reciprocity, age stratification, fictive kin

Anthropologists and Aging

Early ethnographers concentrated on the status of elderly people in a given culture and their overall treatment by other **AGE-SETS**. More recently, anthropologists have turned their attention to the life experiences of elderly people. At first, they focused on gathering cultural knowledge from elders before their way of life was lost to the all-consuming processes of **MODERNIZATION** (Kertzer 1989). Later, anthropologists began recording life histories and personal experiences, and in this way gave a voice to elderly people who may otherwise be ignored (Keith et al. 1994). Today, anthropologists examine aging from a biological, social, and cultural context to determine the influences each of these systems have on the process of aging, and to understand the interrelatedness of these systems.

The study of **AGING** is known as gerontology. It is a multidisciplinary field with specialists from medicine, biology, sociology, psychology, law, and so on, all interested in the process of aging. The "anthropology of aging," as it has become known, brings a cross-cultural perspective to gerontology. This means anthropologists examine how aging is viewed in cultures around the world. They investigate the life stages that influence status, situation, and attitudes toward aging and old age (Fry 1990). For example, among the Ju/'hoansi, food sharing has always been an important part of their adaptation. Food, as well as other necessities, is freely shared. Later in life, this sharing is transformed into caregiving for elders.

Anthropologists have also become advocates for elderly citizens. By addressing what it means to be old in a given culture we may avoid some of the pitfalls of old age, such as stereotyping, marginalization, and over-medicalization.[1]

Anthropological research, by its very nature, is qualitative, and this is certainly evident in studying elderly people. Anthropologists conduct ethnographic fieldwork, living in the culture for an extended period while observing and participating in the community's daily activities. This is known as participant observation.[2] Key informants, often elders themselves, provide anthropologists with personal experiences and discuss cultural values related to aging. Participant observation is an integral research tool in anthropology because it provides anthropologists with insight into the inner workings of the culture, and helps them to understand the views and experiences of its members. Later in this chapter you will encounter an excellent example of participant observation in the research of Dorothy Ayers Counts and David R. Counts who went on the road with North American RVers.

To put this into perspective, anthropologists have asked some important questions when studying aging: Do elderly people live a good life? How do they define a good life? What meaning and importance do elderly people attach to remaining independent and self-sufficient? Are elderly people better off today than in earlier times? How has modernization affected their lives? What role(s) are older people expected to play in a given culture? What does retirement mean? Are elders held in high esteem and valued by other age-sets in their culture? How do they perceive their advancing age, and what coping strategies do they employ? And, how are they cared for as they grow more infirm?

As you can see, anthropologists are interested in the meanings attached to various issues of aging. They ask, "What is old age like in such-and-such a setting?" (Rubinstein 1990: 5).

A Discussion of Growing Old

Humans are not merely biological organisms; we are also cultural beings. Although biological changes certainly play a role in the aging process, like all other facets of life, aging is influenced by the culture and environment in which we live. The meaning of growing old, and even how "old" is defined, can differ markedly from one culture to another. Thus, when investigating aging, we cannot overlook the centrality of culture in our daily lives. For example, the roles and experiences of a person as he or she progresses through life will affect the status and power they hold in later life. This is particularly true when examining material resources; those in possession of material wealth, whatever that wealth may be, usually enjoy a higher quality of life and more opportunities to participate in the economic, political, and social institutions of their culture in their later life.

Old age is most often associated with changes in physicality, diminished cognitive function, and shifting social and economic roles (Blaikie 1999). As people grow older, they begin to lose their health and strength, and may no longer be able to fully participate in the productive activities of their culture. This means they must tailor their activities to their abilities. The young radio announcer will have to give up her job eventually, either because of physical or mental infirmities, or mandatory retirement. How the rest of her life unfolds will be determined by the status afforded elderly people in her culture. This status will play a role in the opportunities afforded her, the quality of life she will enjoy, and the level of care and attention she will receive. This becomes apparent when addressing whether elderly people are considered non-contributing consumers of scarce resources, or valued members of a community with wisdom, skills, and resources to share. Thus, the way old age is perceived can have a psychological, economic, political, and social impact on elderly people.

A discussion of aging may seem unimportant to students just beginning their adult lives; however, growing old does have implications for young people. First, growing old is an inevitable fact of life, and how we view the process and what steps we take to deal with this inevitability, even when we are still young, will have a bearing on the quality of our lives as we grow older. Second, and perhaps more significant to society at large, is the way young people perceive older people—their parents, grandparents, even strangers. The tendency in North America to shift the elderly to the periphery of society and to feel impatient with their slowness, their attitudes garnered from a different time and generation, and their seeming "unworldliness" may have a dramatic impact on relationships between young people and elderly people. Yet, these relationships are important because they create a connection between generations and serve as a stabilizing force within the culture. In many cultures, it is the elders who are the keepers of the cultural knowledge; they pass this knowledge on to the next generation, teaching them the values, beliefs, and social and behavioural norms of their culture. Thus the elderly can serve as a powerful enculturative force. This enculturation is reciprocal. Older people also learn from the young—new ideas, new ways of doing and thinking that keep a culture from growing stagnant.

COPING STRATEGIES

In order to thrive in the later stages of life, elderly people learn coping strategies that ease the transition from one stage to the next and ensure a satisfying life (Henderson 1990). Acceptance is one strategy—acceptance that age-related changes in physical strength and health are inevitable. For example, a person of advanced age may no longer be able to participate in rigorous sports or continue detail-oriented crafts and hobbies (e.g., crocheting). To deal with these changing abilities, this person might find new opportunities to replace old ones.

The stereotype of elderly people as passive observers sitting on the periphery of life, dependent on others to provide for their economic, social, and emotional well-being is giving way to an image of vibrant seniors enjoying leisure activities, and refusing to be marginalized on the edge of society. In North America, popular activities such as RVing have created a **SUBCULTURE** of nomadic seniors who have become a major economic force (Counts & Counts 1998). Old age may also be associated with greater spiritual and emotional strength, and ritual healing powers (Rosenberg 1997). According to Fry et al. (1997), the ability to continue functioning, even in a changed capacity, and continuing to maintain an interest in meaningful daily activities is paramount for a "good old age."

Another coping strategy is to recognize that social roles and relationships will also change. Friends and family members may die, leaving the elderly person with limited companionship. This may come at the same time as retirement from the paid workforce or working at subsistence activities in a community, leaving the elderly person with a smaller social network. This is unfortunate since recent studies suggest that maintaining a large network of friends improves the health and longevity of elderly people. In some cultures, special bonds with grandchildren are forged at this time.

Changes in physical and social reality encourage elders to re-evaluate their self-concept and life position, to take pride and joy in who they are now and what they can accomplish today, rather than who they were and what they used to do. This re-evaluation provides a new sense of self-worth closely tied to continuing self-determination, independence, and free will. These adaptive strategies determine whether or not a person is enjoying a successful aging.

In the following section, aging is examined in four cultural environments and one relatively recent subcultural formation: the Ju/'hoansi of the Kalahari Desert in Africa, the Yanomami of Venezuela, the Masai of Kenya, and the Chinese in Shanghai and Hong Kong. North American RVers, a relatively recent subcultural creation, are also investigated.

THE JU/'HOANSI

The Ju/'hoansi live in the Kalahari Desert of Botswana and Namibia. Until the mid-twentieth century, most Ju/'hoansi were nomadic foragers. Given the mobility of this lifestyle, the elderly, as they grew more infirm, would have had difficulty keeping up. Although there is no ethnographic evidence of abandonment, it may have happened occasionally when caregivers were no longer able to carry a frail person as the band moved to a new campsite.[3]

Today, the Ju/'hoansi are sedentary people, living in small villages scattered across the western Kalahari Desert. They are mainly small-scale herders and gardeners, although they still make short forays into the desert to hunt and gather. The lifespan of the Ju/'hoansi has increased since they became sedentary (Keith et al. 1994). Settled life has meant elders no longer have to move around so much, they have ready supplies of soft foods, and they can be taken to nearby medical facilities if they become seriously ill.

Independence is highly valued, although the Ju/'hoan lifestyle requires a co-operative interdependence for social and economic well-being. Elderly Ju/'hoansi continue to contribute to the household, gathering firewood, water, grass (for roof repair), and food that is readily available close to the village. Elders may also supervise children while the parents are involved in productive activities and keep animals from wandering through the village (Keith et al. 1994). They continue these tasks until they are no longer physically able to do so.

Chronological age appears to have little meaning to the Ju/'hoansi. Old age is divided into three categories: *n!a* who are elders; *m≠da !ki* who are very old; and, *m≠da kum kum*, which means old to the point of helplessness (Lee 2003). No ceremonies are held to mark the transition

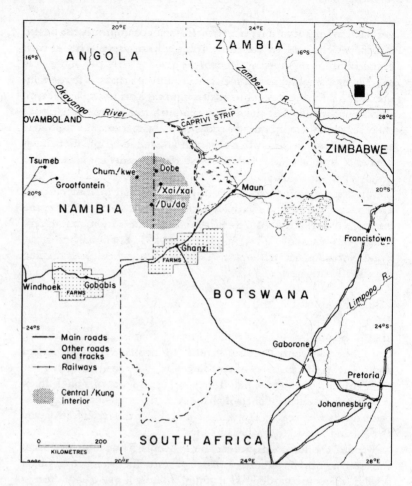

Ju/'hoansi territory

to "old," but by the age of 50, all Ju/'hoansi carry the honorific *n!a* in their name.[4] These terms do not indicate any decline in social status, just the state of their health.

The Ju/'hoansi regret the inevitable decline in physical strength and health, and loss of independence. Children and elderly are not quite whole in the eyes of the Ju/'hoansi because they need assistance to meet their daily needs. The Ju/'hoansi define various stages of life in physiological terms: "he can no longer hunt," or "he can no longer chew meat" (Keith et al. 1994: xxviii). Well-being in the Ju/'hoan culture means possessing continued strength and vitality, being free of sickness, and having the ability to do physical labour. Healthwise, elderly Ju/'hoansi tend not to seek help from the Western-style medical facilities; rather, they turn to the traditional healer in the village. Indeed, the healers are usually elderly men, giving them a prominent position in Ju/'hoan society (Lee 2003).

Elderly Ju/'hoansi live with their kin. They are not segregated in special care facilities or retirement homes, as happens in North America, nor is age segregation evident in Ju/'hoan communities; children, adults, and the elderly freely interact. Even the most ill spend time socializing and are often in the centre of village activities. Caring for the elderly is so enshrined in the Ju/'hoan culture that modernization processes, such as a settled way of life and taking up herding cattle instead of foraging, has not affected this practice. As the daughter of a Ju/'hoan elder said: "It hasn't changed things. We took care of our elders then and we still take care of them" (Lee 2003: 94). Obviously, Ju/'hoan outlook and rationale regarding caring for the elderly, and indeed the process of aging, is still tied to their traditional beliefs. As mentioned earlier, their systems of **EGALITARIANISM** and food sharing are extrapolated to elder care. Children and other kin members are expected to care for their parents and any other elders in the village who need assistance.

Elderly Ju/'hoansi do not see themselves as burdens; rather, they share a sense of entitlement to assistance from their children. As well, caregiving is not genderized in Ju/'hoan society. Both male and female children care for their parents, although women may perform special services such as hair grooming. Not only do they provide for the necessities of life, but the children also spend time visiting with their elders, and a special bond between grandchildren and their grandparents may develop.

Ju/'hoan elders are fairly autonomous, just as they were when young. They can choose their activities, the food they will eat, and the people they will associate with. Most significant, they do not face the fear of poverty when old as do so many North American elders. They do not fear personal violence or theft, and they are not lonely since they live with family members. Lee (2003) estimates that between four and eight people look after each elder.

Despite the positive atmosphere for the aged, Ju/'hoan elders love to complain—what Lee (2003) calls the discourse of neglect. Although old age is joked about, especially regarding sexual prowess (or lack thereof), the care they receive is a source of constant complaint. Lee (2003) believes this complaining serves as a levelling mechanism and ensures good treatment by warning caregivers not to ease up on their support: "caregiving requires constant lubrication, and complaining greases the wheels" (p. 102).

Thus, Ju/'hoan elderly enjoy respect and attention from their juniors, and personal independence. They continue to participate in the economic, political, social, and spiritual life of the community as long as they are physically and mentally able to do so. Their loud complaints are designed to remind family members that their care is important and must be continued, and that no one should think they are doing an adequate job. Although the complaining is great fun, it hardly seems necessary since the Ju/'hoansi value their elders and believe it is important to care for them.

"My own children do not look after me. See the clothes I am wearing—these rags I'm wearing—I get them from my own work, my own sweat. None of them have done anything for me. Because they do not look after me, I, their parent, say, they are 'without sense.'"

JU/'HOAN ELDER KASUPE
(LEE 2003: 101)

YANOMAMI

The Yanomami are foraging horticulturalists (gardeners) who live in villages scattered throughout the Amazon forests of Brazil and Venezuela. They hunt, gather, and fish, although their gardens provide most of their food.[5] Members of approximately 125 villages interact with each other sporadically, albeit not always in a positive manner. Until recently, the Yanomami managed to remain fairly isolated from the outside world.

In this study we will focus on the Xilixana Yanomami who live in the rainforests of Brazil. Until 40 years ago this group of approximately 140 individuals was isolated from outsiders (Peters 1998). Today, they frequently encounter other people (e.g., Western missionaries, Brazilian farmers and ranchers). In 1987, miners swept into the area, bringing with them social ills (e.g., prostitution), new diseases, and increased warfare. Exploitation and the ensuing destruction of the Brazilian rainforest has had a lasting impact on the Yanomami.

Like the Ju/'hoansi, the Yanomami regret the changes in their physicality as they age—grey hair is quickly plucked in younger Yanomami. Few Yanomami live to see old age, given the difficulties of living in a tropical environment and being plagued by constant warfare and epidemics of tuberculosis and measles. Those who do survive face changes as they grow older. For a man, hunting prowess begins to diminish after the age of 40, and as he grows older, he spends more time planting and weeding in the fields. When his wife enters menopause he may take a second wife to bear more children. This second family often rejuvenates the man, at least for a time, and he may take up hunting again. Older men, known as *bata* or seniors, with many children have more influence in the village, especially if they also have political skills and shamanistic powers. They manage the affairs of the village by seeking consensus between all the adult men, rather than by issuing orders (Peters 1998).

As a Yanomami woman grows older, her responsibilities toward her husband diminish, especially if he has taken a second, younger wife. She may even move her hammock to be nearer one of her grown children. As long as she is physically able to do so, she works in the fields with a daughter, takes care of her grandchildren, spins cotton, and performs other domestic duties. Her status as an elder member of the community is often higher than when she was younger and of child-bearing age. She is not endangered when another village attacks, and she can travel to enemy villages without being harmed. Indeed, elderly women are sometimes used as messengers between villages. Elderly women are responsible for recovering the bodies of villagers who have been killed in enemy territory during a war.

Although healthy, mobile Yanomami elders are valued and respected by their families, this attitude changes as they grow increas-

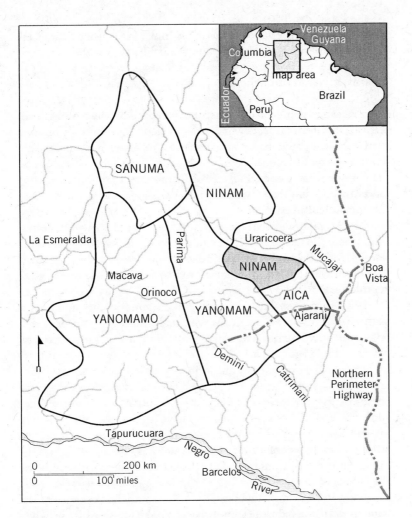

Yanomami territory

ingly infirm. Unhealthy and frail people are considered liabilities, no longer able to contribute to, and even impeding, the normal cycle of village life. Indeed, Peters (1998) witnessed children teasing the visually challenged and infirm in their village. The degree of care the very elderly Yanomami receive is dependent on the willingness of a spouse or daughter to look after them. Regardless, they are considered a burden, and their death is welcomed by the family.

Thus, the social environment for older Yanomami men is quite positive; they hold power and status. Even women, who do not hold a position of power when younger, enjoy more freedom and status as they grow older. However, the social environment for the very weak and frail elderly is dismal. This attitude toward the frail should not be construed as a lack of affection for parents. When Peters (1998: 70) asked one of his informants whether he thought of his parents who had died many years earlier, the man answered: "When someone calls "*paye*" (father) in the yãno I sometimes think of my father. When I am hungry I sometimes think of my mother, who gave me food."

MASAI

The Masai are semi-nomadic pastoralists living on the savannahs of Kenya and Tanzania. Traditionally, they relied almost entirely on their cattle herds for sustenance and disdained foraging, agriculture, and living in permanent settlements. Today, although their pastoralist lifestyle is remarkably enduring, colonialist policies that limited grazing lands and current development projects have forced some Masai to take up agriculture.

The Masai organize their communities around an age-grade system, where the males are divided into three groups: youths, warriors (*moran*), and elders. Bauer (1987) calls these age-sets the essence of Masai culture. The passage from warrior to elder is marked with great ceremony. Once a Masai becomes an elder, at about age 30, he can marry and begin establishing a polygynous family compound known as the *kraal*. Unlike most cultures, where advanced age is not acknowledged with any ceremony, among the Masai a man's passage into total elderhood (old age) is marked with ritual.

Masai elderly men exert authority over other Masai and have certain privileges that others do not, such as imbibing alcohol. They may admonish the warriors not to fight with each other or steal each other's cattle. Elderly Masai women (*engoko*) have a great deal of freedom to say and do as they please; many enjoy teasing, joking, and telling ribald stories to young people. They may also serve as peacekeepers and the moral voice of the community. As with elderly people in many cultures, the elderly of the Masai love to recount nostalgic stories of the "good old days," in this case, when every Masai had cattle. Yet those Masai women Hodgson (2001: 46) interviewed spoke fondly of their family and viewed them as a symbol of wealth: "I am surrounded by my grandchildren and great-grandchildren. I am wealthy in this way."

Few Masai men become widowers because they have several wives of varying ages. Thus, elderly Masai men are cared for by their much younger wives. Elderly women, even if not widowed, depend on their sons or grandsons to support them in old age, although it is the wives of these sons and grandsons who provide the personal care for elderly mothers-in-law. Thus, the women live in multi-generational households (Cattell 1997).

According to Hodgson (2001), modernization and development projects have affected generational relationships among the Masai. The men seem to feel the generational rift the most, resenting the loss of their authority. They bemoan the selfishness and "sassiness" of their adult children. The women feel neglected by their sons, who in the past always cared for their mothers with the utmost respect. Indeed, mutual

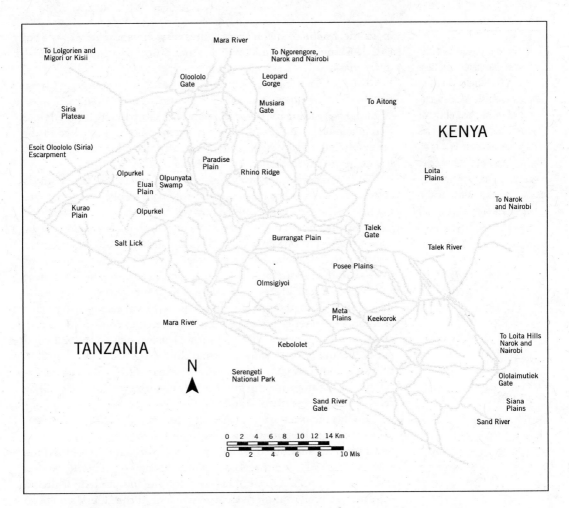

Map showing the Masai territory spanning the border region of Tanzania and Kenya, including Serengeti National Park, the Mara River, and numerous plains and gates.

Labels on map:
To Lolgorien and Migori or Kisii; Mara River; To Ngorengore, Narok and Nairobi; Oloololo Gate; Leopard Gorge; Siria Plateau; Musiara Gate; To Aitong; KENYA; Esoit Oloololo (Siria) Escarpment; Paradise Plain; Rhino Ridge; Loita Plains; Olpurkel; Olpunyata Swamp; Eluai Plain; To Narok and Nairobi; Kurao Plain; Olpurkel; Talek Gate; Burrangat Plain; Talek River; Salt Lick; Posee Plains; Olmsigiyoi; Meta Plains; Keekorok; Mara River; TANZANIA; N; Kebololet; To Loita Hills Narok and Nairobi; Serengeti National Park; Ololaimutiek Gate; Sand River Gate; Siana Plains; Sand River; 0 2 4 6 8 10 12 14 Km; 0 2 4 6 8 10 Mls

Masai territory

respect (*enkanyit*) is a central value among the Masai and serves to define appropriate social protocols and ideals (Hodgson 2001; Cattell 1997). Reciprocity is also a strong motivator. The Masai believe adult children owe their parents for a lifetime of support.

The position of the aged in Masai society is fairly positive. The men possess significant status and are ensured of support from their young wives, while the women can count on their sons to care for them. The aged in Masai villages spend their days playing with children, enjoying the sun on warm days, and staying close to the fire when it is cold. They continue to participate in the economic, social, and religious activities of the village as long as they are able or interested.

CHINESE[6]

Examining aging and the aged in China presents somewhat of a challenge: China is a vast nation, and the Chinese represent a great deal

The mixed love, fear and awe of the children for their father was strengthened by the great respect paid to age. An old man's loss of vigour was more than offset by his growth in wisdom. As long as he remained in possession of his faculties the patriarch possessed every sanction to enable him to dominate the family scene. (FAIRBANK 1959: 36)

of ethnic, regional, and economic diversity. Thus, the experiences of elderly Chinese living in Shanghai, rural China, and Hong Kong may differ markedly.

Despite changing economic, political, and social policies in China, familial care of elderly parents is still firmly entrenched in Chinese thinking. According to this philosophy, those who have fulfilled their family and work responsibilities deserve to relax and be cared for by others in their old age (Ikels 1989). Traditionally, caring for the elderly has been the responsibility of adult sons.

In recent decades, the welfare of elderly Chinese and their families has been threatened by the one-child policy. This policy limits couples to one child, where before they may have had several children to rely on in old age. The policy has weakened the family structure and is causing some concern among citizens and state authorities. As a patriarchal society, the Chinese have always preferred sons, partly because sons were expected to care for their aged parents, and partly because these sons were responsible for performing ancestor rites once the parents died. This filial preference has led to incidences of female infanticide and abortion of female fetuses after amniocentesis confirmed the sex. To prevent this practice, state authorities have modified the one-child policy in rural areas to allow a second child if the first one is a girl. In this way, if both are girls, the oldest can be married out and an uxorilo-cal[7] husband can be married in, thereby ensuring the parents will be cared for in old age (Sankar 1990).

The family is a haven for elderly Chinese, following the Confucian ethic which venerates elders (Henderson 1990), although to be valued and supported, elders must still provide some functions within the family. In 1982, 70 per cent of Hong Kong elderly lived in multi-generational households (Ikels 1989). On mainland China, a 1988 study found that more than 70 per cent of the elderly still lived with an adult child (Sankar 1990). This reflects the cultural ideal of an extended family, although housing shortages in places like Shanghai may have some impact on this residence pattern. Co-residence appears most common among the wealthy who have extra space, and the poor who accommodate, regardless of crowding. This trend is reversed in Beijing, where Chinese elderly prefer living alone (Sankar 1990 from Yuan 1987).

RECIPROCITY and intergenerational support are powerful components in the Chinese family (Sankar 1990). Parents care for their children when they are young and the children, in turn, care for their aged parents. Nonetheless, elderly people are expected to continue to contribute to the household economy as much as possible, even when extremely old. For example, an elderly woman may raise a pig and then sell it on the private market, with the money added to the household income (Sankar 1990 from Davis-Friedmann 1983). Other elders contribute through producing crafts and performing domestic chores.

Dementia does not hold the same stigma in China as it does in North America; indeed, it is considered a normal part of aging (Ikels 1997). Cognitive deficiencies are overlooked if the person still behaves well. The illness or impairment most feared by the Chinese is paralysis from a stroke, which would incapacitate them and place a heavy burden on their families. Like the Ju/'hoansi, elderly Chinese, both rural and urban, mainland or Hong Kong, tend to seek help for chronic illnesses from a healer, only turning to licensed doctors if absolutely necessary.

AGE STRATIFICATION and inequality is evident among the elderly in China. The economic situation of elderly Chinese has a great deal to do with the way they lived earlier in their lives, particularly whether they had a state-pensioned job or in recent years developed successful economic enterprises. In urban centres, pensions provide adequate economic resources for those over 60 (average age of retirement), and indeed, some elderly are affluent. The patriarchal power of the male head of an affluent Chinese family is still evident. Even though younger members of the family may be running the family businesses, the patriarch's opinions are heeded. It also appears that the elders are actively involved in family functions and indeed are enveloped in the social fabric of the family. They may live near or with some of the younger family members out of choice rather than necessity.

For those less affluent, such as rural farmers, choices are more limited. When no longer able to farm, they are reliant on other family members taking over the farm and providing them with the necessities of life. Elderly women often provide child care for their adult children and are paid for it while others perform household chores. Indeed, the presence of a grandmother in the household is considered an economic advantage.

In Hong Kong the elderly population is primarily urban and industrialized. Elderly people are described as doing well or doing poorly (Ikels 1989). If they do not complain and gossip or try to control their children's lives, then they are easy to get along with and are doing well. Those who are doing poorly are usually in bad health, have little wealth or security, and few family members to care for them. They are often difficult to get along with and are always nagging family members. At a societal level in Hong Kong, frail elders tend to be fairly marginalized.

The Chinese government has taken on the role of ensuring support for some elderly. Prior to the 1980s, generous subsidies were provided to urban populations, including health benefits, pensions, and welfare for those without families (Ikels 1997). Since then, the head-long march into the market economy has led to some erosion of these services. The situation is more serious in rural China. To ease the problems rural elderly Chinese may face in the coming decades, the Chinese government is encouraging the creation of pension plans and subsidized home care for the most incapacitated elderly.

Before the revolution, childless elderly people often turned to **FICTIVE KIN** for mutual support and obligation. Ikels (1997) found that today some Chinese elderly practice neighbourhood reciprocity—neighbours take care of each other when necessary. Childless elderly couples may even adopt a relative's child who will care for them in the future. Those without children and no means of support are supported by the state (Sankar 1990).

The new realities of modernized China challenge the pivotal Chinese value of filial piety. As China moves ever deeper into the market economy, the importance of family support will likely diminish while Western-style institutional facilities will become more prevalent. Yet, the family is the basic economic and social unit, and despite changing circumstances within China, families will continue to be a vital support network for elderly Chinese citizens.

NORTH AMERICAN RVERS[7]

Let's go RVing! The call of the road! Home is where I park it! These are slogans that two to three million North American seniors live by as they follow the American dream of freedom and independence. These modern-day nomads have left behind sedate retirement and taken to the highways of North America in search of adventure. Indeed, RVers[8] interviewed by Counts and Counts (1998: 24) see themselves as "adventurous, self-reliant, flexible, friendly, and gutsy." They also credit RVing with keeping them healthy, happy, and vibrant. As one long-time RVer stated, "People stay young on the road" (Ibid.). The nomadic RV subculture meets the needs of seniors in search of a meaningful later life. It provides a sense of freedom, community, an invigoration of their mental and physical status, and allows them to search out new experiences.

RVers are not an homogeneous group; indeed, it is impossible to characterize RVers because they are so diverse. They come from all walks of life and search for different things from life while RVing. Some are retired couples, others are singles, some are fairly young, while others are quite aged. Some are fairly well off, while others live on limited budgets. Each of these groups face different concerns. For example, singles experience more loneliness than couple RVers, and elderly RVers have to deal with the limitations advancing age places on their nomadic lifestyle.

RVers adopt various lifestyles. Boondockers are RVers who do not use membership RV parks with hook-ups and other amenities—they park wherever, often in isolated regions, supermarket parking lots, or roadside rest areas for free. Boondockers place great stock on being completely free from restrictions concerning where and when they travel. Full-timers identify more with "Zen affluence"—having few material possessions, but everything they need. This lack of ownership gives full-timers a sense of liberation—"not to be possessed by possessions" (Counts & Counts 1998: 73).

An RVer social gathering.

Negative images of RVers as being rootless, irresponsible gypsy tourists who use up scarce resources without contributing anything are perpetuated by people who have little knowledge or understanding of this way of life. Retired RVers face a double stigma—that of being old and RVers. Both groups tend to be marginalized by mainstream North Americans. Part of the hostility toward this group may stem from the way RVers challenge the stereotype of elderly retirees spending their days hidden away in a rocking chair, simply existing until they die. Many RVers do not take offence to the label "gypsy"; indeed, they embrace it as a symbol of freedom and adventure. Contrary to popular opinion, RVers do give back to the greater community. They volunteer to build houses and help in areas where disasters have struck. RVers also bring economic revenue into a community while using few resources, or causing settled communities any problems.

A strong sense of community and the importance of mutual aid and sharing appear to permeate RVer society. Indeed, many RVers who have felt isolated and alienated in suburbia feel perfectly at home and welcome in RV parks. The reciprocal nature of RVers means they will accept help with gratitude, but the opportunity to help someone else is also important. The most common food-sharing ritual among RVers is a potluck supper, especially during festivals and holidays such as Thanksgiving. Food sharing also serves as a resource redistribution mechanism, without upsetting the egalitarian ideal of RVers.

Elderly RVers who have difficulty travelling may spend more time in one spot, only moving seasonally, or they may even set up a home base in a parking lot or choose one of the retreat parks established for the very elderly or ill. Nonetheless, Counts and Counts (1998) found that despite the inevitable end to their RVing, most RVers hope to continue their unique lifestyle until the day they die.

Conclusion

Growing old obviously means many things to many people. The aging process is progressive and pervasive, which means we do not one day wake up old. Rather, as we age, our physical, social, and cultural realities change. To age successfully, we must develop strategies for adapting to these changes, as do those around us.

Although the cultures and subculture examined in this chapter are quite diverse, there appear to be several underlying themes that come through when discussing aging. In every culture elders express a heartfelt desire to continue doing what they have always done—whether that is hunting, farming, making quilts, working at professional jobs, keeping house, and so on. If their lifestyle changes in later years, then they want it to be their choice. Their identity and sense of well-being comes from this independence and feeling of control over their lives.

A second resounding theme is the importance of maintaining close ties with family and friends. Elderly people want to remain in their normal social environment and not be marginalized on the edge of society and left out of the daily activities they enjoy. In most cultures, elderly people continue to participate in social and economic affairs for as long as they are able to do so, and in this way remain contributing members of society. Small-scale societies, such as the Ju/'hoansi, Yanomami, and Masai, do not have a formal retirement; elders continue to contribute to the household economy, albeit in changing capacities. Chinese elderly, like North Americans, do retire from paid work, but they too continue to contribute to the household economy in other ways, such as performing child care and domestic chores. In families with abundant economic resources, the elderly Chinese patriarch may still wield control over the family enterprises. North American RVers may appear to opt out of normal life, but in fact they find a sense of community with other RVers and their mobility allows them to visit family and friends whenever they please.

Among the Yanomami and Hong Kong Chinese, it appears that very old and frail people are considered a burden. Given the tendency to place North American elderly who have become infirm into nursing homes, it appears we have the same attitude. Mainland Chinese also seem to be heading away from family care to more institutionalized care, although the Chinese families I met still continue to envelop their aged relatives into the family fold.

Regardless of advancing age and infirmity, elderly members of a community are rarely abandoned. Elders are globally considered vessels of wisdom and cultural knowledge, or "living libraries" that can be drawn on by the people in the community (Haviland et al. 2005). Old age can also be a time of leisure and enjoyment, when advancing age frees people from strenuous economic activities and affords them more freedom for leisurely activities, such as RVing.

The discussion of coping strategies used by elderly people to deal with advancing age actually trivializes what can be a very traumatic and heart-wrenching time for them—a time of changes that are neither wanted nor welcomed. To varying degrees, family members and communities at large appear relatively sensitive to the problems their elders face as they age.

In conclusion, growing old is inevitable, but how we view aging, and how we live the many stages of life will determine how we deal with the "culture of oldness."

Questions for Consideration

1. In North American society we tend to place our elderly into institutionalized care "for their own good." Is this the best way to treat elderly people? Can you identify any alternatives that would be agreeable to our lifestyles?

2. Analyze the stereotypes you hold toward elderly people. Why do you hold these views? Do you have a close relationship with someone who is elderly? Do they fit these stereotypes?

3. Plot the stages of your life. What are your plans for the later stages, and how are you preparing for old age (not just economically)? Given the nature of your society today, what status can you expect to hold when you grow old? How does the status of elderly members of a community affect the quality of their life?

NOTES

1   Over-medicalization is the tendency, particularly in Western countries, to treat the natural processes of aging with medications and various invasive and unnecessary procedures. (For example, doctors suggested that my husband's frail, 98-year-old grandmother should have a spot surgically removed from her face because it might become cancerous some day.)

2   See the introduction to this text for a detailed discussion of participant observation.

3   Despite reports of abandonment among foraging peoples, such as the Inuit of Canada, this was a measure taken only under the most desperate of circumstances.

4   *N!a* means old, big, and great.

5   Plantains (cooking bananas) are their major food.

6   Some of the information provided in this discussion is drawn from the author's observations and interviews during a recent visit to China.

7   This examination of RVers is taken from Counts and Counts (1998).

8   RVers are defined by Counts and Counts (1998) as those living in their RVs. This group does not include vacationers or "snowbirds."

References

BLAIKIE, A. (1999). *Ageing and popular culture*. Cambridge: Cambridge University Press.

BAUER, E. (1987). Mystique of the Masai. *The World and I* (pp. 497–513). In E. Angeloni (Ed.), *Annual Editions Anthropology: 05/06*. Toronto: McGraw-Hill.

CATTELL, M.G. (1997). African widows, culture and social change: Case studies from Kenya. In J. Sokolovsky (Ed.), *The cultural control of aging: Worldwide perspectives* (2nd ed., pp. 71–98). Westport, CT: Bergin & Garvey.

COUNTS, D.A., & COUNTS, D.R. (1998). *Over the next hill: An ethnography of RVing Seniors in North America*. Peterborough, ON: Broadview Press.

DAVIS-FRIEDMANN, D. (1983). *Long lives: Chinese elderly and the communist revolution*. Cambridge: Massachusetts: Harvard University Press.

FAIRBANK, J.K. (1959). The nature of Chinese society. In F. Schurmann & O. Schell (Eds.), *China Readings 1: Imperial China* (pp. 34–46). Harmondsworth, Middlesex, UK: Penguin.

FRY, C.L. (1990). The life curse in context: Implications of comparative research. In R.L. Rubinstein, J. Keith, D. Shink, & D. Wielund (Eds.), *Anthropology and aging: Comprehensive reviews* (pp. 129–149). Boston: Kluwer Academic Publishers.

FRY, C.L., DICKERSON-PUTNAM, J., DRAPER, P., IKELS, C., KEITH, J., GLASCOCK, A.P., & HARPENDING, H.C. (1997). Culture and the meaning of a good old age. In J. Sokolovsky (Ed.), *The cultural control of aging: Worldwide perspectives* (2nd ed., pp. 99–123). Westport, CT: Bergin & Garvey.

HAVILAND, W.A., FEDORAK, S., CRAWFORD, G., & LEE, R. (2005). *Cultural anthropology* (2nd Cdn. ed.). Toronto: Thomson Nelson Learning.

HENDERSON, J.N. (1990). Anthropology, health and aging. In R.L. Rubinstein, J. Keith, D. Shink, & D. Wielund (Eds.), *Anthropology and aging: Comprehensive reviews* (pp. 39–68). Boston: Kluwer Academic Publishers

HODGSON, D.L. (2001). *Once intrepid warriors: Gender, ethnicity, and the cultural politics of Maasai development*. Bloomington: Indiana University Press.

IKELS, C. (1989). Becoming a human being in theory and practice: Chinese views of human development. In D.I. Kertzer & K.W. Schaie (Eds.), *Age structuring in comparative perspective* (pp. 109–134). Hillsdale, NJ: Lawrence Erlbaum Associates, Publishers.

IKELS, C. (1997). Long-term care and the disabled elderly in urban China. In J. Sokolovsky (Ed.), *The cultural control of aging: Worldwide perspectives* (2nd ed., pp. 452–471). Westport, CT: Bergin & Garvey.

KEITH, J., FRY, C.L., GLASCOCK, A.P., IKELS, C., DICKERSON-PUTNAM, J., HARPEND-ING, H.C., & DRAPER, P. (1994). *The aging experience: Diversity and commonality across cultures*. Thousand Oaks: Sage Publications.

KERTZER, D.I. (1989). Age structuring in comparative and historical perspective. In D.I. Kertzer & K.W. Schaie (Eds.), *Age structuring in comparative perspective* (pp. 3–20). Hillsdale, NJ: Lawrence Erlbaum Associates, Publishers.

LEE, R.B. (2003). *The Dobe Ju/'hoansi* (3rd ed.). Toronto: Nelson Thomson Learning.

LI, Z. (2006, March 12). *China faces elderly dilemma*. Retrieved March 12, 2006, from the World Wide Web at http://www.chinadaily.com.cn/english/doc/2004-08/21/content_367466.htm.

PETERS, J.F. (1998). *Life among the Yanomami*. Peterborough, ON: Broadview Press.

ROSENBERG, H. (1997). Complaint discourse, aging and caregiving among the Ju/'hoansi of Botswana. In J. Sokolovsky (Ed.), *The cultural control of aging: Worldwide perspectives* (2nd ed., pp. 33–55). Westport, CT: Bergin & Garvey.

RUBINSTEIN, R.L. (1990). Introduction. In R.L. Rubinstein, J. Keith, D. Shink, & D. Wielund (Eds.), *Anthropology and aging: Comprehensive reviews* (pp. 1–7). Boston: Kluwer Academic Publishers.

SANKAR, A. (1990). Gerontological research in China: The role for anthropological inquiry. In R.L. Rubinstein, J. Keith, D. Shink, & D. Wielund (Eds.), *Anthropology and aging: Comprehensive reviews* (pp. 173–199). Boston: Kluwer Academic Publishers.

YUAN, F. (1987). The status and role of the Chinese elderly in families and society. In J.H. Schulz & D. Davis-Friedmann (Eds.), *Aging China: Family economics, and government policies in transition* (pp. 36–46). Washington, DC: The Gerontological Society of America.

YOUNGMAN, J. (2003). *Map of the Masai Mara*. Retrieved March 12, 2006, from the World Wide Web at http://www.masai-mara.com/mmvm.htm.

Suggested Reading

COUNTS, D.A., & COUNTS, D.R. (1998). *Over the next hill: An ethnography of RVing Seniors in North America*. Peterborough, ON: Broadview Press.

A delightful account of a growing subculture in North America—the RVers. Anthropologists D.A. Count and D.R. Count join the nomadic caravans for a season to understand the culture of people who have "retired" and live in recreational vans for at least part of each year.

CHAPTER NINE

What Impact Has Missionism Had on Indigenous Cultures?

Introduction

Anthropologists have always been keenly aware of the importance of religious beliefs and practices in any society. Although **RELIGION** is difficult to succinctly define since its meaning can vary significantly from one group to another, it is reasonable to suggest that religion is a survival mechanism, giving people the strength to cope with reality and a sense of some control over their lives. Religion is also dynamic—it changes internally, albeit slowly, to meet the needs of members of a culture. These changes can occur more rapidly if outsiders introduce a new belief system into a culture. Missionaries, the agents of institutionalized religions such as Buddhism, Christianity, and Islam, have spread around the world with the goal of converting indigenous groups to their beliefs and practices. In the process, they have brought about dramatic changes in the world views and cultural systems of indigenous peoples. Thus, religion has also been a powerful instrument of external change.

KEY TERMS: religion, missionism, indigenous peoples, syncretism, pantheon, culture change

The subject of religious conversion is controversial; many people, including most anthropologists, decry the destruction of traditional beliefs and the ensuing cultural disruptions. However, missionaries and members of institutionalized religions feel it is imperative to spread the teachings of their religion. In this chapter we will explore the cultural changes that missionary activities have wrought and the implications of religious conversion on the stability of traditional cultures. To limit this study to manageable parameters, the spread of Christianity to the Mardu Aborigines of Western Australia, the Gebusi of Papua New Guinea, and the Soloman Islanders will be the focus of our discussion.

Anthropologists and Missionism

Van der Geest (1990), a missionary-turned-professional anthropologist recognizes an ambiguous relationship between missionaries and anthropologists. Anthropologists generally abhor the goal of **MISSIONISM**—to convert **INDIGENOUS PEOPLES** to Western beliefs and practices. Cultural relativism, the hallmark of anthropology, refutes the ethnocentric idea that there is only one true way of thinking and living, and that all people must be converted to this way. Yet, van der Geest (1990: 588) cautions against stereotyping contemporary missionaries as destroyers of traditional beliefs, knowledge, values, and practices, bent on destroying material culture (e.g., artwork related to pagan ritual) and disrupting and alienating people from their own culture.

These absolutes fail to recognize that many missionaries and their sponsoring churches have come to terms with their colonial past when these stereotypes may have been true. Today, missionaries use their energies to assist people in their struggles against repressive regimes and work tirelessly to improve the standard of living of indigenous peoples. Van der Geest (1990) also makes the valid point that anthropologists are similar to missionaries in several ways. For example, the intrusive nature of anthropological "occupation" in a foreign culture, and anthropologists inadvertently becoming agents of culture change by their mere presence in a foreign culture are similar to the reality of missionism.

A Discussion of Missionism

Missionary pursuits are not a new phenomena. In the early centuries following its inception, Christianity spread from Palestine and the Mediterranean to Western Europe, south India, and northeastern Africa, and more recently to the Americas and Australasia (Wolffe 2002). Incursions into sub-Saharan Africa and Asia are also ongoing.

Missionism can take many forms. In its early history, proselytizing[1] was the main focus with the aim of converting people to Christianity. Early missionism was an effective instrument for assimilating non-Western cultures into Western ideas and practices (Cudd 2005). Indeed, missionism has been accused of being an agent of cultural imperialism—the imposition of one culture over all others, ultimately destroying or significantly changing a traditional culture. Missionism is a form of imperialism in that missionaries seek to replace a peoples' traditional belief system (that missionaries consider false) with their institutionalized religion, leading to a new way of life and, ultimately, salvation (Niezen 1997). For example, at Fiske Seminary in Persia, early missionaries encouraged Nestorian women to renounce Islamic female seclusion practices, such as purdah (see Chapter 10). These changes to their cultural traditions caused friction between Nestorians and the dominant Muslim culture and led to persecutions and the eventual decline of the Nestorians (Tomasek 1999).

By the mid-twentieth century, development-oriented missionary work—establishing local infrastructures (e.g., building roads and hospitals, digging wells) and providing medical and educational services—became a common strategy, still with the goal of converting the locals to Christianity, but with a more humanitarian focus. Indigenous peoples were more likely to listen to the messages of missionaries if these messages were offered along with development assistance, such as digging wells for clean water or building schools and clinics (Marx 2005).

In recent years, some evangelist Christian groups have returned to proselytizing. Evangelists in India travel from village to village, holding prayer meetings and preaching to outdoor gatherings of villagers in an attempt to convert the people to Christianity (Baldauf 2005). Missions are often involved in providing international aid, especially after major ecological or natural disasters. In some instances this aid has come with conditions. Following the Indonesian tsunami, American evangelist agencies travelled to India, Indonesia, and Sri Lanka purportedly to offer humanitarian aid but they also distributed Christian literature, prompting the US National Council of Churches to protest this behaviour as unethical (Ibid.). Indeed, this insensitive proselytizing to traumatized people angered local Christian groups who feared a backlash against Christians in Sri Lanka, which already suffers from serious religious tensions (Rohde 2005). Other Christian groups abide by the Red Cross guidelines that aid work should not be used to further any political or religious agendas.

Those who advocate missionism during times of stress suggest that this is when people are most ready to hear about Christianity and are most in need of a message of hope. They believe "missionary work and aid work 'is one thing, not two separate things'" (Rohde 2005: A1). Missionism can be summed up as "God sends for the Church to carry out His work to the ends of the earth, to all nations, and to the end of time" (World Council of Churches 2003: 606). To that end, missionism, proselytizing, and conversion are all justified in their eyes.

Medical missionism has given missionaries a great deal of power over people suffering from diseases. However, even in the early twentieth century debates raged regarding the ethics of conversion under the guise of offering medical aid. Indeed, some medical missionaries have viewed medical work as merely "a tool for evangelization" (Macola 2005). Western medicine is often incompatible with traditional healing practices and the proselytizing can undermine social, cultural, and political authority in the community, as well as disrupt traditional religious beliefs. On the other hand, there is little doubt that Christian-based organizations have provided desperately needed services to areas of the world stricken with devastating diseases. An excellent example of this truly humanitarian work is that of John Tucker, with the US-based Catholic Markoll Missioners, who has worked in Cambodia since 2001 providing shelters and medical care to children with HIV and AIDS (Fraser 2005).

Some of these methods, such as development projects or effecting change in an oppressive community, are benevolent but other tactics, such as "conversion for aid," are at best insidiously coercive. Missionaries have been criticized for showing little regard or respect for traditional belief systems, and their actions may disrupt or even rupture the community (Cudd 2005). This is certainly evident in the missionary endeavours among the Mardu of Australia.

THE MARDU ABORIGINES

The Mardu Aborigines were hunter-gatherers who lived in the Western Desert of Australia (Tonkinson 1991).[2] They were fairly isolated from the outside world until the mid-1960s, and as a consequence their traditional lifestyle remained relatively untouched. Of all their myriad social and cultural features, religion appears the most powerful element of their existence. Indeed, their religious beliefs, and in particular the Dreaming, permeated every aspect of their lives.

The Dreaming or Dreamtime was a time of creation involving mystical figures, such as Rainbow Snake, Lightning Brothers, and Cloud Beings, who went on epic adventures. These Dreaming beings created the world around them and populated the world with part-human, part-animal, and part-divine beings, and became the founding ancestors of the Mardu (Arden 1994). These ancestral spirits are believed responsible for renewing the land and the cycle of seasons.

Belief in the Dreamtime is found among all Australian Aborigine groups, which suggests the belief system is ancient and may have come to Australia with the first humans (Baglin & Moore 1970). The Mardu perform rituals and obey the Law of the Dreaming beings to maintain order in their universe and ensure the continuance of life. This Law controls all aspects of Mardu life—their subsistence strategies, kinship, reciprocity, and social organization.

When the Mardu came in contact with Europeans, their sense of autonomy and their conceptualization of life based on the Dreaming was badly shaken. As Baglin and Moore (1970: 90) state: "they have lost their past without gaining a future." First, their traditional subsistence patterns were altered as Europeans encroached on their land. As a result, by the mid-1960s, the last of the Mardu had moved off the desert to a town called Jigalong. With no means of support in the town, the Mardu were forced to rely on government rations.

The so-called Mission Era lasted from 1946 to 1969 (Tonkinson 1991). A Protestant mission was established in Jigalong in 1945, and Mardu children were taken to live in mission dormitories, where attempts were made to eliminate their Mardu culture. If the children spoke their traditional language, they were beaten. They were taught Christian dogma and forced to reject their culture, and in particular the Dreaming and the Law. Despite the missionaries' efforts, the Mardu clung to their Dreaming beliefs, and they continued to hold frequent rituals, such as initiations and big meetings, to reaffirm their beliefs and teach their children.

The Mardu social structure was also affected by missionary interference. The missionaries objected when Mardu men tried to claim 12-year-old girls betrothed to them based on the Dreaming Law. As well, some Mardu women, aided by the teachings of the missionaries, objected to polygynous marriages. Although from a Western perspective this seems a positive step, this new freedom from the Dreaming and the Law led to increased sexual promiscuity among the young, as well as more unmarried mothers. Some young people began ignoring their parents' wishes and chose their own marriage partners, often breaking the Law and entering into what the Mardu considered incestuous relationships. In one instance, missionaries called the police when the Mardu carried out a traditional punishment based on the Law that involved spearing and clubbing the miscreant.

As the Dreaming Law lost its prominence, the Mardu in Jigalong suffered from increasing social problems, including poverty, conflict, alcoholism, and unemployment (Tonkinson 2002). Most of the Mardu felt these problems came from abandoning the Dreaming Law. With increasing exposure to a Western-style education system, television, music, and literature, and access to alcohol and gambling, the Dreaming Law continued to lose its influence, especially among the young. The Mardu community became split, with some people willing to modernize, such as hospitalizing boys for circumcisions, while others refused to compromise the Dreaming Law.

In the end, the missionaries were unsuccessful in destroying the traditional religion of the Mardu, and in 1969 they gave up trying to convert their "unredeemably sinful character" (Tonkinson 1991: 166). The missionaries were unsuccessful because they refused to respect or even understand the power of the Dreaming and the Law. Ironically, after the missionaries left Jigalong, some of the children who had grown up in the mission dormitories began incorporating Christianity into the Dreaming Law (Arden 1994).

Christian proselytising fell on barren ground here, seemingly unable to dislodge an indigenous religious system so pervasive and integrated that it was synonymous with, and inseparable from, the fabric of life itself. (TONKINSON 2002: 6)

In the 1980s, some of the Mardu returned to their ancestral lands and began hunting, gathering, and fishing once again (Bird & Bleige Bird 2003). By 1986, they had established several outstations to assist any Mardu wishing to return to the desert and the Law. However, the number of Mardu who have returned to their traditional life is still low, and even these Mardu are never far from outside influences. Today, the Mardu are caught between two worlds: traditional desert life and the Western world. Many Mardu wish to maintain their core beliefs in the Dreaming and the Law, yet others have renounced both.

THE SOLOMON ISLANDS

Faced with aggressive missionaries, some indigenous groups have blended their religious beliefs with those foisted on them, and in this way have managed to maintain at least some autonomy through the process of remoulding their belief system. This is known as **SYNCRETISM**, and is readily evident in places such as the Caribbean where indigenous groups have blended aboriginal, African, and Christian (mainly Roman Catholic) beliefs and practices into *vodun*[3] (voodoo) cults.

There is some question as to whether religious conversion is as successful as one might believe. In the Solomon Islands, Harmon (1998) found that despite 150 years of Christian missionary work, the pagan belief system still thrives "underground." Many evangelical Christian groups have visited these islands and attempted to convert the people to Christianity. Yet ancestor worship and magic are still practised: "Jesus is invoked for public consumption—but as soon as illness or natural disaster strikes, or good fortune is desired or envy consumes the individual, the spirits are called upon. Belief in elements of the old religion is so profound they transcend all generations, clans and conversions" (Harmon 1998: 20).

During European colonization in this region, the traditional belief systems of the indigenous peoples were banned and their leaders imprisoned (Harmon 1998). Presbyterian missionaries bound the hands and feet of islanders who did not attend Sunday church service and had them publicly flogged. Yet, these harsh measures did little to stamp out pagan beliefs, and even the indigenous Christian preachers admit to a continuing belief in ancestor spirits and magic.

The missionaries' intolerance for the ancient beliefs and practices of the Solomon Islanders continues today. On the island of Malaita, the South Seas Evangelical Church holds power over the islanders and tightly controls their everyday behaviour. The islanders are not allowed to chew betel nuts, smoke, drink alcohol, eat pork or scaleless fish, nor become sexually involved with anyone outside of marriage. Despite these restrictions, and although missionaries have tried to wipe out the traditional belief system and replace it with Christianity, pagan[4] religions continue to thrive on the Solomon Islands.

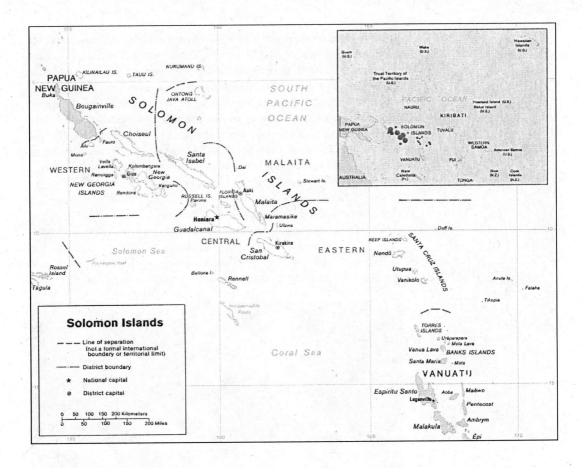

THE GEBUSI

The Gebusi live in small villages deep within the dense rainforest of Papua New Guinea (Knauft 2005). They are small-scale horticulturalists, fishers, and hunter-gatherers. Until the 1960s, the Gebusi had little contact with outsiders, including anthropologists, although occasional contact brought some modern conveniences into the community, such as steel tools and clothing.

The essence of Gebusi culture is *kogwayay*, which means togetherness, friendship, and similarity. Knauft (2005) found the Gebusi people in the 1980s to be vibrant and friendly, violent and pragmatic, and consumed with the spirit world and fears of sorcery. Their lives revolved around rituals, such as song-fests and divinations, spirit seances, and male initiation rites. Their animistic religious system was deeply tied to a **PANTHEON** of animal and other spirits within the forest, and their shamanistic practices were used to harness spirits to help manage everyday human affairs.

All-night spirit seances in which they communicated with the spirits through spirit mediums helped them to make decisions concerning when to begin a hunting expedition, perform a ritual, fight an enemy, or accuse someone of sorcery. The Gebusi believed that deaths caused by sickness, accidents, or suicide were due to sorcery. Male spirit mediums were responsible for determining who the sorcerer was, and if identified, the sorcerer was executed. Beyond community decisions, these seances were an opportunity for forming social bonds among the participants. At night the men gathered in a longhouse near the spirit medium who went into a trance. The spirit of the medium left his body, and then a soul from the spirit world entered. Through the spirit medium, the spirit sang songs, and the men formed a chorus that repeated each line of the song. The song-fest continued all night long. Although Gebusi women were excluded from the spirit seance, the primary spirits were beautiful young women who allowed Gebusi men to sing of their sexual fantasies.

When Knauft returned to the Gebusi in 1998 he found much had changed. The entire community had moved to the outskirts of Nomad

A Gebusi dancer at a ritual feast.

Station, a community of more than 1,000 people from several ethnic backgrounds. The Gebusi had been converted to Christianity—Catholic, Evangelical Protestant, and Seventh Day Adventist. Their children were receiving a Western-influenced education, and the women were selling produce from their forest gardens for cash at the market. The Gebusi material culture had not changed substantially, with the addition of only a few more tools, although they now all wore Western clothing—the women never walked around the village bare-breasted as had been the custom in the 1980s. The central longhouse that always served as a focal point of community activity no longer existed, and the essence of togetherness was greatly muted.

Gebusi social life had also changed—joking (especially sexual) and camaraderie were no longer so common as when Knauft first visited. Young people spent Friday and Saturday nights partying or watching videos, and rock music boomed through the community. The Gebusi, to whom time had formerly been a casual concept, now organized their daily lives; much to Knauft's surprise the Gebusi were on time for church services and sporting events.

The traditional songs and spirit seances of their animistic belief system had been replaced with church services. The role of the spirit mediums had declined, meaning the people did not have a way to communicate with their spirit world. Christian funerals and burials had replaced death inquests and sorcery accusations. All three of the churches influenced the social and spiritual changes among the Gebusi. The Roman Catholic Church was considered the "softest" church, only requiring the Gebusi to believe in God, attend church services, avoid fighting, and not drink kava, a mildly alcoholic drink. The Evangelicals were more stringent: they forbade the Gebusi from smoking or participating in pagan rituals. The Seventh Day Adventists took a strict stance against dancing, smoking, drinking, traditional rituals, eating scaleless fish or pork (something the Gebusi loved), nor could the Gebusi do any work or participate in entertainment on Saturday, the worship day.

With the advent of Christianity, much of the vibrancy of the Gebusi culture was lost: their traditional beliefs, poetry, symbolism, music, and complex spirit world all disappeared. Instead they had become passive recipients of an outside religious authority. On the other hand, the Gebusi previously attributed many deaths to sorcery, and sought revenge by murdering an accused sorcerer. Now, the Gebusi rejected their belief in sorcery, and the homicide rate dropped to zero. Women, always on the edge of the Gebusi spirit world, now fully participated in Christian services, though they were still subordinate in a patriarchal society.

Knauft (2005) suggests the Gebusi were uniquely open to outside influences, and attracted to a more modern way of life. They were eager to improve their economic (market and consumer goods), social (school and employment opportunities), and moral (church) conditions.

Conclusion

The impact of missionaries and missionism on indigenous peoples is multi-faceted. There can be little doubt that missionaries are agents of change, but this does not imply only negative change. As we have seen in the three cases presented in this chapter, responses to missionism vary, from outright rejection, to a blending of old and new beliefs, to total acceptance.

CULTURE CHANGE is inevitable and comes from many quarters, including missionary movements. In the case of the Gebusi, we are seeing an adoption of a new way of life based on the introduction of a new religion. Unlike the people of the nearby Solomon Islands, who dealt with missionism by creating a syncretic belief system, the Gebusi wholeheartedly embraced their new religion—whether Catholic, Evangelical Protestant, or Seventh Day Adventist. The changes in their religious beliefs were just one element of the modernization processes ongoing in the Gebusi world. For the Mardu Aborigines, their Dreaming Law was so firmly entrenched that they resolutely refused the missionary advances, and indeed, their traditional beliefs have led many to reject, at least partly, the modern world. Regardless of the success or failure of missionary activities, there is little doubt that missionism exacts dramatic changes on people and their culture.

Questions for Consideration

1. How did the missionary activities disturb the traditional worldview and way of life of the Mardu? Did they have any positive impact on the Mardu? Why do you think the Mardu Dreamtime was strong enough to resist Christian missionism when so many other traditional belief systems have been destroyed?

2. Choose a cultural group and examine the missionary influences on this group. Create a chart of the changes and impacts that missionary activities had on this group. From the perspective of the people in the culture, were these influences mainly positive or negative?

3. In your opinion, is missionary work unethical? Explain your answer.

4. Did the Gebusi gain more or lose more when they gave up their traditional animistic belief system?

5. The Solomon Islanders have attempted to blend their ancient beliefs with Christianity. How successful have they been? Do you think they can maintain this blending?

NOTES

1 Preaching a particular religious doctrine.
2 The past tense is used here because most Mardu have left the desert and no longer make their living as hunter-gatherers, though Mardu people still live in Australia.
3 Closest to Creole spelling.
4 Usually refers to indigenous religions that existed before the advent of Christianity, such as Wicca.

References

ARDEN, H. (1994). *Dreamkeepers: A spirit-journey into Aboriginal Australia.* New York: Harper Collins Publishers.

BAGLIN, D., & MOORE, D.R. (1970). *People of the dreamtime: The Australian Aborigines.* New York: Walker/Weatherhill.

BALDAUF, S. (2005, April 1). A new breed of missionary; A drive for conversions, not development, is stirring violent animosity in India. *The Christian Science Monitor,* 1. Retrieved October 23, 2005, from the World Wide Web at http://www.infotrac.galegroup.com.

BIRD, D.W., & BLIEGE BIRD, R. (2003). *Mardu children's hunting strategies in the Western Desert, Australia.* Retrieved Sept. 26, 2004, from the World Wide Web at http://www.umit.maine.edu/~rebecca_bird/chags.pdf.

CUDD, A.E. (2005). Missionary positions. *Hypatia, 20,* 164. Retrieved October 23, 2005, from the World Wide Web at http://www.infotrac.galegroup.com.

FRASER, B. (2005, October 1). Getting drugs to HIV-infected children in Cambodia: A Catholic missionary group struggles to provide homes and drug treatment for HIV-infected children in Cambodia and the government seeks to expand treatment countrywide. Early results are promising, but challenges loom as costs rise. *The Lancet, 366,* 1153. Retrieved October 28, 2005, from the World Wide Web at http://www.infotrac.galegroup.com.

HARMON, J.B. (1998, August 21). Ignoring the missionary position. *New Statesman 12,* 20–21. Retrieved October 26, 2005, from the World Wide Web at http://www.infotrac.galegroup.com.

KNAUFT, B. (2005). *The Gebusi. Lives transformed in a rainforest world.* Toronto: McGraw-Hill.

MACOLA, G. (2005, July). [Review of book *The steamer parish: The rise and fall of missionary medicine on an African frontier*]. *The Journal of African History, 46,* 36. Cambridge: Cambridge University Press.

MARX, G. (2005, July 31). Missionary pilot speaks the gospel in Haiti. *Chicago Tribune.* Retrieved October 30, 2005, from the World Wide Web: http://www.infotrac.galegroup.com.

NIEZEN, R. (1997). Healing and conversion: Medical evangelism in James Bay Cree Society. *Ethnohistory, 44*(4), 463–491.

ROHDE, D. (2005, January 22). Mix of Quake aid and preaching stirs concern. *The New York Times*. Retrieved October 23, 2005, from the World Wide Web at http://www.infotrac.galegroup.com.

TOMASEK, K.M. (1999). Review of Mary Lyon and the Mount Holyoke missionaries. *Journal of Interdisciplinary History, 30*(1), 143–145.

TONKINSON, R. (1991). *The Mardu Aborigines: Living the dream in Australia's desert* (2nd ed.). Toronto: Holt, Rinehart and Winston, Inc.

TONKINSON, R. (2002). *Spiritual prescription, social reality: Reflections on religious dynamism*. Retrieved January 22, 2005, from the World Wide Web at http://www.anthropology.arts.uwa.edu.au/__data/page/27090/tonkinson_2002.pdf.

WOLFFE, J. (2002). Introduction. In J. Wolffe (Ed.), *Global religious movements in regional context* (pp. 1–9). Milton Keynes, UK: Ashgate in association with The Open University.

WORLD COUNCIL OF CHURCHES (2003, October). A statement on the missionary calling of the church. *International Review of Mission, 92*, 606. Retrieved October 29, 2005, from the World Wide Web at http://www.infotrac.galegroup.com.

VAN DER GEEST, S. (1990). Anthropologists and missionaries: Brothers under the skin. *Man, 25*(4), 588–601.

Suggested Readings

TONKINSON, R. (1991). *The Mardu Aborigines: Living the dream in Australia's desert* (2nd ed.). Toronto: Holt, Rinehart and Winston, Inc.

A well-written and interesting ethnography on the Mardu Aborigines—a little-known indigenous group of hunter-gatherers with a very strong sense of spirituality and a complex belief system.

WALLACE, A.F.C. (1966). *Religion: An anthropological view*. New York: Random House.

A classic work in anthropology that considers religion from an anthropological perspective.

VAN DER GEEST, S. (1990). Anthropologists and missionaries: Brothers under the skin. *Man, 25*(4), 588–601.

A thought-provoking article on the similarities as well as the differences between anthropologists and missionaries.

CHAPTER TEN

Is the Practice of Purdah and Wearing the Hijab Oppressive to Women or an Expression of Their Identity?

Introduction

The image of an Afghan woman hurrying through the streets draped from head to toe in voluminous folds of thick blue cloth, with not even her eyes visible, resonates among Westerners. These women are wearing the hijab and observing the ancient custom of purdah. To us (Westerners), purdah and the hijab are symbols of female oppression, tangible evidence that women in some parts of the world are still treated like second-class citizens, forever submissive and secluded from the public eye. Is this true? Do women who follow purdah and wear the hijab consider themselves oppressed, and is purdah viewed in the same manner in all states that practice it?

KEY TERMS: gender stratification, purdah, hijab, multicultural

In this chapter we will address gender stratification through the age-old custom of purdah. Purdah will be examined from an historical, religious, social, and economic perspective. As you will see, the meaning of purdah varies from one area to another. For this reason we will take a cross-cultural approach, visiting several regions of the world: Palestine, Iran, Sudan, Pakistan, and Afghanistan. One of the most controversial and confusing aspects of purdah is the hijab, the covering of a woman's head, and *jilbaab*, the covering of a woman's body. Since the questions we are asking become less straightforward when examining hijab, the main focus in this chapter will be on hijab—what it means to people who follow this custom and to those who resist it.

Anthropologists have grown increasingly conscious of a new voice in the study of humankind—that of the people being studied. In this case, the thoughts and opinions of the women who follow purdah and wear various forms of hijab will be heard, as it is their interpretation of purdah that is most significant. Internet sources are drawn on in this chapter, since it is here, rather than in most academic papers, that Muslim women have found a timely forum for expressing their views on hijab and its meanings. Finally, this chapter is not only about whether purdah and hijab are oppressive, it is also about the *perception* of oppression that many Westerners hold.

Anthropologists and Gender Stratification

Anthropologists are interested in gender stratification and its impact on the social structure of cultural groups. Just as gender is a cultural construct, gender stratification is also culturally defined. GENDER STRATIFICATION reflects inequality between males and females. This inequality may be in the form of access to wealth and resources, power for self-determination, and the prestige and status afforded to individuals according to their gender. Anthropologists have found that the gender that controls production and distribution of consumable products is usually the dominant gender. Where women are relegated to domestic chores only, they possess relatively little status and male dominance is the norm. Indeed, anthropologists have found that some degree of female gender stratification exists in all modern-day societies.

To determine the degree of gender stratification, anthropologists measure the social and political positions that women can hold in the culture, the economic independence they are able to achieve, and the decision-making power that they have over their own lives and bodies. This leads us to the question of whether purdah exemplifies a form of gender stratification.

A Discussion of Purdah and Hijab

The Persian word **PURDAH** means curtain (Khan 1999); it can also mean screen or veil (Arnett 2001). Most people associate purdah with clothing that completely covers a woman, but purdah actually means the seclusion of women, whether beneath concealing clothing or by isolation in their homes. To Muslims, following purdah symbolizes the importance of feminine modesty.

The reasons for purdah are myriad: religious beliefs, views on proper female behaviour, social status, and a sense of honour and respectability (de Souza 2004). The Quran appears to sanction female seclusion: "And when you ask his wives for anything, ask it of them from behind a curtain (*hejjab*). That is purer for your hearts and their hearts." According to the Quran, then, purdah is considered a code of behaviour that sustains a woman's privacy, protects her reputation, and prevents sexual exploitation (Geissinger 2000). Muslim clergy believe that good Muslim women will wear hijab to protect their virtue and help men control their sexual appetites. Indeed, the desire to ensure that females remain sexually pure—virgins until marriage, and faithful to their husbands after marriage—is the most common reason cited (Khan 1999). Many Muslim women living in the West feel that observing purdah and in particular wearing the hijab isolates them from the Western tendency to objectify women.

One of the main reasons for purdah relates to maintaining control over wealth and property (de Souza 2004). Women are the mothers of sons who will inherit property and wealth from the patriarch; the paternity of these sons must be ensured. Thus, in some states, purdah is deemed more important for the wealthy upper classes that have property to protect than for the poorer lower classes. If this is the case, purdah becomes a symbol of status—only wealthy women can afford to practice purdah, while women who must work to help support their families find it difficult to practice purdah. Observing purdah is also a symbol of the Muslim world's rejection of Western morals and political ideology; wearing the hijab has become a political statement. Since purdah is both religious and cultural, the degree of purdah will obviously differ from one culture to another.

The modest covering of a woman's head and body is known as the **HIJAB**. Hijab comes from the Arabic word *hajaba*,[1] which means to hide or conceal from view (Ali n.d.). To many women, hijab is the truest expression of being a Muslim. Guidance regarding proper dress comes from interpretations of the Quran and Hadith.[2] Today, the hijab also announces the inherent differences between Islamic states and the West.

Many cultural groups practice hijab, although the form of hijab adopted varies considerably, depending on the culture and the reasons for practising it. The Azerbaijan wear a head scarf to cover their hair,

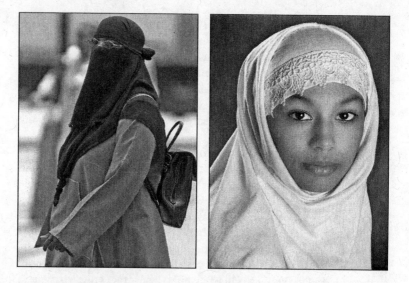

These two Moroccan women are wearing head scarves that symbolize their Muslim faith and Muslim cultural identity.

while women of the Rashaayda Bedouin wear a married woman's mask. Iranian women wear the chador, a loose, shapeless garment and veil, and Pashtun Afghan women wear the body-enveloping *burqa*. There are many other expressions of hijab, such as the Indian sari, Sudanese *tobah*, Iraqi *abbayah*, Turkish *yashmak*, North African *djellabah* and *haik*, and Egyptian *milaya*[3] (Fernea & Fernea 2000; Alvi, Hoodfar, & McDonough 2003). These coverings are tangible expressions of cultural practices that hold deeply rooted meanings in each of these societies.

The practice of veiling is not unknown in Western society—witness the white veil covering a bride during a Christian wedding ceremony. This veil symbolizes chasteness and purity. Until recently many women wore veiled hats to Sunday church service, and black veils and hats or scarves to funerals. Indeed, until the 1960s, Catholic women were required to cover their heads when in church. Many cultural groups have traditionally worn head scarves, such as Canadian Doukhobors and Hutterites. Catholic nuns also wear habits that exemplify a form of purdah and hijab.

Although purdah requires women to wear concealing clothing when they leave the house, it also refers to female seclusion, such as living in a separate part of the house—what Young (1996) calls segregation of the sexes. This segregation is practised among the Rashaayda Bedouin, who recognize private domestic spaces for women and open public spaces for men. In a much different example of female seclusion, until the early twentieth century it was common to bind the feet of Chinese girls, ostensibly to make their feet more attractive. In actuality, foot binding prevented females from walking any distance, which meant the women remained secluded in their homes.

Having separate space for males and females is not unusual, even in the West. In the 1960s, as a young girl living on the Canadian prairies, I remember entering a local elementary school through the "girls" entrance, which was next to the "boys" entrance. The town pool room or billiard hall was only for men, whether by an unwritten code of conduct or a town bylaw, I am unsure. The beer parlour (bar) had a room for "gents" and a room for men and their female escorts. In the early 1970s, there were two entrances, one for women and one for men, at a pub in the townsite of Banff National Park. Thus, the practice of secluding women or at the very least separating males and females was common in twentieth-century Canada, especially outside cosmopolitan centres.

In some cases, purdah has been used to keep women from participating in the socio-economic and political life of the society. Among the Yusufzai Pakhtun of the Swat Valley in northeast Pakistan, women remain secluded inside domestic compounds, only leaving to attend weddings, funerals, and circumcision rituals. If they do leave their homes, they must be accompanied by other women or a male family member (Lindholm & Lindholm 2000). This practice means women spend most of their lives within the domestic sphere and are unable to obtain employment or an education, or participate in other activities within their community.

Purdah is also an expression of modest behaviour that befits a woman's station and reflects positively on her family. Many Muslim women feel wearing hijab is a symbol of their purity and modesty. The Quran (24: 30–31) states: "And say to the believing women that they should lower their gaze and guard their modesty; and that they should not display their beauty and ornaments except what must ordinarily appear thereof; that they should draw their veils over their bosoms and not display their beauty except to their husbands." Besides modestly covering a woman's body, the clothing must be loose and shapeless, and opaque so as not to draw any attention.[4] Despite the seeming oppression, many Muslim women see the hijab as a submission to their God and faith, not to men (Bullock 2001). Fernea and Fernea (2000: 239) call the hijab "portable seclusion," which enables a woman to affect an aura of respectability and religious piety, thereby bringing honour to the woman and her family.

HISTORY OF PURDAH

The origin of purdah remains unclear, although it may have developed in ancient Persia. Regardless of its origin, purdah was practised long before the beginning of Islam. In fact, purdah did not spread to the Middle East until the Arab conquest of the region in the seventh century. Ancient Babylonian[5] women were masked and chaperoned by a male relative when they left the house. They were also segregated in a separate part of the household. Similarly, Assyrian women were hidden behind screens in their houses (Arnett 2001). Indeed, the first known reference to hijab was found in an Assyrian legal text in the thirteenth century BCE (Shirazi 2001).

Women from Pakistan ... [wore] comfortable *salwar kameez*—silky tunics drifting low over billowing pants with long shawls of matching fabric tossed loosely over their heads. Saudi women trod carefully behind their husbands, peering from behind gauzy face veils and 360-degree black cloaks that made them look, as Guy de Maupassant once wrote, 'like death out for a walk.' Afghan women also wore 360-degree coverings, called *chadris*—colorful crinkly shrouds with an oblong of embroidered lattice work over the eyes. Women from Dubai wore stiff, birdlike masks of black and gold that beaked over the nose.

EYEWITNESS ACCOUNT BY JOURNALIST GERALDINE BROOKS (1994: 21) AT THE CAIRO AIRPORT

Evidence of purdah and hijab has also been found in classical Greece, Byzantium, Persia, and India among the Rajput caste (Women in World History Curriculum 1996–2005). In Assyrian, Greco-Roman, Byzantine[6] and pre-Islamic Iran empires, purdah was a mark of prestige and status, and in India, purdah was practised as early as 100 BCE to protect royal women from unwanted gazes (Khan 1999). Records suggest the practice of hijab began in Islamic society after the wives of Muhammad were insulted by people thinking they were slaves (Fernea & Fernea 2000).

By the eighth century, female seclusion was well entrenched in Iran and the Eastern Mediterranean among the upper classes (Khan 1999). In India, purdah was strictly adhered to during colonial rule. Indeed, during this era Muslim women lost the right to inherit property and wealth, and retain income they earned, bringing the rights of Muslim women more in line with Hindu women and British women of the time. In essence, colonial rule destroyed the matrilineal societies of southern India (Khan 1999).

In the late nineteenth and early twentieth centuries, many liberals and intellectuals pushed for an end to hijab and purdah—this era became a hallmark for social progress. However, as the twentieth century progressed, hijab enjoyed a revival, especially in areas where people felt Islam was being threatened by Western influence. Hijab soon became a righteous symbol of Islam.

Today, the wearing of hijab is compulsory in Saudi Arabia, Iran, Zamfara State in Nigeria, and Kelantan State in Malaysia (although not in government offices). Punishment for not following the Islamic law of hijab can be severe. In countries where hijab is expected but not law, such as Egypt, Algeria, Kuwait, and Palestine, women have been attacked for not wearing the hijab. In other Muslim countries conditions remain volatile, with some segments advocating hijab, while others have rejected the custom. Regardless, women find themselves at the centre of the debate, often enduring harassment and discrimination regardless of whether they wear hijab or not, depending on the current political and ideological atmosphere.

PURDAH AS OPPRESSION

Some scholars suggest that Muslim women occupy a subordinate position in Middle Eastern countries (Read & Bartkowski 2000). They use purdah, and in particular, hijab, to justify their claims. Others, who have taken an emic[7] perspective, have found that oppression and subjugation may not be so evident to Muslim women, and that the reason they continue to wear hijab varies from one group and even one individual to another.

Read and Bartkowski (2000) conducted a study of two dozen Muslim women living in Austin, Texas. Half wore the veil and the other half were unveiled. They found that the unveiled women viewed the veil (hijab) as a mechanism for patriarchal domination of women. "The veil is used to control women" (p. 408). Both groups felt hijab was directly related to men's sexuality and lack of control: "Men can't control themselves, so they make women veil" (p. 408). Many of the unveiled respondents sought to weaken the link between hijab and religion. "Women are made to believe that the veil is religious. In reality, it's all political" (p. 408).

Narratives from veiled women rationalized wearing the hijab for religious reasons: "I wear the hijab because the Qur'an says it's better" (p. 403). Another woman believed "the veil represents submission to god" (p. 403). Religion was not the only reason given for wearing the hijab; hijab can also be a cultural marker—a statement of a Muslim's ethnic and cultural distinctiveness: "The veil differentiates Muslim women from other women. When you see a woman in hijab, you know she's Muslim" (p. 404). Even the unveiled women considered hijab to be an important cultural marker: "Some Muslim women need the veil to identify them with the Muslim culture" (p. 409).

Although the veiled women in this study did not explicitly discuss the idea that men's sexual activities must be controlled, they did allude to the problem: "If the veil did not exist, many evil things would happen. Boys would mix with girls, which will result in evil things" (p. 404). The sense of female distinctiveness was articulated by one woman: "Women are like diamonds; they are so precious. They should not be revealed to everyone—just to their husbands and close kin" (p. 404). Contrary to the Western perspective that hijab restricts women, the veiled women in Read and Bartkowski's (2000) study felt that the veil liberated them. To these women, hijab has overlapping religious, gender, and ethnic significance.

Opponents see purdah as oppressive, depriving women of the right to gain an education, economic independence, and fully participate in community life. They see purdah as one more way to marginalize and subjugate women. Interestingly, feminist writers on purdah suggest that women are veiled to mute their sexual desires and their potential danger to men (Bonvillain 1998), while women who wear hijab (e.g., the American Muslim women in Read & Bartkowski's [2000] study), believe it is men's sexual desires that are being controlled. Opponents also point out that hijab originated before Islam and outside the Middle East. Therefore using religious scripture to support wearing hijab is false reasoning, and interpretations of the scriptures and hadiths are highly questionable.

The feminist perspective goes against the religious elites who strongly favour hijab. They associate the hijab (or veiling) with religious devotion and obedience to the tenets of Islam (Read & Bartkowski 2000). A recent resurgence of the hijab has been noted among educated Muslim women who wish to announce their strong faith and traditions: "Young Muslim women are reclaiming the hijab, reinterpreting it in

light of its original purpose—to give back to women ultimate control of
their own bodies" (Mustafa n.d.: 1). One of the most common supports
for hijab is the freedom gained from a sense of anonymity. "Wearing the hijab has given me freedom from constant attention to my
physical self," says Naheed Mustafa, a journalism student at Ryerson
Polytechnic University. A Canadian-born Muslim, she began wearing
the traditional hijab head scarf at the age of 21. While others tend to
see her as either a terrorist or an oppressed woman, she feels liberated—free from unwanted sexual advances and the politics of Western
"gender games." Indeed, empirical evidence seems to suggest that men
do interact differently with women in hijab. Supporters of purdah also
suggest seclusion can offer women protection and safe haven, a place
where they can relax and enjoy their favourite activities.

PALESTINE

During the intifada[8] of the 1980s in Gaza, Hamas extremists
attempted to impose hijab on Palestinian women (Hammami 1990).
These women, who had enjoyed relative freedom to choose whether
or not to wear hijab, and in what form, now found their dress code
under increasing scrutiny and pressure to conform to the Hamas'[9]
interpretation of hijab.

Although the hijab was fairly common among older Palestinian
peasant women, many educated urban women had given up wearing
any form of hijab by the 1950s (Hammami 1990). Even those still wearing hijab saw it as a symbol of group identity, not as genderized. For
some, hijab was a symbol of resistance to Israeli occupation in Gaza.
Regardless of how the hijab was viewed, most Palestinian women were
against forced imposition of hijab. The Hamas, however, sought to
"restore" hijab as part of a movement to return to a moral and social
order closer to their (Hamas) interpretations of Islam and the way
Muslims should live and worship. Hamas considered the hijab a reflection of traditional Islamic piety and political affiliation. Women who
refused found themselves the target of attacks by "religious" youths,
who threw stones at them and shouted verbal abuse. The original religious and modesty aspects of hijab seemed lost. Only the intifada was
important, and the hijab became a sign of a woman's political commitment to the intifada.

It is important for readers to recognize that Palestinian women
resisting the pressure were not against hijab as such, but wanted the
right to choose to wear hijab. They also resisted the patriarchal control Hamas wielded, and feared that hijab was only a first step in an
offensive against Palestinian women's rights. Safety was also an argument used for wearing the hijab—protecting Palestinian women from
attacks by soldiers and activist youths. Hooligans, acting under the
auspice of Hamas, broke into a school and demanded that the girls

wear the hijab in May 1988, and in September 1988 a group of males attacked girls at the Ahmad Shawqi school in Gaza City for not covering their heads (Hammami 1990).

When the attacks on women spread to Jerusalem, the Unified National Leadership of the Uprising (UNLU) political leaders in Gaza finally came to the aid of Palestinian women. After a particularly ugly incident in which two women were harassed and accused of being collaborators, the UNLU condemned the attacks in a statement, and the attacks stopped for a time (Hammami 1990). Unfortunately, in 1990 the Hamas resumed the hijab campaign with a vengeance, only now they were advocating full body coverage. Hamas also issued orders that women were to have a male relative with them when leaving the house. Despite this resurgence, Palestinian women have continued to resist patriarchal domination during the intifada. Hammami (1990: 25) feels that, in this case, hijab is being used as an instrument of oppression, "a direct disciplining of women's bodies for political ends."

IRAN

The story of women and hijab in Iran has taken a convoluted path. The veil was banned by Reza Shah Pahlevi in 1936 (Talvi 2002) as part of the Women's Awakening of 1936–41. This project opened up educational and employment opportunities for Iranian women—if they gave up their veils (Amin 2002). Nonetheless, the concept of a male "guardian" for all women was still extolled, thereby preventing any true sense of equality. Following the project's failure, women experienced a backlash from men; some unveiled women were even attacked by religious extremists.

By the 1960s and 1970s, Iranian women under the rule of the Shah enjoyed a degree of independence. They were able to obtain an education and work in traditionally male professions. However, this does not mean Iranian women were free from oppression. Indeed, Iranian women who continued to wear the veil were arrested and their veils were forcibly removed until dress codes became more open and women were allowed to wear the veil if they so chose. Then the political atmosphere changed in the 1970s and Iranian women began wearing the chador (black, loose-fitting robes). When the Shah was deposed in 1979, and the Islamic Revolution swept the country, the chador became compulsory, and women were once again punished—this time for not wearing hijab (Talvi 2002). Under the Ayatollah Khomeini, religious and cultural fundamentalism forced women to veil and take on more traditional female roles. Women were seen as pivotal to changing Iran's moral code, and those who resisted were mocked and called "unchaste painted dolls" (Women in World History Curriculum 1996–2005). Witnesses recounted the terrors of executions by public stoning of women who broke the strict laws of Islamic appearance and conduct (Talvi 2002).

One woman put it this way: "It [the hijab] is not an issue for me.... In my community [Abassan] it's natural to wear it. The problem is when little boys, including my son, feel they have the right to tell me to wear it." (HAMMAMI 1990: 26)

Today, wearing the chador is still mandatory in Iran. Even foreign women who visit Iran must follow the Islamic Republic of Iran's law of hijab and have their visa entrance photos taken wearing the hijab (Shirazi 2001). When Faegheh Shirazi visited her home country of Iran in 1997, graffiti slogans such as "Death to the improperly veiled woman" covered the walls of buildings, reminding her that hijab was not only a cultural and religious custom to Iranians, but an ideology that permeated every aspect of their lives. Propaganda on the virtues of the veil was everywhere: television programs, newspaper and magazine articles and ads, and even stamps had the word *hijab* inscribed on the lower left corner.

Although wearing the hijab has been the custom in several periods of Iranian history, in modern Iranian society, choice is no longer an issue, suggesting that at this point in time purdah and the hijab are also instruments of oppression in Iran.

SUDAN

The Rashaayda Bedouin are nomadic pastoralists who live in northeastern Sudan. They practice both purdah, in the form of sexual segregation of space, and hijab, in the form of wearing veils and masks that also serve as cultural identity markers (Young 1996). When journeying from one camp to another, Rashaayda women don masks decorated with silvery-lead beadwork and their best dresses. The masks, which are tubes of black cloth flared at the lower end, cover their noses, mouths, and cheeks. The upper end fits so snugly around the face that it is difficult for the woman to open her mouth widely. The Rashaayda distinctive clothing styles are used to identify different stages of a person's life cycle. Young girls cover their heads, shoulders, and chests with a large piece of cloth, while boys wear a knit cap. Older girls add a virgin's veil and a black gown, and once married, they wear the woman's mask (*ginaa'*).

The Rashaayda Bedouin organize their lives around men's and women's space. The tent and areas around the tent are women's space, while the open desert and open areas in market towns are men's spaces (Young 1996). This division of space limits opportunities for Rashaayda women to participate in economic activities. They cannot keep herds or sell any goods at market because the desert and market are public spaces for men only. Women own the tents, but must follow certain space restrictions even within the tent, which is divided into a woman's side on the west, and a man's side on the east, usually with a curtain dividing these spaces.

The Rashaayda Bedouin are definitely a patriarchal society; many of the practices of the Rashaayda favour men, such as inheritance rights. Because women are not allowed to move through unenclosed spaces alone, this sexual division of space undoubtedly limits a woman's ability to acquire any wealth or independence. These customs appear to be a by-product of Rashaayda Arab traditions—in many Arab groups it is shameful for women to be in men's spaces for any length of time.

To suggest that women are oppressed in Rashaayda society is misleading. They do experience economic and mobility restrictions, but they are readily acknowledged as integral to the household corporation. They earn respect and prestige from their domestic skills at weaving and cooking, by being a generous hostess, and by being a good mother. Women also have power because they own the tents, and men are dependent on their wives for shelter and food. Thus, Rashaayda Bedouin women are valued participants in the corporate household and wield significant power within the domestic spaces.

PAKISTAN

Pakistan, particularly among groups such as the Yusufzai Pakhtun of the Swat Valley in the northeast Frontier Province, is an extremely male-dominated society. Lindholm and Lindholm (2000) spent nine months among the Pakhtun, where they found that women endured one of the strictest forms of purdah. As a result, relationships between men and women are fairly hostile. (The word for husband is *kwawund*, which also means God.) Men avoid showing any affection for their wives in order to keep them cowed and submissive. Purdah requires the women to remain unseen by men outside their immediate family, and they must wear the chador whenever leaving the confines of their homes. Lindholm and Lindholm (2000) found that the Pakhtun men fear the sexuality and power of Pakhtun women, and react by overly controlling the movements and freedom of women.

Pakhtun women are secluded in their domestic compounds, never leaving except for special occasions such as weddings or to visit a saint's tomb. Even then they must be accompanied by other women—never can they be outside alone. As one male put it, "The woman's place is in the home or the grave" (Lindholm & Lindholm 2000: 452). Years ago punishment for breaking purdah, or being found alone with a man, was swift and brutal: the woman's husband could cut off her nose or kill her in order to cleanse his honour. An adulteress was stoned to death, as prescribed by Islamic law. Today, punishments for breaking purdah are much less harsh, although adulterous wives are still killed.

Despite the obvious oppression experienced by Pakhtun women, Lindholm and Lindholm (2000) tell an interesting story of how these incredibly strong women manipulate the rules of purdah. On one occasion when all the females of a household had been forbidden from leaving the compound to receive cholera inoculations, one of the women (likely an older head woman) devised a plan to have each of the household women anonymously stick their bare arms through a doorway and receive the shot—without setting foot outside the compound or breaking purdah.

Shah and Bulatao (1981) found that 82 per cent of urban women and 47 per cent of rural women observed some form of purdah, although in some urban centres, the most educated Pakistani women no longer wear the chador, opting for a piece of veiling draped over their heads and modest Western dress. Urban women also enjoy more freedom to visit with friends or shop in commercial districts. Men are unsure of this change, often lamenting this trend as a sign of men becoming weak.

It appears the Pakhtun identity is fuelled by a sense of male supremacy, the importance of maintaining strict purdah, and an ideology of women's sexual power. Their fear of women has led to an androcentric culture organized around male dominance and oppression of women.

AFGHANISTAN

The image of an Afghan woman scurrying through the streets, completely concealed beneath a *burqa*, is difficult for Westerners to reconcile with their sense of personal freedom and human rights. Afghan women under the control of the Taliban had to be concealed beneath the *burqa* at all times when they were in public spaces. Only close family members—husbands, children, fathers, and siblings—and other women were allowed to see a woman without her *burqa*. Afghan women were also forbidden to work outside the home or pursue an education. Indeed, many were under house arrest. Feminists liken the lives of Afghan women under the rule of the Taliban to "gender apartheid" (Geissinger 2000).

Although Westerners usually associate the *burqa* with the Taliban, resurgence of the hijab actually began in the 1970s; the Taliban simply made the custom a law. However, much has changed since the overthrow of the Taliban. Women have returned to school and university, and have once again taken up professional positions. Yet, their lives are far from peaceful or safe; warlords who have traditionally practised ethnically motivated rape are now in positions of power sanctioned by the United States.

As mentioned earlier, many Afghan women continue to wear the *burqa* even though the Taliban has been overthrown. This is due to the historical and cultural significance of purdah. Despite outside influences, Afghanistan remains a highly patriarchal society where women obey their husbands—it is part of their culture (Women in World History Curriculum 1996–2005). To the men, women are socially immature and likely to behave irresponsibly. To protect the family honour, strict regulation of purdah is necessary. Thus, social and familial pressures continue to perpetuate the practice of purdah among Afghan women.

WESTERN PERCEPTIONS OF PURDAH AND MUSLIM WOMEN

Since September 11, 2001, Muslims in North America have found themselves under intense scrutiny, including the way they dress—what Alan Lebleigez, an EU parliament member called Islamaphobia (Bishr n.d.). Discrimination and harassment of women dressed in hijab in supposedly

MULTICULTURAL, "free" countries such as the United States has shocked the Muslim community, and once again brought home their status as that of "others." Purdah has become symbolic of this otherness.

Although there have been many responses in the Muslim community to increased stereotyping and discrimination, one relevant to this discussion is an increased self-assertion of their Muslim identity, including wearing traditional clothing such as the hijab. However, the hijab makes Westerners feel uncomfortable because they see this practice as oppressive. An incident in Quebec, Canada, in 1995 reinforces the fact that a negative image of purdah and hijab is still evident in the West (Bullock 2001). Thirteen-year-old Emilie Ouimet was sent home from her Montreal high school for wearing the hijab. School officials and others suggested that hijab was not proper Canadian attire.

Readers might ask, how could something like this happen in a multicultural country like Canada? The answer lies in the uneasy truce between religion and the secularization of Canadian institutions, such as schools. Culturally, Westerners cannot seem to move beyond the image of hijab as oppressive. We continue to express the concern that women who wear hijab must have been pressured or coerced into doing so by male relatives or religious leaders. Despite our official policy of multiculturalism, when it comes to cultural traditions such as the hijab, there is a sense that Muslims must comply with Western behaviour. Muslim women have been accosted by other Canadians and accused of bringing "backwardness" to Canada. Even some Muslim women have decried the hijab, wanting Muslims to modernize. Returning to the incident in Quebec, forcing this young women to conform to Canadian ideals of dress (whatever that might be) and give up a symbol of her Muslim identity is a form of discrimination and is as oppressive as forcing a woman to wear the hijab.

In March 2004, France banned conspicuous religious symbols and attire in schools—children were no longer allowed to wear Islamic head scarves, Christian crosses, Jewish skull caps, or Sikh turbans (IRNA 2005). Some states in Germany have passed similar legislation. Muslim women, along with supporters from other religious communities, protested this move, demanding their religious freedom and a right to express their beliefs. Human rights activists and EU parliament members are demanding that EU countries respect the freedom of faith and dress (Islamonline.net). In some countries where veiling was abandoned, such as Egypt and Turkey, educated urban women of middle class or higher are now returning to the practice of hijab. In large part, this is a reflection of renewed interest in their religious and cultural identity, and a desire to publicly affirm their Muslim identity and announce Muslim resistance to Western domination.

This return to traditional dress has been met with opposition, even in Muslim countries. In Turkey, scarves have been banned from educational institutions and state offices. Young women have been arrested in

"Take those clothes off, you don't have to wear that. You're in Canada now," shouted the elderly lady on the bus. She waved her arms around, partly to get my attention and partly to express her anger. Normally I would have replied with something witty, but being in a state of shock, all I could come up with was, "I know where I am."

"Then take them off. You make me feel hot!'

"I'm wearing this by choice," I replied.

"No you're not. You're being controlled. You're being controlled by males!"

Her striking words about my hijab (Islamic head-dress) caught me off-guard. I felt certain that this woman was not just repeating an old stereotype. This was what she really believed!

SARA ZAHEDI (N.D.)

Turkey for wearing a head scarf to class (Geissinger 2000). Women have also been expelled from government positions. In Uzbekistan men with beards and women with scarves have been harassed and even arrested, while in Tunisia, women have been fired for wearing scarves. These and many more examples of such discrimination have been justified as an effort to stamp out fundamentalism and terrorism.[10]

Debate among Islamic groups continues to rage today. Some groups, such as the Women's Action Forum (WAF) in Pakistan, actively reject attempts to impose hijab on women, while others hold fast to the tradition and the importance of submitting to God's will. Conversely, demonstrations to protect the right of women to wear the hijab have touched many corners of the world. European women and activists have gathered at state buildings to demand religious freedom of expression. At a Wayne State protest, scarves became a weapon against ignorance and a symbol of solidarity (Capeloto 2004). Non-Muslim women donned the scarves alongside Muslim women in defence of a growing worldwide campaign to show support for the right to wear hijab.

Conclusion

The practice of purdah is a complicated issue. Hijab represents three major tenets in a Muslim woman's life: religious faith and obeisance of religious commandments; cultural identity representing status, class, kinship, and culture membership; and political consciousness and activism. Although the custom is often symptomatic of a patriarchal, oppressive society, it is also a way for women to affirm their religious beliefs and their respectability. In many ways, wearing hijab is a liberating practice—de-emphasizing the beauty and sexuality of a woman, and drawing attention to her self-worth.

Unfortunately, most of the literature takes a negative and rather limiting stance on purdah, whether the history of the custom is being examined or contemporary practices discussed. It is only when we ask the women themselves what purdah means to them and why they choose to continue the practice that we learn there are many facets to purdah, and that it means many things to the people who follow the custom.

The key here seems to be that of choice, and pertains mainly to hijab. If a woman chooses to wear hijab, then this is her will. However, if the practice is forced on her, either through insidious social pressure, familial demands, or threats of punishment, then it is oppressive. With regards to female seclusion, the issues are more clouded. It appears that women obey seclusionary rules to keep peace with parents, husbands, and religious leaders. Choice does not seem to play a significant role in the equation. Does this mean secluded women are oppressed—victims of gender exclusion and inequality? Only these women can answer that, and they have not yet spoken.

The issue should not be whether women are wearing the hijab, in whatever form, but whether they have access to the same resources and opportunities as men. From the material presented in this chapter, readers should realize that many women choose to wear the hijab. The reasons for this choice are myriad, and to a certain extent are connected to oppression, but not the oppression of the veil; rather the oppression of societies that fail to offer women equal status and treatment. A woman who feels safer covered in folds of cloth so that men will not leer at her or make unwanted advances is being oppressed by men, not the veil. A woman who feels she will only be taken seriously as a human being with something to offer the community if she is anonymously hidden behind concealing clothing is being oppressed by societal views, not the veil. This type of oppression is worldwide, and as serious an issue in the West (if not more so) than anywhere else in the world.

"If I don't stand up for Muslim women's right to wear hijab when they want to, who's going to stand up for me when I'm attacked?"

A NON-MUSLIM SUPPORTER (CAPELOTO 2004: 1)

Questions for Consideration

1.   Do you consider forcing young Muslim women to remove their head scarves or other religious symbols as oppressive? Why or why not? Are students free to wear religious symbols at your institution?

2.   Research the meaning of purdah to Muslims, then compare it to the meaning held by most Westerners. How are these views influenced by our cultural environments?

3.   Why do you think wearing the hijab has increased in some countries in recent years? Does this revival have to do with religious zeal, politicalization of the hijab, or could there be some other reason?

4.   Ultimately, this chapter was about gender stratification, although readers should recognize this oppression does not come from purdah but rather that purdah is a symptom of global female oppression. Examine your own society. How are women limited in their opportunities, or "inconvenienced" by the attitudes of society?

5.   Although this chapter focused on female purdah, in some cultures there are male purdah rules as well. Identify purdah requirements for men in Egypt, Pakistan, and Sudan.

6.   Create a chart identifying arguments for and against purdah. Which argument is stronger in your opinion?

7.   Compare the five states examined in this chapter. Which systems of purdah seem oppressive and which do not?

NOTES

1   *Hajaba* has also been defined as a barrier (Fernea & Fernea 2000).

2   Muslim holy book and Muslim prophetic narratives (second-hand reports of Muhammad's personal traditions and lifestyle), respectively.

3   The name and spelling of clothing items associated with hijab vary depending on the source.

4   In contemporary Cairo this admonishment seems to be ignored by young women— their colour-coded coverings are extremely form fitting, accentuating their figures, and appear to have become more of a fashion statement than a religious symbol.

5   Eighteenth to sixth century BC.

6   CE 300–1450.

7   Insiders' perspective.

8   Intifada is an Arabic word meaning shaking off illness or shivering. It can also mean abruptly waking from a sleep or from an unconcerned state. In a political context, intifada symbolizes the Palestinian uprising against Israeli occupation of their lands (Intifada.com n.d.).

9   Islamic Resistance Movement, also known as Mujama's.

10 Egypt banned school girls from wearing scarves for a time; the federal government of Kelanton, Malaysia, banned wearing of a face veil by government workers; Kurds in northern Iraq discourage the wearing of scarves (Geissinger 2000).

References

ALI, M.C. (n.d.). *The question of hijab: Suppression or liberation?* The Institute of Islamic Information and Education. Retrieved September 8, 2005, from the World Wide Web at http://www.usc.edu/dept/MSA//human-relations/womeninislam/whatishijab.html.

ALVI, S.S., HOODFAR, H., & MCDONOUGH, S. (2003). *The Muslim veil in North America: Issues and debates.* Toronto: Women's Press.

AMIN, C.M. (2002). *The making of the modern Iranian woman: Gender, state policy, and popular culture, 1865–1946.* Gainesville: University Press of Florida.

ARNETT, S.P. (2001). Purdah. *Women's History Resource Site.* King's College History Dept. Retrieved September 8, 2005, from the World Wide Web at http://www.kings.edu/womens_history.purdah.html.

BARR, J., CLARK, I., & MARSH, M. (n.d.). *The veil and veiling.* Women, the visual arts, and Islam. Retrieved March 14, 2006, from the World Wide Web at http://www.skidmore.edu/academics/arthistory/ah369/finalveil.htm.

BISHR, H. (n.d.). *Pro-hijab campaign in EU parliament.* Retrieved September 11, 2005, from the World Wide Web at http://www.prohijab.net/english/islam-online-article3.htm.

BONVILLAIN, N. (1998). *Women and men: Cultural constructs of gender.* Upper Saddle River, NJ: Prentice Hall.

BROOKS, G. (1994). *Nine parts of desire: The hidden world of Islamic women*. New York: Anchor Books.

BULLOCK, K. (2001). *You don't have to wear that in Canada*. Retrieved September 9, 2005, from the World Wide Web at http://www.soundvision. com/news/hijab/hjb.canada1.shtml.

THE BURKA. (n.d.). Burqa image. Retrieved March 14, 2006, from the World Wide Web at http://images.google.ca/imgres?imgurl=http://www. shasekh.com/galeria/mis_imagenes/burka.jpg&imgrefurl=http:// www.shasekh.com/galeria/fotos.htm&h=1052&w=763&sz=90&tbn id=NRFt3NpnRKcJ:&tbnh=149&tbnw=108&prev=/images%3Fq%3 Dburka%26hl%3Den%26lr%3D&oi=imagesr&start=2.

CAPELOTO, A. (2004). *Hijab campaign: Women don scarfs in solidarity with female Muslims*. Retrieved September 11, 2005, from the World Wide Web at http://www.freep.com/news/nw/terror2001/scarf18_ 20011018.htm.

DE SOUZA, E. (Ed.). (2004). Introduction. In *Purdah: An anthology*. Oxford: Oxford University Press.

FERNEA, E.W., & FERNEA, R.A. (2000). Symbolizing roles: Behind the veil. In J. Spradley & D.W. McCurdy (Eds.), *Conformity and conflict: Readings in cultural anthropology* (10th ed., pp. 233–240). Boston: Allyn and Bacon.

GEISSINGER, A. (2000). *Hijab: An issue of global concern for the Islamic movement*. Retrieved September 14, 2005, from the World Wide Web at http://www.muslimedia.com/archives/movement00/hijab-glob. htm.

HAMMAMI, R. (1990). Women, the hijab and the intifada. *Middle East Report, 164/165*, 24–28.

INTIFADA.COM (n.d.). Introduction. *The intifada in Palestine*. Retrieved September 11, 2005, from the World Wide Web at http://www.intifada/com/palestine.html.

IRNA. (2005). *Pro-hijab campaigners lobby in European parliament*. Retrieved September 11, 2005, from the World Wide Web at http://www.irna. ir/en/news/view/menu-234/0505100391115018.htm.

ISLAMONLINE.NET. (2005). *Pro-hijab campaign in the parliament*. Retrieved September 11, 2005, from the World Wide Web at http://www.prohijab.net/english/islam-online-article 3.htm.

KHAN, S. (1999). *A glimpse through purdah: Asian women and the myth and reality*. Oakhill, UK: Trentham Books.

KHAN, S. (2005). *Banning hijab in.Canada: It can happen anywhere*. Retrieved September 15, 2005, from the World Wide Web at http://soundvision. com/Info/news/hijab/hjb.canada.asp.

LINDHOLM, C., & LINDHOLM, C. (2000). Life behind the veil. In E. Ashton-Jones, G.A. Olson, & M.G. Perry (Eds.), *The gender reader* (pp. 451–41). Needham Heights, MA: Allyn & Bacon.

MUSTAFA, N. (n.d.). Naheed Mustafa: Hijab (veil) and Muslim women. *Islamic Information and News Network*. Retrieved September 8, 2005, from the World Wide Web at http://www.usc.edu/dept/MSA/human-relations/womeninislam/hijabexperience.html.

READ, J.G., & BARTKOWSKI, J.P. (2000). To veil or not to veil? A case study of identity negotiations among Muslim women in Austin, Texas. *Gender and Society*, 14(3), 395–417.

SHAH, N.M., & BULATAO, E.Q. (1981). Purdah and family planning in Pakistan. *International Family Planning Perspectives*, 7(1), 32–37.

SHIRAZI, F. (2001). *The veil unveiled*. Gainesville: University Press of Florida.

TALVI, S.J.A. (2002). *The veil: Resistance or repression?* [Book review essay]. Retrieved September 11, 2005 from the World Wide Web at http://www.lipmagazine.org/articles/revitalvi_212.shtml.

WOMEN IN WORLD HISTORY CURRICULUM. (1996–2005). Historical perspectives in Islamic dress. *Women in the Muslim world: Personalities and perspectives from the past*. Retrieved September 8, 2005, from the World Wide Web at http://www.womeninworldhistory.com/essay-01.html.

YOUNG, W.C. (1996). *The Rashaayda Bedouin: Arab pastoralists of Eastern Sudan*. Toronto: Harcourt Brace College Publishers.

ZAHEDA, S. (n.d.). Hijab harassment. *Islam for Today*. Retrieved March 14, 2006, from the World Wide Web at http://www.islamfortoday.com/hijabcanada5.htm.

Suggested Readings

BROOKS, G. (1994). *Nine parts of desire: The hidden world of Islamic women*. New York: Anchor Books.

An extremely perceptive book that deals with the issue of purdah and wearing the hijab in several Middle Eastern countries.

SHIRAZI, F. (2001). *The veil unveiled: The hijab in modern culture*. Gainesville: University of Florida Press.

This book is a non-academic and engrossing treatment of purdah and the hijab that actually examines hijab as part of everyday or popular culture. Shirazi attempts to dispel some stereotypes of Muslim women without resorting to theoretical perspectives, which makes this book a refreshing read for almost anyone.

CHAPTER ELEVEN

How Do Anthropologists View Same-Sex Marriages and Changing Family Structure? How Do We Define Marriage?

Introduction

On June 28, 2005, the Canadian parliament passed Bill C-38, becoming only the fourth country in the world to legitimize same-sex marriages.[1] The bill changed the definition of marriage to a union between two people rather than between a man and a woman. The long battle leading up to this historic vote was both disturbing and divisive. The struggle for same-sex marriage came to a head in 2003, when Ontario's Court of Appeal ruled that the current Canadian definition of marriage was unconstitutional. This opened the door for gays and lesbians to legally marry, at least in Ontario. British Columbia soon followed, and prior to the passing of Bill C-38, seven provinces and one territory had legalized same-sex marriage.[2]

KEY TERMS: same-sex marriage, homosexual, sexuality, *berdache*, third gender, pederasty, marriage, polygamy, household, brideprice, brideservice, dowry, monogamy, polyandry, group marriage, family, common-law family, gender identity, androcentrism

At first, I wasn't sure if Gebusi males engaged each other sexually at all. Groups to the east of the Gebusi were known to practice male-male sexuality, but peoples farther to the west did not. I thought that my Gebusi friends were more likely to be in the former camp than the latter, but how could I know? Their interactions were certainly full of suggestive jokes. A young man might shout in jest, "Friend, your phallus was stroked, and it came up!" But beneath the surface, how much was orgasmic fire and how much was playful smoke?[3] I suspected that male trysts took place near the outhouse at night during séances and festive dances. To find out if this was true, I found myself sitting near the appropriate longhouse exit during these events so I could see who went out and if they "hooked up." But I felt vulgar as I did so—as if I was snooping around or being a voyeur. Yet I didn't want to "project" sex between men onto the Gebusi

The issues surrounding **SAME-SEX MARRIAGE** are complex. First, the religious and conservative sector morally objects to homosexuality as a lifestyle. Second, there is strong opposition from many walks of life to changing the "traditional" definition of marriage as between a man and a woman. Those opposed to same-sex marriages and the redefinition of marriage fear the whole concept of marriage is being threatened, and that ultimately family structure and society will break down. Yet, as anthropologists point out, same-sex marriages have been accepted in other cultures without dire consequences.

Anthropologists recognize that marriage is viewed in many ways around the world and is a dynamic institution that has changed considerably over time. Thus, to cite any one form of marriage as "traditional" is misleading. In this chapter we will consider what marriage means and the way marriage has been culturally constructed to meet the needs of various groups of people. Marriage, regardless of its form, creates a family; we will also attempt to define family and investigate its roles in human social organization. Throughout the chapter, cultural examples of opposite and same-sex marriages will be examined from an historical and anthropological perspective.

Anthropologists and Same-Sex Marriage

Until recently, the issue of same-sex relations and/or marriage has not earned much attention from anthropologists. Indeed, there seems to have been a stigma attached to studying homosexuality as a behaviour regulated by desire, especially as it is found in the West. This stigma translates into a lack of funding for ethnographic research into **HOMOSEXUAL** behaviour. The reasons for this oversight or "slighting" are manifold. Anthropologists, like everyone else, are the product of the culture in which they were raised. In North America, and indeed most Western states, homosexuality has been frowned upon and in many instances legally banned; therefore, American anthropologists have avoided the subject.[4] According to Murray (1997: 2), most early anthropological studies of **SEXUALITY** briefly noted "gender variant roles" then neatly categorized the behaviour within notions of "hermaphrodites."[5] For example, most anthropological studies of homosexuality in North American aboriginal groups have emphasized gender variant roles, with little investigation of sexual behaviour or desires. Indeed, Murray (1997) feels that new terminology, such as "Two-Spirits" replacing **BERDACHE**, is an attempt to de-sexualize alternative gender roles. There are exceptions, of course, such as the extensive research of Alfred Kroeber in a survey of the *berdache* in California aboriginal groups.

Outside of the Western world, there is more information on homosexual behaviour. Anthropologists in Muslim societies have written about male-male love and sex. James Peacock investigated Javanese theatrical troupes in his book *Rites of Modernization* (1968) and Unni Wika wrote an article on the Omani *khanith* (Murray 1997). Wika's study of the *khanith* introduced the important anthropological concept of a **THIRD GENDER**. Unfortunately, anthropologists neglected to study **PEDERASTY**, the predominant form of male homosexuality in Muslim societies. Today, some anthropologists, such as Bruce Knauft (2005), openly report evidence of homosexuality among their study groups.

As is evident in this narrative, the intensely personal and sensitive nature of sexual behaviour, and in particular homosexual behaviour, can have an impact on whether anthropologists are able to evaluate the true extent of homosexual behaviour in a cultural group. Only through prolonged fieldwork, such as conducted by Knauft (2005), and stubborn persistence will the whole story be told.

Contemporary anthropologists have turned their attention to homosexuality and same-sex marriages, and indeed, have entered the public commentary on these contentious issues, arguing on both sides. Like Knauft (2005), Wood and Lewin (2006) found that homosexual behaviour had been channelled into normative social behaviour and given ritual significance in many small-scale Melanesian cultures. Wood and Lewin (2006: 135) suggest that when homosexual relations "are

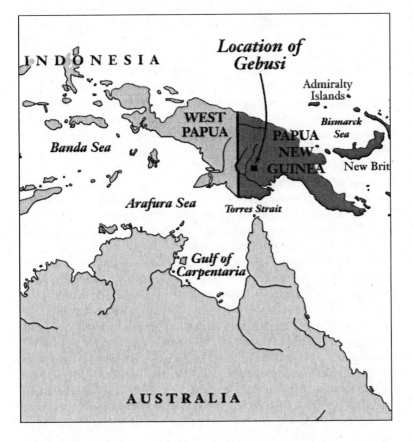

Location of Gebusi in Papua New Guinea

if it wasn't documented—and other anthropologists would want to know one way or the other…. Unfortunately, my Gebusi friends seemed unable to talk about the subject in a serious way. Any sober query was quickly turned into a joke. At several feasts, I ultimately did see pairs of males slip out toward the outhouse, cavort with each other in the night shadows, and return a few minutes later…. [These trysts] tended to be between a teenage boy and a young initiated man.

Wahi [informant] later verified for me the substance of these sexual practices: the teenager manipulates the phallus of the elder counterpart and then orally consumes the semen. As was also the case with groups farther east, this insemination had an important cultural function: it supplied the uninitiated bachelor with male life force for his masculine development…. Wahi also verified that, as a rule, men who had been married for a significant time—like Swiman, Yaba, and Dogon—did not engage in trysts with other males even though they might joke about it quite realistically. In effect, they relived their earlier experiences through their sexual banter."[6] (KNAUFT 2005: 70–71) subject to cultural elaboration they almost always fit into a pattern of initiation into secrets, male exclusivity, and a low status for women."

Despite the general lack of reliable, well-researched data on homosexuality, and indeed, heterosexuality, anthropologists have excelled in the study of marriage and the formation of family and household. In the following discussion, forms of marriage, their roles in creating family and household entities, same-sex marriages, and opposition to other than "traditional" marriages is discussed.

A Discussion of Heterosexual and Homosexual Marriage

Anthropologists have encountered many forms of marriage in global communities, and if there is one thing they have learned, it is that marriage means many things to many people. Thus, developing an inclusive definition of marriage remains a challenge. Haviland et al. (2005: 197) defines **MARRIAGE** as "a relationship between one or more men (male or female) and one or more women (female or male) who are recognized by the group as having a continuing claim to the right of sexual access to each other." This rather convoluted definition of marriage recognizes that, globally, there are many forms of marriage, including same-sex marriage. It is also important to recognize that marriage is a cultural construct designed to meet the needs of a group of people, unlike mating, which is a biological behaviour.

Opponents of same-sex marriage have raised the spectre of other forms of marriage becoming legal in Western countries—most specifically **POLYGAMY**. What they really mean is polygyny—the marriage of a man to more than one woman at the same time. This is only one example of misinformation surrounding the same-sex marriage debate. Polygyny, as a legitimate form of marriage, will be discussed in some detail later in this chapter.

The question often arises, is marriage a religious or a social institution? Anthropologists respond that it is both, and much more. Long before the institutionalized religions[7] of today, people were joining together in what even the most limited definition would consider a marriage. They were doing so for many reasons—to regulate sexual behaviour and create families, of course, but even more significant were the economic benefits of marriage. Marriage creates the most basic of economic units, the **HOUSEHOLD**. From the household flows a great deal of economic activity, such as tilling the land, raising the livestock, and in more recent times earning wages and establishing businesses. Marriage serves to define the roles and responsibilities of each spouse. For example, in a foraging band, women usually gather the wild vegetables while men hunt wild animals and fish farther afield. In this way each spouse complements the other in economic duties. Marriages also generate wealth in the form of **BRIDEPRICE**, **BRIDESER-**

VICE, and **DOWRY**. Among the Nuer, bridewealth cattle are paid to the bride's family, thereby formalizing the marriage contract. Brideprice also symbolizes the transfer of the bride from her father's household to the groom's, and ensures that any children born of the union belong to the groom's kin (Evans Pritchard 1951).

Westerners consider marriage a joining of two people, but in most cultures marriage is the joining of two families to create an economic and political support network. Among the Ju/'hoansi marriage is a major form of inter-group alliance that is social and economic. The kin network formed by the marriage of two people offers security for both families: "If one has good relations with in-laws, at different waterholes, one will never go hungry" (Lee 2003: 86). Marriage alliances are also political—they help maintain peace within and between groups.

In sum, marriage functions to curtail and regulate human sexuality. It serves to define gender roles, whatever they may be, and provides a stable environment for procreating and raising children. Marriage also functions to create social, economic, and political networks between families, creating an expanded kinship network. Marriage, then, like all the systems of culture, is a form of social control.

FORMS OF MARRIAGE

Polygyny is an age-old and time-honoured marriage pattern in many regions of the world. Indeed, 70 per cent of the world's populations prefer polygynous marriage (Murdock 1967), and if we were going to identify a truly "traditional" marriage, then it would be polygyny, not heterosexual **MONOGAMY**. Polygyny is particularly common among pastoral and farming communities where the women do the bulk of the work. Among the Kapauku of Papua New Guinea, men marry as many wives as they can afford. The wives till the fields and raise the pigs, thus generating wealth for the family household (Pospisil 1963). Among the Masai, a pastoral people in Kenya, a man's wealth is determined by the number of herds he owns, which is dependent on the number of wives he acquires. Each wife cares for her own herd, which she holds in trust for her future sons. Therefore, the more wives the man has, the more wealth at the family's disposal (Llewelyn-Davies 1974). In Canada, the Blackfoot First Nations practised polygyny during the seventeenth-century fur trade era. When the Blackfoot men acquired horses[8] they were able to dispatch many bison. The hides needed to be tanned quickly, but this was too much work for one woman, resulting in some men taking second or third wives to improve their economic status: "The more wives a man had, the more women's labour he controlled. His wives provided him with additional children whose labour he also managed" (McMillan 1988: 140–141).

All of these cultures and many other polygynous peoples view wealth generation as a primary reason for marriage. Despite the inherent value of polygynous marriages, they are not as common as they might be, given that a man must possess considerable wealth to pay the brideprice for each wife. Those that cannot do so remain monogamous. Indeed, monogamy is the most common form of marriage worldwide, although as previously stated, polygyny is the most preferred.

Polygyny is not legal in Western states, although it is practised in isolated pockets, such as the Rocky Mountains of the United States and Canada. Contrary to Western perceptions, polygyny usually does not exploit women. Indeed, women in polygynous marriages often enjoy more freedom and independence than women in monogamous marriages. Each woman in a polygynous marriage has her own dwelling, where she lives with her young children, and she may enjoy considerable economic independence. Although outside forces (e.g., missionary incursions) have attempted to eliminate polygyny, it continues to provide an ideal wealth-generating system.

The Kapauku, Masai, and Blackfoot polygynous practices all highlight the important economic functions of marriage. This runs counter to the "love and roses" concept that Westerners cling to, but if we look carefully at our own marriage patterns, we will see that economics plays a vital role in our societies as well. For example, do we look for minimum-wage earners or professionals as preferred marriage partners? Is the double-income family an attractive lifestyle choice? And, is the option of one parent staying home to raise the children while the other brings in sufficient income appealing?

Although we might think we know why polygyny would appeal to men, it is difficult for Westerners to imagine the appeal for women. Let us begin with demographics. In virtually all cultures and regions of the world, there are more women than men;[9] polygyny enables all women to marry. In more traditional cultures, where women take their identity and security first from their fathers, then their husbands, and in later life, their adult sons, being married and producing sons is vital. Generally, a man must have acquired sufficient wealth to afford the brideprice for more than one wife; being married into a wealthy family gives the woman, as well as the man, great prestige and means she will enjoy a higher standard of living. As mentioned, the female's labour capabilities are a major reason for marriage; in a polygynous marriage her workload is lightened because of her co-wives, who also provide companionship.

Polygyny is an ideal system for enhancing the economic well-being of men and women, but it is not without its own set of problems. The most obvious problem is jealousy between wives and clashing personalities, which can make the household a battleground. This is evident in the Nuer of Sudan, where jealousy among co-wives is quite common (Hutchinson 1996). However, this competition is not about a husband's attention and affection. Rather, it is related to acquisition of a fair share of resources, the roles and duties of each wife, and other benefits to which each wife feels she is entitled. Among the Rashaayda of eastern Sudan, a wife who feels she is being unfairly treated can complain to her brothers, who will back their sister. If she decides to divorce her husband, the brothers will support her until she remarries (Young 1996).

There are several other recognized forms of marriage, specifically polyandry and group marriage. **POLYANDRY** is the marriage of one woman to two or more men at the same time. Less than a dozen cultures are known to have practised polyandry. This rarity is mainly due to the high mortality of males, and the limitations placed on procreation in a polyandrous marriage, which runs counter to the values of most cultures. In Tibet, fraternal polyandry has sometimes been practised, where a group of brothers marry one woman to keep the farm intact and limit the number of offspring. **GROUP MARRIAGE** involves several men and women in a communal setting having sexual access to each other. Group marriages are rare, and tend to break up fairly quickly. A third type of relatively rare marriage, although gaining increasing recognition in the Western world, is same-sex marriage.

SAME-SEX MARRIAGE

Same-sex marriage involves marriage of individuals who are of the same biological sex. In many parts of the world, such as western Africa, same-sex marriage serves to solve problems in situations where opposite-sex marriages do not offer a solution. To illustrate this point, we will examine several cultures that accept same-sex marriages, but to begin, we will investigate some historical cases of same-sex marriages.

Same-sex relationships, including same-sex marriages, have a long history and wide geographical distribution (Lahey & Alderson 2004). In the southern Fujian province of China during the Yuan and Ming dynasties (CE 1264–1644), men married male youths in elaborate ceremonies (Hinsch 2004; McGough 2004). When the marriage came to an end, the older man in the relationship paid a brideprice to acquire a wife for the young man. In a similar vein, Japanese Samurai warriors entered battle with their apprentice warrior-lovers at their side (Eskridge 1996: 3). A formal exchange of written and spoken vows legitimized the relationship, which was based on romantic love and loyalty. Besides the sexual aspects of these relationships, the samurai provided "social backing, emotional support, and a model of manliness for the apprentice" (Ibid.). The apprentice, in turn, was expected to become a good student of samurai manhood. In medieval Europe same-sex relationships were recognized, even celebrated, in several societies. Records of ancient Rome and Greece show evidence of homosexual unions. In the Hellenic period, Greek men (*erastes*) and youths (*eromenos*) entered into same-sex marriages. These marriages required the father of the youth to give his consent to the union (Pickett 2002).

Two women celebrate their marriage.

Many North American aboriginal groups, such as the Ojibwa, Lakota, Yuma, and Winnebago, also recognized and accepted unions between Two-Spirit[10] individuals (Williams 1986). Two-Spirit marriages have also been recorded in the West Indies, and among the Aztec, Maya, and Inca civilizations (Eskridge 1996). Two-Spirits were androgynous[11] males or females who took on the roles, dress, and behaviour of the opposite sex. The Two-Spirits gained social prestige for their spiritual and intellectual qualities, and often possessed shamanic or special ceremonial powers. For example, Two-Spirits in several California groups were responsible for burial and mourning rituals (Bonvillain 1998). Same-sex marriages among the Mohave of the southwestern United States were institutionalized and socially accepted. A young man at the age of 10 participated in a ritual dance where he was proclaimed a Two-Spirit (*alyha*). The boy was ritually bathed, given a woman's skirt to wear, and acquired a woman's name. According to Williams (1986) the Two-Spirit marriage closely emulated "regular" marriage in that it served to divide duties based on gender—the man took on the roles of a male and the Two-Spirit took on the roles of a woman.[12] Two-Spirits never married other Two-Spirits. In some groups, such as the Lakota and Zapotec, the Two-Spirit was likely a second or third wife, while the husband had a female wife to produce children.

The main reason for Two-Spirit marriages appears to be economic—Two-Spirits could take on the roles of both a man and a woman, and in the process enhance the social status of a group. By the late nineteenth and early twentieth centuries Two-Spirits had almost disappeared, mainly due to the influence of Europeans settling in North America, who refused to accept the existence of more than two genders and declared homosexuality a violation of natural and divine laws (Bonvillain 1998).

Woman-woman marriage was a common practice in northern Nigeria (e.g., Yoruba, Yagba, Akoko, Nuper, and Gana-Gana cultures) (Herskovits 2004). These marriages took many forms; sometimes a barren woman married a young girl who then mated with the barren woman's husband to produce children. In other cases, a wealthy older woman (female husband) married a young woman. Traditional marriage rituals, including offering a brideprice to the father of the girl, were always observed in these marriages. The young woman mated with a man to produce children for the female husband. These marriages were viewed with favour.

Among the Dahomean people woman-woman marriages were quite complicated, with no less than 13 different forms (Herskovits 2004). Most commonly practised among the upper classes, older women acquired commoner or slave girls for their wives. The female husband paid a brideprice, and built a house for the new bride. The older woman then chose a man, either from acquaintances or her husband's family, to mate with the young woman, live with her, and produce children. Each of these marriages provided options for acquiring children for women unable to do so on their own.

One of the most extensively documented same-sex relationships was found among the Azande of Sudan (Evans Pritchard 1974). Military men took "boy wives" as their marriage partners. A brideprice was paid to the parents of a boy, and brideservice was also performed. This marriage was both sexual and economic, in that the boy performed household and sexual duties. Some men had both female wives and boy wives—they took the boy wives into war with them to take care of the camp, while the female wife produced children. This type of marriage was legally and culturally sanctioned by the Azande.

Canada is not the only modern state to recognize same-sex marriages; many European countries have also granted rights to same-sex couples (BBC News 2005). In 1989, Denmark became the first country to offer same-sex couples rights on par with heterosexual married couples, although they could not marry in a church. In 1996, Norway, Sweden, and Iceland passed similar legislation, followed by Finland in 2002. The Netherlands granted full civil marriage rights, including the right to adopt, to gay couples in 2001, becoming the first country to do so. Belgium followed suit in 2003. Then in 2005 Spain granted gay couples the right to marry and adopt children (Lahey & Alderson 2004).

Other European countries have enacted legislation that grants gay and lesbian couples certain rights: Germany allows same-sex couples to register for life partnerships; France allows a civil contract called the Pacs; Luxembourg recognizes civil partnerships; and Britain passed legislation on December 21, 2005, that gives registered same-sex couples similar rights to married couples, such as pensions, joint property, and social security (Demian 2005). In other parts of the world, New Zealand has passed a law recognizing civil unions between same-sex couples. With the exception of south Australia and Victoria, Australia recognizes same-sex partnerships. However, the current prime minister, John Howard, amended the marriage laws in 2004 to ban same-sex marriages and same-sex couples from adopting. In Asia, attempts in Taiwan, China, the Philippines, and Cambodia have so far been stymied by opponents in the legislature, although many politicians and even monarchs (Cambodia) support legislation to legalize same-sex marriages.

On the other side of the spectrum, new legislation in the United States clearly defines marriage as being only between a man and a woman, and many states have banned same-sex marriages. There are a few exceptions: Vermont has granted same-sex couples the same legal status as civil marriages, and on May 17, 2004, Massachusetts gave same-sex couples the right to full civil marriage (Burns 2005).

In contemporary small-scale societies, same-sex marriages often solve economic or social problems within a group. Researchers have documented woman-woman marriages in more than 30 African groups, for example, the Nuer of Sudan, Lovedue, Zulu, and Sotho of South Africa, the Yoruba and Ibo of West Africa, and the Nandi of East Africa (Carrier & Murray 1998). Woman-woman marriage among the Nuer of Sudan involves a woman of some economic means offering brideprice to acquire a wife for help with domestic duties. The women are not involved in any sexual relationship; rather, the woman brought into the household will have sex with other men, and any children born of these liaisons belong to the household.

The Nandi of western Kenya also practise a form of woman-woman marriage. The Nandi are a pastoralist and farming people. The men own both the land and the herds, which they share equally with their wives. The wives hold this wealth in trust for their sons (Obler 1980). A woman past child-bearing age, who has not borne any sons, is in a difficult situation—she does not have sons to inherit a share of her husband's property. To deal with this problem, the woman may marry a younger woman who can then provide her with sons through sexual liaisons with other men. The older woman, now known as a female husband, is expected to assume the gender identity, dress, and behaviour of a man. By doing so, she raises her status in the community to that of a man. Sexual activity between the two women is strictly forbidden; indeed, the female husband is expected to give up sex, including with her male husband. Readers may wonder why a young woman would enter into such an arrangement. Often she has given birth to an illegitimate child and can no longer make a good marriage, or her family may not have any status in the community. By marrying a female husband her status is raised, and any children she produces are ensured of a secure future.

OPPOSITION TO SAME-SEX MARRIAGE

To many, the continued quest to legalize same-sex marriages in the Western world is seen as a threat to the very foundations of civilization—the honourable institution of marriage, the biological need to reproduce, and the social condition of parenting (Weeks, Heaphy, & Donavan 2001). It is important to recognize that the debate swirling around same-sex marriages is just one more manifestation of our difficulty with defining the place of homosexuals in Western society.

The most vocal opposition comes from the religious right. They view same-sex marriages as a violation of the teachings of a supernatural being (e.g., God), and allowing same-sex marriage sanctifies deviant and immoral acts that go against religious teachings. If same-sex marriages are legalized, then in a way this bestows societal approval on a way of life long maligned. There is also a fear that religious institutions may be forced to perform same-sex marriage ceremonies if they become legal. The harshest criticism suggests that allowing same-sex marriages opens the doors to other forms of deviant marriage, such as polygyny, incestuous marriages, and marriages with animals. For the latter two, obviously these objections are based on fear and ignorance, and as mentioned previously, polygyny has been a successful form of marriage the world over, except in Western countries.

Those who support the right of same-sex couples to legally marry counter these objections by stating religion does not have a place in legal institutions such as marriage, and that granting same-sex couples the right to marry is a matter of equality. They also suggest that being able to make long-term commitments in a marriage encourages stability and a relationship with one partner. Proponents believe that banning same-sex marriages is a form of discrimination against an identifiable group that has been marginalized for too long.

Opponents also express concerns that "traditional" family structure will be jeopardized if same-sex marriages are allowed, and children could become confused about their own sexual identities if raised in a same-sex situation. Proponents dispute the family concerns, arguing that same-sex couples can and do provide the same nurturing atmosphere as heterosexual couples, and are involved in procreation via adoption and surrogacy. The issue of family deserves further consideration.

FAMILY

Opponents of same-sex marriages worry that the traditional institution of family is jeopardized by these unions. Is this true? How do we define a

FAMILY? Is it a nuclear unit composed of a mother (female), father (male) and 2.2. children? Or is it a young unmarried woman with a newborn baby and a 10-year-old basset hound? Is it a middle-aged Chinese man with his wife, their daughter, his wife's parents and her brothers and sisters, spouses, and children? Is it a woman and her children married to a polygynous husband who has three other wives and many children? Or is it two men raising their three children from previous heterosexual relationships? As with marriage, a family can mean many things to many people.

All of the previous examples, no matter how diverse their circumstances, represent a family. Yet, the traditional institution of family is in a constant state of flux, sometimes known as a "crisis of the family" in the West. What this means is the traditional family is being challenged, and the definition of family now encompasses alternative family structures—what Weeks, Heaphy, and Donovan (2001: 9) call "families of choice." Indeed, in some areas of the United States, single-parent families outnumber nuclear families. Blended families, the result of divorce and remarriage of adults with children from previous marriages, have also become extremely common. The fastest growing demographic in Canada is the **COMMON-LAW FAMILY**. These and other forms of family illustrate the ability of the so-called family institution to adapt and change its structure as society changes. This expansion of the concept of family has caused a great deal of concern and confusion among people with a firmly entrenched idea of what should comprise a family.

Opponents to same-sex marriages often express concerns about the well-being of children being raised in same-sex families. They raise the issues of gender identity and behaviour, and sexual orientation. Questions concerning the "fitness" of gay and lesbian parents have also been broached, yet studies by Flaks et al. (1989) found that lesbian mothers seemed more concerned with good mothering than heterosexual mothers.

Research into the development of **GENDER IDENTITY** in Western states has found that children living in same-sex marriages experience little confusion about their gender identity, and appear happy and comfortable with their gender. Behavioural studies found no difference in various behaviours, such as toy preference, favourite television shows and characters, activities, interests, and choice of future career, regardless of whether their mothers were lesbian or heterosexual. According to studies on sexual orientation, the vast majority of children identified themselves as heterosexual, and no evidence of an increase in gays and lesbians from same-sex families have been found. Peer relationships also appear normal among children of same-sex parents; they develop close friendships with same-sex peers as do children from heterosexual homes.

CHANGES IN MARRIAGE

Culture change is an inevitable part of human society. Technology is the most obvious change, but our beliefs and patterns of behaviour also change, albeit more slowly. The process of expanding the definition of marriage is an example of culture change at work. It is also an example of the most difficult and, some would say, most painful type of culture change, where people slowly alter their ideas of what is right and wrong.

Has marriage changed? Despite the protestations of traditionalists, marriage has changed considerably, even within the last century (Sullivan 2004). Marriage has shifted from an **ANDROCENTRIC** institution to one that is now much more egalitarian. The "til death do us part" section of many vows has been rendered irrelevant when more than half of all marriages end in divorce; therefore, marriage is now a temporary situation, especially in the West. It has also become more of a companionate institution, especially in the West, for people to share emotional bonds, rather than only to co-operate in economic affairs and produce children. It has changed from a system for segregating families, "races," religions, and classes to a way to transcend these barriers through intermarriage. Acceptance of same-sex marriage as a legitimate form of marriage is merely the most recent manifestation of this culture change.

Conclusion

In this chapter we have taken an inclusive, culturally relativistic look at marriage, and examined the issues surrounding same-sex marriages. To remain culturally relativistic while examining such a sensitive subject as marriage is extremely difficult for many people, including anthropologists. Marriage speaks to the heart of our society. It is more than a civil, social, political, or religious union: it is central to our sense of well-being and existence. This is why the debate over same-sex marriages elicits such a passionate response from people, both those who oppose any change in the definition of marriage as they know it, and from those who seek greater recognition of their identity through the right to marry.

In Western countries, same-sex relationships are predicated on love and commitment, as are heterosexual marriages. The desire to marry and be recognized by other citizens as legally joined together originates with the Western ideal of marriage. Gay and lesbian couples want the same rights of recognition and respect as heterosexual couples.

Will legally recognized same-sex marriages ever become a full reality in the Western world? Perhaps, since it has already happened in Canada and several European countries. As people become more aware of different ways of life, through the efforts of people such as anthropologists, they also become more accepting. As well, the gay rights movement has been gaining strength and becoming a powerful political voice since the 1960s. They are no longer willing to remain marginalized on the edge of accepted society.

Yet, we have a long way to go before homosexuality and same-sex marriages are accepted. Moral and religious issues still factor heavily in the debate, despite the recognition of civil rights, and likely will for some time to come. Even if we step outside the civil and religious arguments, many of which are valid, there is still the matter of deep-seated sentiments attached to marriage that tend to be fairly rigid and difficult to change or expand. As Sullivan (2004: xxx) expresses it: "in this culture war, profound and powerful arguments about human equality and integrity have clashed with deep convictions about an ancient institution."

Questions for Consideration

1. Why do you think there is always a battle between liberal and conservative elements in society? Does this conflict promote healthy dialogue or does it divide society? How have the opposing views stymied and advanced the rights of gays and lesbians?

2. In your opinion, what constitutes a family? How does your definition fit with the diverse family structures of the twenty-first century in your country? Develop an inclusive definition of family. Does your definition offer the possibility of same-sex families?

3. Politicians and religious leaders worry about the breakdown of the family unit and society. Do you think allowing gays and lesbians to marry will result in the breakdown of family and society? Why or why not?

4. Like female circumcision, polygyny has often been used as an example of gender oppression and exploitation. Research this practice in several cultures (e.g., the Turkana, Nuer). Based on your findings, do you agree or disagree with the Western opinion? Explain the reasoning behind your answer.

5. "Obviously, any examination of marriage requires an element of cultural relativism or it will simply degenerate into a judgment of the superiority of one marriage form to another." Comment on this statement.

6. Culture change is an inevitable part of human society. As you know, changing one system of culture often has an impact on the other systems of a culture. Identify some of the changes in our economic, social, political, and religious institutions that may arise if same-sex marriages are legitimatized.

7. Research the North American Two-Spirit. Are there any groups that still recognize and welcome Two-Spirits? Is their disappearance an example of culture change or cultural imperialism?

8. Do you believe same-sex marriages will ever be legalized in all Western countries? Give reasons for your answer. If this happens, will the functions and roles of heterosexual marriage be affected in any way?

NOTES

1 The Senate passed Bill C-38 on July 19, 2005. On July 2, 2005, Spain legalized same-sex marriages and the right of same-sex couples to adopt, becoming the third country to legalize same-sex marriages after Belgium and the Netherlands.

2 British Columbia, Manitoba, Nova Scotia, Newfoundland, Ontario, Quebec, Saskatchewan, and the Yukon.

3 Knauft (2005) calls this homosocial behaviour.

4 Anthropological journals contained nothing about modern gay men until the 1990s, and as of 1997, there were no articles on the global nature of homosexuality in anthropological journals (Murray 1997).

5 Term used to describe people with ambiguous genitalia or biological sex.

6 Knauft later found out this was not altogether true—some married men also participated in homosexual acts.

7 For example, Christianity, Islam, and Judaism.

8 When the Spanish came to Meso-America, they brought horses with them. Some of these horses escaped and wild horse herds spread across the continent.

9 Males have a higher mortality rate at birth than females, and those who survive birth engage in more dangerous activities, such as hunting and warfare, which also takes a toll.

10 As discussed earlier, many anthropologists use the term "Two-Spirits" to identify the previous term, *berdache*. To avoid confusion, the term used in the literature is followed here.

11 A mixing of masculine and feminine characteristics.

12 In the case of a female Two-Spirit, she would marry a woman, and take on the roles of a man.

References

BBC NEWS. (2005, June 30). *Gay marriage around the globe*. Retrieved June 30, 2005, from the World Wide Web at http://news.bbc.co.uk/1/hi/world/americas/4081999.stm.

BONVILLAIN, N. (1998). *Women and men: Cultural constructs of gender* (2nd ed.). Upper Saddle River, NJ: Prentice Hall.

BURNS, K. (Ed.). (2005). *Gay marriage*. Farmington Hills, MI: Thomson Gale.

CARRIER, J.M., & MURRAY, S.O. (1998). Woman-woman marriage in Africa. In S.O. Murray and W. Roscoe (Eds.), *Boy-wives and female husbands: Studies of African homosexualities* (pp. 255–257). New York: St. Martin's Press.

DEMIAN. (2005). *Marriage traditions in various times and cultures*. Retrieved June 31, 2005, from the World Wide Web at http://www.buddybuddy.com/mar-trad.html.

EVANS PRITCHARD, E.E. (1951). *Kinship and marriages among the Nuer*. Oxford: Oxford University Press.

EVANS PRITCHARD, E.E. (1974). *Man and woman among the Azande*. London: Faber and Faber.

ESKRIDGE, W.N. (1996). *The case for same-sex marriage*. Retrieved August 31, 2005, from the World Wide Web at http://www.simonsays.com/titles/0684824043/sameex1c.html.

FLAKS, D.K., FICHER, I., MASTERPASQUA, F., & JOSEPH, G. (2004). Lesbians choosing motherhood: A comparative study of lesbian and heterosexual parents and their children. In A. Sullivan (Ed.), *Same-sex marriage: Pro and con* (pp. 246–249). New York: Vintage Books.

HAVILAND, W.A., FEDORAK, S.A., CRAWFORD, G., & LEE, R.B. (2005). *Cultural anthropology*. Toronto: Thomson Nelson.

HERSKOVITS, M.J. (2004). A note on "woman marriage" in Dahomey. In A. Sullivan (Ed.), *Same-sex marriage: Pro and con* (pp. 32–35). New York: Vintage Books.

HINSCH, B. (2004). Husbands, boys, servants. In A. Sullivan (Ed.), *Same-sex marriage: Pro and con* (pp. 29–30). New York: Vintage Books.

HUTCHINSON, S. (1996). *Nuer dilemmas: Coping with war, money and the state*. Berkeley: University of California Press.

KNAUFT, B. (2005). *The Gebusi: Lives transformed in a rainforest world*. Toronto: McGraw-Hill.

LAHEY, K., & ALDERSON, A. (2004). *Same-sex marriage. The personal and the political*. Toronto: Insomniac Press.

LEE, R.B. (2003). *The Dobe Ju/'hoansi* (3rd ed.). Toronto: Thomson Nelson Learning.

LLEWELYN-DAVIES, M. (1974). *Masai women* [Video]. Disappearing World Series. Granada Television International.

MCGOUGH, J. (2004). Deviant marriage patterns in Chinese society. In A. Sullivan (Ed.), *Same-sex marriage: Pro and con* (pp. 24–28). New York: Vintage Books.

MCMILLAN, A.D. (1988). *Native peoples and cultures of Canada: An anthropological overview*. Vancouver: Douglas & McIntyre.

MURDOCK, G.P. (1967). *Ethnographic atlas*. Pittsburgh: University of Pittsburgh Press.

MURRAY, S.O. (1997). Explaining away same-sex sexualities when they obtrude on anthropologists' notice at all. *Anthropology Today, 13*(3): 2–5.

OBLER, R.S. (1980). Is the female husband a man? Woman/woman marriage among the Nandi of Kenya. *Ethnology, 19,* 69–88.

PEACOCK, J.L. (1968). *Rites of modernization: Symbolic and social aspects of Indonesian proletarian drama.* Chicago: University of Chicago Press.

PICKETT, B. (2002). Homosexuality. In E.N. Zalta (Ed.), *The Stanford Encyclopedia of Philosophy.* Retrieved Sept. 3, 2005, from the World Wide Web at http://plato.stanford.edu/archives/fall2002/entries/homosexuality.

POSPISIL, L. (1963). *The Kapauku Papuans of West New Guinea.* New York: Holt, Rinehart and Winston.

SULLIVAN, A. (2004). Introduction. In A. Sullivan (Ed.), *Same-sex marriage: Pro and con* (pp. xxii–xxx). New York: Vintage Books.

WEEKS, J., HEAPHY, B., & DONOVAN, C. (2001). *Same sex intimacies: Families of choice and other life experiments.* London: Routledge.

WILLIAMS, W.L. (1986). *The spirit and the flesh.* Boston: Beacon Press.

WOOD, P., & LEWIN, E. (2006). Gay and lesbian marriage. Should gays and lesbians have the right to marry? In W.A. Haviland, R.J. Gordon, & L.A. Vivanco (Eds.), *Talking about people: Readings in contemporary cultural anthropology* (pp. 134–142). Toronto: McGraw-Hill.

YOUNG, W.C. (1996). *The Rashaayda Bedouin: Arab pastoralists of Eastern Sudan.* Toronto: Harcourt Brace College Publishers.

Suggested Readings

KNAUFT, B. (2005). *The Gebusi: Lives transformed in a rainforest world.* Toronto: McGraw-Hill.

A forthright and clearly written ethnography that does not shy away from issues of human sexuality among the Gebusi.

SULLIVAN, A. (Ed.). (2004). *Same-sex marriage: Pro and con.* New York: Vintage Books.

A comprehensive reader that presents solid arguments for and against same-sex marriages from an anthropological perspective.

CHAPTER TWELVE

Has the Medium of Television Changed Human Behaviour and World Views?

Introduction

Often called one of the greatest inventions of the twentieth century, television burst into our homes some 50 years ago.[1] Since then the technology has flourished and become a regular part of our daily lives. Today, television is a powerful enculturative force in contemporary societies around the world. Indeed, some researchers claim that television has dramatically impacted on the way we view our world.

In this chapter we will investigate some of the ways television and other forms of media influence and reflect the attitudes of the audience. More specifically, we will consider how television is a reflection of society, using the phenomenally successful television franchise, *Star Trek*. Television may also influence society. To examine this assertion, we will consider how watching television has modified behaviour in public spaces, particularly classrooms and movie theatres. Since television has become the global medium of the late twentieth and early twenty-first centuries, and continues to be the number one leisure activity in most regions of the world, we will briefly examine television in Brazil, Hong Kong, China, and Sri Lanka.

KEY TERMS: popular culture, media anthropology, blended family, teleconditioning, homogenization

Anthropologists and the Media

Culture is learned, shared, symbolic, and integrated, encompassing our whole way of life, including that which has been labelled, almost disdainfully, as **POPULAR CULTURE**. If culture is defined as our whole way of life, then ignoring popular culture means ignoring a significant part of our life. Indeed, on a day-to-day basis, popular culture, of which television is a part, has a much greater impact on the public than high culture (e.g., opera, art galleries, or Shakespearean plays). Television is a cultural product that cuts across gender, age, class, ethnicity, localities, and so on, bringing the same messages to diverse groups of people (Kottak 1990).

Academics, including anthropologists, who trivialize the impact of television on everyday culture are missing the point: television is culturally significant. A 1986 *TV Guide* survey found that 68 per cent of the American people enjoyed watching television more than food, liquor, sex, vacations, money, or religion (Kottak 1990). Television programming then, is worthy of study, because these programs and the act of watching them have meaning for the audience. Visual culture of the twentieth and twenty-first centuries is an unprecedented communications medium that is vital to contemporary society (Newcomb & Hirsch 2000).

Anthropologists have traditionally shied away from studying their own cultures, especially modern, complex North American society, which they have left to sociologists, economists, and others. Hence, the institutions of these cultures, such as the media, have been neglected. The position that the media, and in particular television, was beneath regard began to change in the 1980s and 1990s when **MEDIA ANTHROPOLOGY** emerged, and many anthropologists expanded their understanding of culture and society. As Kottak suggests, anthropologists who study popular culture in contemporary societies have the opportunity to transform the familiar into the exotic (DaMatta 1990). Some anthropologists have expanded their research on the impact of television beyond English-speaking countries, and are attempting to demystify television and address the effect of media on human behaviour.

A Discussion of the Medium

Television is a powerful cultural medium that provides eager audiences with escapist forms of entertainment in the guise of dramas, comedies, and musical variety shows. Beyond its entertainment value, the medium also serves to inform. Documentaries, news programs, and infomercials have created an educated populace that is more aware of the world outside their community than any previous generation. The medium may also attempt to condition or influence the audience by tailoring information to shape the audience's perceptions.

In the 1940s and 1950s, television became "a magical doorway into images and experiences that both nurtured and stretched the limits" (Toerpe 2001: 441). Television programming has expanded considerably since those first snowy images appeared on the air in the 1950s, becoming "a social, economic, cultural, and ideological institution" (D'Acci 2004: 374). Today, television has diffused to most parts of the world, and although American television remains dominant, many other countries also have their own programming suited to their cultural values.

TELEVISION AS A REFLECTION OF CULTURE

Television is a reflection of society—it represents and reflects family, gender, ethnicity, age, class, sexuality, nationality, religion, and so on (D'Acci 2004). The social ideal of a traditional family in the 1950s, with a stay-at-home mother, a working father, and several well-manicured children was reflected in programs such as *Father Knows Best*, *Leave it to Beaver*, and *I Love Lucy*, all of which sell the American dream of an ideal life (Kottak 1990). Today, these shows appear quaint and out of touch with the reality of life in the twenty-first century, when the majority of women work outside the home, and many families have only one parent living with the children. In the 1970s and 1980s, shows such as *The Brady Bunch* represented a new social phenomenon, the **BLENDED FAMILY**, the product of divorced adults marrying and joining two sets of children. During this era, the acceptance of African American families into mainstream society was reflected in shows such as *The Cosby Show* that portrayed African American people in non-stereotypical roles (Havens 2004).

Soap operas, such as *The Young and the Restless* and *One Life to Live*, are daytime dramas that focus on domestic life, albeit in a fantasy world of money and opportunity. They dramatize the trials and tribulations of life, such as divorce, illness, financial woes, and sibling rivalry (Pulliam 2001). Although often considered second-class entertainment, or lowbrow television, soap operas deal with social issues such as abortion and homosexuality, and regularly address domestic violence, child abuse, racism, alcohol and drug abuse, sexual harassment, and interracial marriages. These are the everyday problems of everyday people. Medical issues, such as breast cancer and AIDS, have also been addressed on shows such as *General Hospital*, followed by public awareness announcements to reinforce the storyline.

North America is not the only region where these daytime dramas are popular. The favourite programs in Brazil are *telenovelas* (soaps), although they differ slightly from their American counterparts in that there is eventually an ending to these shows. Kottak (1990) suggests that watching these *telenovelas* creates a social solidarity among the audience comparable to religious worship. Television programs in Brazil emphasize the importance of the extended family, and most shows take place in domestic spaces (e.g., the home) rather than the workplace or other public setting (Kottak 1990). In Sri Lanka, the most popular television programs are dramas and one-off plays (Richards & Mahendra 2000). These programs depict issues of importance in Sri Lankan society, such as family life in rural and urban settings, poverty, and alienation. For example, *Prabhataya* depicts a rural, impoverished family that struggles to survive as family members work for a well-to-do coconut planter. In China, with the largest viewing audience[2] in the world, local programming reflects Chinese culture[3] and tends to show it in a positive light.

Popular American comedies, such as *Murphy Brown* in the 1980s, and *Friends* in the 1990s, elevated single life to a higher status. *Friends* drew attention to the difficulties young people experience today in finding meaningful employment, while *Murphy Brown* dealt with the challenges of single parenthood for a professional woman. The increasing professionalization of women in the workplace and the "new" issues of womanhood, such as relationships, empty nests, and career pressures, made shows such as *Ally McBeal* popular in the 1990s.

By the end of the 1990s, American television daringly addressed alternative lifestyles. The immensely popular television programs *Will and Grace* and *Six Feet Under* revealed the lives of several gay men and their friends, one from a comedic perspective, the other as a quirky drama. Regardless of tone, both shows reflected the changing attitudes about homosexuality in North America, and also served to expand awareness of gay and lesbian people and the lives they might lead. Whether the shows' portrayals were realistic or not, is not the issue—at least people gained a sense that homosexuals live meaningful lives.

STAR TREK

The long-running and extremely popular *Star Trek* series is a reflection of mainstream North American values.[4] This series incorporates several themes that are considered important to North American viewers: exploration and adventure; the ability to overcome all obstacles using technology and heroism; curiosity about other people and other ways of living; friendship and loyalty to one's friends and colleagues; the importance of strong, wise leadership; and the hope for a future world where warfare, racism, and greed have disappeared. Above all, the *Star Trek* series emulates the fundamental principle of anthropology, cultural relativism, in the guise of the Prime Directive. *Star Trek*, then, emulates the anthropological respect for alien cultures and other ways of living.

The *Star Trek* series has also undergone changes that are a reflection of the changes taking place in North American societal values. The original series in the *Star Trek* franchise came on the scene in 1966 with Captain Kirk and Mr. Spock as the lead characters. In this show, which lasted only three seasons but has since become a cult icon, the indomitable spirit of adventurers and explorers, "to boldly go where no man has gone before," was emphasized. Even this slogan is obviously a reflection of the era, using the gender-exclusive term "man" to refer to all of humankind.

The 1960s perception of women is readily evident throughout the original series. The dashing Captain Kirk treated the few peripheral women on the show as sexual playthings who also brought him coffee, and occasionally needed to be rescued. Yet, Captain Kirk personified the American hero—always obeying military orders, though able to take the initiative to perform heroic deeds and solve seemingly insurmountable crises. The challenges of space travel symbolize the need for humans to always have challenges, to explore (and conquer) or risk stagnation.

Star Trek appeared on the surface to be more open-minded when it came to ethnicity. Despite the Cold War of the 1950s and 1960s, two main characters, Chekov from Russia and Sulu from Asia, symbolized a better world in the future. Nonetheless, the evil Klingons (often compared to Russians in manner and attitude) epitomized the dangers enlightened and presumably American humans faced.

In the second series of the franchise, *Star Trek: The Next Generation,* which came on the scene in 1987, much of the chauvinistic behaviour had disappeared. Several of the main cast members were women (Doctor Beverly Crusher, and empath Deanna Troy) and were treated as equals. The captain, Jean-Luc Picard, maintained a strictly no-nonsense demeanour (so much so that the first season was too stiff), but even in the ensuing seasons, as he loosened up, and despite the warm and caring relationships that developed between crew members, there was little evidence of sexual exploitation.[5] The opening slogan became "to boldly go where no one has gone before," making it more gender inclusive.

The ethnic diversity of the United States was also given more prominence in the *Next Generation* series, with cast members of African American heritage holding prominent roles. Much was made of the fact that Jean-Luc Picard was French, not American, and that several of the crew members (e.g. Troy and Worf) were from other planets. One of the African Americans, Geordi Laforge, also had a physical impairment that seemed to be an advantage rather than a handicap. Through the eyes of Data, the ship's android, the show examined the question of what it means to be human—a product of the questioning atmosphere of the 1980s. The franchise regularly addressed dealing with "aliens"—an analogy to the many immigrants living in North America, and the increasing globalization of the world. Values of equality, respect, and the interest in cultural diversity were played out in each episode. These changes were reflections of a socially maturing audience.

These themes continued on *Deep Space Nine,* which was an isolated,

Prime Directive: "No Starfleet personnel shall ever interfere in the development of a less technologically advanced civilization, and if interference was made accidentally, then all attempts must be made to minimize or reverse the damage." (KATRIN 2002: 1)

multicultural (multi-species) community where people had learned to coexist in peace and relative harmony despite their diversity. The commander of the space station was an African American who in many ways epitomized the characteristics most valued by North Americans: honesty, integrity, a sense of duty, and wisdom to deal with diverse peoples. Commander Sisko loved baseball—the all-American sport. Elements of hero-worship entered the show in later seasons as Sisko became a spiritual icon, which some analysts have compared to the late Martin Luther King.

On a less positive note, the *Star Trek* series undoubtedly promoted cultural imperialism, advancing the righteousness of American culture, institutions, and ideology, reminiscent of the white knight out to save the world. Indeed, the many ethnic groups and even alien cultures on the *Enterprise* ship represented the melting pot philosophy of the United States—everyone will eventually join the crusade of Americanization of the world. Even Worf, a Klingon, represented a long-time enemy race finally coming around.

In the next major series of the *Star Trek* franchise, *Voyager*, the captain and moral compass of the crew was a woman, Katherine Janeway. Captain Janeway epitomized all that is good and honourable in human beings—she was compassionate, moral, self-sacrificing, and always chose to do what was right. Although Janeway maintained a certain distance from her crew, their well-being was all-important to her. This characterization is analogous to the image politicians and government leaders would like to portray to their audience. Like Data, the android in *Star Trek: The Next Generation*, the holographic doctor on *Voyager* also explored the parameters of life and the concept of being human.

The concept of home and hearth, so close to American hearts, was the overriding theme of *Star Trek Voyager*, as the crew overcame all manner of obstacles in their quest to reach home. Along the way, they "saved the world" in nearly every episode, and showed the galaxy how upstanding and outstanding human beings could be. At the outset of the series, rebel Maquis were resisting the power and authority of Starfleet and the Federation, also analogous to American dominance. When both the *Voyager* crew and the Maquis found themselves trapped on the other side of the galaxy, the Maquis were quickly and easily subsumed within *Voyager* culture as both groups worked to find a way home. One wonders if the audience would have stayed tuned if the *Voyager* crew had been forced to join the Maquis instead. Additionally, when Seven of Nine, a former human who had become a drone for the Borg, was captured by Janeway, she too was brought into the fold.

When family is unavailable, people have a tendency to include friends and neighbours in their kinship network. This is known as fictive kinship. On each of the *Star Trek* series, fictive kinship is readily apparent, especially among the officers, where strong bonds of friendship, loyalty, and support systems usually reserved for close family members developed. This sense of kinship is one of the endearing qualities of the franchise and may explain why the newest *Star Trek* series, *Enterprise*, failed—there was little sign of kinship. State societies, such as those found in North America, suffer from fragmentary kinship; *Star Trek* provides an alternative example of a kinship construct.

Today, the *Star Trek* franchise, although steeped in consumerism, has taken on mythic proportions, mirroring the North American ideals of freedom, individuality, and equality among the sexes and ethnic groups, and the superiority of the American way of life.

TELEVISION AS AN INFLUENCE ON SOCIETY

Television also exerts considerable influence on society. Each of the above programs and many others may be a reflection of societal attitudes of the time, but these shows also impart messages to the audience, shaping and influencing their attitudes, beliefs, and behaviour.

Television is a powerful enculturative force (Kottak 1990), helping to shape our children's world view, and as we age, continuing to influence our outlook and behaviour. The Drive Safe campaigns that have become commonplace in the media are an excellent example. Because of the bombardment of high-impact ads, it is no longer "cool" to drink and drive. The same can be said for anti-smoking campaigns that have played a pivotal role in the reduction in the number of smokers, especially among the young. As mentioned earlier, shows such as *Will and Grace* brought homosexuality into the audience's living room, and through comedy has shown North Americans that gays and lesbians are people dealing with similar problems and issues as heterosexuals. Although certainly a reflection of changing attitudes, these programs also help change the unfamiliar and shocking into the familiar, making it part of the mythos of popular culture. In other words, television plays a significant role in determining how the audience will think about themselves and the world around them.

Television may also be used as a controlling device, in that networks and executives may have an agenda that determines what information the audience accesses, and how this information is presented, thereby shaping how we consider the issue. As an example, the difference in ideology presented on CNN and Fox American news programs encourages audiences to form an opinion that fits with one of these ideologies.

Censorship means the audience only hears what the government or other controllers wish them to hear. In China, television was first used as a political, rather than a technological, tool (Huang & Green 2000), and there has been active resistance to foreign television and the infiltration of "Western decadence" (Pan & Chan 2000). Television news programs are still tightly controlled in China, and in the year 2006, access to Internet news sites remains restricted.

Television can also be used to foster a sense of national identity by promoting certain ideologies and history, and limiting outside perspectives (Richards 2000). Lee (2000) suggests that television in Hong Kong has been successful in creating a local Cantonese-based cultural identity that distinguishes them from mainland China. This identity formation has come about through the development of distinct programming, and popularizing of Hong Kong entertainers, creating a sense of identity and social solidarity.

In the 1950s, the Egyptian government recognized the potential for television to create a new Egyptian nation. Egyptians value family-centred entertainment, thus television became an ideal forum for promoting Egyptian culture (MBC 2005). From its beginning, Egyptian television was strongly tied to Arab culture and has been viewed as a vehicle for promoting Arab literature and arts. Besides local soap operas and music, news programs presenting Egyptian viewpoints that serve to shape the audience's perceptions are common in Egypt. Readings from the Quran are broadcast regularly, as are rituals promoting Islamic traditions and values. Since the 1970s, educational programming has grown in importance. Thus, Egyptian television has changed over time in response to the economic, political, religious, and social circumstances of the nation, yet continues to emphasize what is important to Egyptians. Abu-Lughod (2002) considers Egyptian television an instrument for social development and an aid in modernization.

Television has become a focal point for advertising consumer products. As Kottak (1990: 23) succinctly states: "the main purpose of commercial television is neither to entertain nor to enlighten, but to sell." Although ostensibly advertisements are designed to inform the public that certain goods are available, the actual goal is to create consumers and encourage increased consumption (Ruggiero 2001). In India, the real growth in television has been in advertising (Kumar 2000). Multinational corporations began recognizing the growth potential in Asian economies, and as soon as government restrictions were lifted, began their advertising campaigns. In China, domestic advertising began in 1979 with the advertising of a local brand—Xingfu Cola—which first appeared during a woman's basketball game on Shanghai Television (Huang & Green 2000), and later in the year foreign advertisements first appeared on television.

Some researchers have voiced concerns that overexposure to television may cause aggression and violence among young people, and perhaps a "numbing" to the consequences of violence—what Bushman and Huesmann (2001) call cognitive desensitization. The heavy emphasis on violence in programs, such as *The Sopranos*, and the escapist nature of sitting in front of a television are considered emotionally and intellectually damaging, and may limit our ability to cope with reality (Gans 1974). Indeed, Gerbner and Gross (1976) suggest that the more time people spend watching television, the more they may confuse the real world with the fictional worlds created for television. This finding may have some bearing on the fear that being repeatedly exposed to violence on television could lead impressionable young people to become violent—what Gerbner and Gross (1976) call the "cultivation effect" that creates a distorted perception of reality. The prevalence of shows related to criminal activity and law enforcement, such as *CSI: Miami*, reflects American preoccupation with guns and the ensuing violence that is rampant in most American cities.

Kottak (1990) counters the suggestion that television influences children's aggression and may lead to destructive, dysfunctional behaviour, suggesting that poverty and inequality likely have as much to do with violence as television, although the implications of certain types of people mimicking behaviours from television cannot be discounted. Bushman and Huesmann (2001) do not suggest that violence on television causes aggression, but that it may be one contributing factor. Whether violent behaviour can be fostered by repeated exposure to it on television remains unclear; some studies have irrefutably proven that it does, while other studies have proven that violence on television has little or no influence on aggressive and violent behaviour. That being said, the culture of violence prevalent in the United States is featured on American television, which appears to be promoting violence. If television promotes violence as "normal," then children without any countering influences may grow up thinking violence is a way to solve a problem or retaliate for a perceived wrong, just like their heroes on television.

CLASSROOM BEHAVIOUR

In an insightful article on student behaviour in the classroom, anthropologist Conrad Kottak (2000) suggests that years (perhaps decades) of watching television have modified the way students behave in classroom settings—what Kottak calls **TELECONDITIONING**. He proposes that "televiewing causes people to duplicate in many areas of their lives styles of behavior developed while watching television, and this fuels the culture of postmodernity."[6]

How do students behave in a university classroom? Based on personal experience, students talk and laugh among themselves as the mood takes them; they flip through magazines and campus newspapers; some eat messy snacks, others lunch, then after all this, they leave for a washroom break, or on to more interesting activities (e.g., watching television in the lounge). Many also seem unable to remain in their seats longer than an hour (the length of a typical television program), sneaking out before the class is over.

Kottak (2000) believes college students have come to see the instructor as being much like a television set—something that is on while they do other things, and something that can be "turned off" by leaving. Lamentably, students have become the audience, and the teacher, an entertainer. Indeed, students who miss a lecture or exam for important appointments, like getting their hair done (true story), expect a rerun or "videoed" version at a time more convenient for their busy schedules.

To accommodate the postmodern student, many instructors, myself included, have turned to electronic gadgets, such as PowerPoint slides, to connect with these students. Raised on television, students appear comfortable with these visual cues, although it takes considerable effort to teach them the proper way to take PowerPoint and lecture notes concurrently. At least they do not have as much time to talk, eat, or peruse the university newspaper.

Another example of teleconditioning is the movie theatre—people talk and eat through the movie with little consideration for those around them. They bring their crying babies and jostle them on their knees. They go to the movies despite having a wicked and likely contagious cough, and continually get up to buy more snacks or to visit the washroom. All of these behaviours were learned at home while watching television. Many people (our family included) no longer attend theatres because of this disruptive behaviour, which may eventually have economic implications for the movie industry.[7]

TELEVISION DIFFUSION

The diffusion of North American television around the world has raised some concerns about cultural imperialism and **HOMOGENIZA-TION** (Richards & French 2000), which may threaten local cultures, and certainly have an impact on regional popular culture. This is evident among Mayan people of Guatemala, who maintained their folk or popular culture for a thousand years. Yet, when they gained access to television and radio, the Mayans began forsaking their traditional culture, which may have a profound effect on their cultural systems

(Shuman 1991). Certainly television has increased the expectations of people for material goods, and created a craving for modern technology. Among the Mardu Aborigines of Australia, access to Western television, music, and literature in the 1980s impacted on their social organization, and began displacing the Dreaming Law, which caused confusion for the Mardu (Arden 1994). Many Mardu youth turned to television[8] to escape their hopeless, directionless lives. Indeed, among other Australian Aborigines and indigenous groups around the world, there have been concerns that overexposure to American television will result in the loss of their cultural diversity and autonomy, and a homogenization of their cultures.

Despite such examples, researchers have found that developing countries relatively recently exposed to television are not being homogenized as much as feared. Rather, people tend to prefer local programming with themes important to their own culture, and this local television mediates outside influences. In Brazil, local programs, such as the previously mentioned *telenovelas*, are popular, and have created a pan-Brazilian national culture (Kottak 1990). By 1990, 75 per cent of all Brazilians had at least one television set, even in remote areas via satellite.[9] The impact of television is very obvious in small villages such as Arembepe, Bahia, where the people previously had very little access to news about the outside world. By 1980, with the introduction of television, the world had opened up for the Arembepeiros, and they became aware of others (Kottak 1990).

This does not mean that people in other countries are not interested in foreign programming as well. In 1988, when I was working in Israel, the whole country shut down on Tuesday night when the American program *Alf* was broadcast. On Saturday night after the end of Shabat, young women, particularly those who read American fashion magazines, came downtown wearing party dresses, under the impression that American women always wore such dresses.

Conclusion

Television is much more than an entertainment medium. It is a forum for expressing our values, ideals, and cultural mores. In 50 some years, television has become an integral component of human society, as influential and as powerful as family, peers, churches, and schools. It can create an international sense of sorrow via repeated images of tragedy (e.g., 9/11 terrorist attacks, Southeast Asia's tsunami, the death of Princess Diana, and the political and natural disaster of hurricane Katrina), or galvanize us into action, willing people to become involved in protecting the environment or righting civil injustices. Once in a while, television even inspires us, such as the 1969 American landing on the moon, or global Olympic coverage.

In the twenty-first century, television has become our national medium, responding to pivotal moments in history, creating public forums, and calling on audiences to laugh, cry, get angry, change their minds, or even expand their minds, and join together in a show of social solidarity. Television and those who create it respond to the cultural milieu, constantly interpreting and reinterpreting society's needs and interests. The evening ritual of tuning into *The Tonight Show*, *Lost*, or *Monday Night Football* can create a sense of shared experience and community.

The medium, although mainly a form of entertainment, has become a powerful symbol of culture, and has served as a link between global communities. Television has played an influential role in society, modifying our collective behaviour, and influencing the way we think and feel. Above all, television has dramatically increased our awareness of the world around us and the people who live in this world.

Questions for Consideration

1.   Observe the behaviour of students in your classroom. How many of the behaviours identified in this chapter did you observe? Do these behaviours disturb your concentration? Conduct the same observations in a movie theatre.

2.   How accountable should we hold television networks regarding violence on television? Do you believe violence on television could incite violence in viewers?

3.   Should advertisers be held accountable for the accuracy of their ads? And should celebrity spokespersons be held accountable for the testimonials they offer?

4.   How do you feel about censorship of the news? Should some information, if deemed too disturbing or frightening, be withheld from the general public? If yes, think of some instances where censorship would be ethically appropriate. If no, why do you think censorship is never appropriate? In fictional TV are there topics, in your opinion, that should not be discussed on television even in an adult sit-com or drama?

5.   In Chapter 6 the diffusion of the Western ideal of body image to other parts of the world and the changes in body image that have resulted from this diffusion is discussed. How has the media played a role in this diffusion?

6. Log your television watching activities for a week. What types of programs do you most consistently watch (e.g., dramas, sports, comedies, etc.). What does your choice of programming indicate about your personality and interests?

7. While you watch television, what other activities are you involved in?

8. Do you ever find your attitude about certain issues changing or expanding because of something you watched on television? Provide examples.

9. Do you think watching television has affected or modified your behaviour? The behaviour of your friends?

10. Prepare a chart listing the economic, political, social, and religious roles television performs.

11. Choose a popular and long-running television show and conduct an analysis of the societal values and norms reflected in the show (similar to the *Star Trek* analysis).

12. Choose a country and investigate television. What roles does television play in this country (e.g., cultural medium, political propagandist, etc.).

13. What would we lose if television disappeared from our lives? What would we gain? Create a chart listing pros and cons, then state your conclusion—would we better off without television?

14. How much influence does commercial advertising have on your spending habits? How do you respond to unappealing or annoying commercials?

NOTES

1   When various regions of the world gained television broadcasts varies considerably, although the development of television technology began in the 1930s.
2   By 1998 some 3,000 channels broadcast to about one billion viewers in China (Huang & Green 2000, citing the China Broadcast Yearbook; China Journalism Yearbook; the World Factbook—China 1999).
3   There are at least 56 indigenous cultures in China, making it difficult to represent all Chinese cultures on television.
4   See Kottak (1990) for an additional analysis of the *Star Trek* series and its reflection of North American societal values.
5   Some would say that Deanna Troy's revealing and clinging uniforms were still evidence of sexual inequality.

6   Kottak (2000) defines postmodernity as the state of flux we find our world in today. We are a media-saturated people who are constantly on the move, and must deal with new, shifting, and multiple identities. This has created a sense of uncertainty regarding rules of conduct and boundaries of behaviour.

7   Statistics are already showing a dramatic drop in movie attendance. Although the reasons given for this change are usually poor quality movies or access to movie rentals (as well as the fact that neighbourhood theatres have closed, leaving only the option of multi-plex theatres, often located in the suburbs and outskirts of cities), teleconditioning and the ensuing disruptive behaviour should be further investigated as a factor.

8   They also turn to sex, alcohol, and gambling for the same reason.

9   Sixty to eighty million Brazilians watch the commercial network, *TV Globo*, which produces its own shows, every night.

References

ABU-LUGHOD, L. (2002). Egyptian melodrama: Technology of the modern subject? In F.D. Ginsberg, L. Abu-Lughod, & B. Larkin (Eds.), *Media worlds: Anthropology on new terrain* (pp. 115–133). Berkeley: University of California Press.

ARDEN, H. (1994). *Dreamkeepers: A spirit-journey into Aboriginal Australia*. New York: Harper Collins Publishers.

BUSHMAN, B.J., & HUESMANN, L.R. (2001). Effects of televised violence on aggression. In D.G. Singer & J.L. Singer (Eds.), *Handbook of children and the media* (pp. 223–254). Thousand Oaks, CA: Sage Publications, Inc.

D'ACCI, J. (2004). Television, representation and gender. In R.C. Allen & A. Hill (Eds.), *The television studies reader* (pp. 373–388). New York: Routledge.

DAMATTA, R. (1990). Foreword. In *Prime-time society: An anthropological analysis of television and culture*. Belmont, CA: Wadsworth Publishing Company.

GANS, H.J. (1974). *Popular culture and high culture: An analysis and evaluation of taste*. New York: Basic Books, Inc.

GERBNER, G., & GROSS, L. (1976). Living with television: The violence profile. *Journal of Communications, 26*, 173–199.

HAVENS, T. (2004). "The biggest show in the world": Race and the global popularity of *The Cosby Show*. In H. Newcomb (Ed.), *Television: The critical view* (pp. 442–456). New York: Oxford University Press.

HUANG, Y., & GREEN, A. (2000). From Mao to the millennium: 40 years of television in China (1958–98). In D. French & M. Richards (Eds.), *Television in contemporary Asia* (pp. 268–291). Thousand Oaks, CA: Sage Publications.

KATRIN, L. (2002). *Star Trek Voyager Info*. Retrieved September 25, 2005, from the World Wide Web at http://www.startrek-voyager.info/mission.html.

KOTTAK, C.P. (1990). *Prime-time society: An anthropological analysis of television and culture*. Belmont, CA: Wadsworth Publishing Company.

KOTTAK, C.P. (2000). Teleconditioning and the postmodern classroom. In J. Spradley & D.W. McCurdy (Eds.), *Conformity and conflict: Readings in cultural anthropology* (10th ed., pp. 92–97). Boston: Allyn and Bacon.

KUMAR, K.J. (2000). Cable and satellite television in India: The role of advertising. In D. French & M. Richards (Eds.), *Television in contemporary Asia* (pp. 111–129). Thousand Oaks, CA: Sage Publications.

LEE, P.S.N. (2000). Hong Kong television: An anchor for local identity. In D. French & M. Richards (Eds.), *Television in contemporary Asia* (pp. 363–384). Thousand Oaks, CA: Sage Publications.

MBC [THE MUSEUM OF BROADCAST COMMUNICATIONS]. (2005). *Egypt*. Retrieved January 11, 2006, from the World Wide Web at http://www.museum.tv/archives/etv/E/htmlE/egypt/egypt.htm.

NEWCOMB, H., & HIRSCH, P.M. (2000). Television as a cultural forum. In H. Newcomb (Ed.), *Television: The critical view* (6th ed., pp. 561–573). New York: Oxford University Press.

PAN, Z., & CHAN, J.M. (2000). Building a market-based party organ: Television and national integration in China. In D. French & M. Richards (Eds.), *Television in contemporary Asia* (pp. 233–263). Thousand Oaks, CA: Sage Publications.

PULLIAM, J.M. (2001). All my children. In R.B. Browne & P. Browne (Eds.), *The guide to United States popular culture*. Bowling Green, OH: Bowling Green State University Popular Press.

RICHARDS, M. (2000). Television, development and national identity. In D. French & M. Richards (Eds.), *Television in contemporary Asia* (pp. 29–42). Thousand Oaks, CA: Sage Publications.

RICHARDS, M., & FRENCH, D. (2000). Globalisation, television and Asia. In D. French & M. Richards (Eds.), *Television in contemporary Asia* (pp. 13–28). Thousand Oaks, CA: Sage Publications.

RICHARDS, M., & MAHENDRA, S. (2000). Television, culture, and the state in Sri Lanka. In D. French & M. Richards (Eds.), *Television in contemporary Asia* (pp. 313–324). Thousand Oaks, CA: Sage Publications.

RUGGIERO, V.R. (2001). *Thinking critically about ethical issues* (5th ed.). Mountain View, CA: Mayfield Publishing Co.

SHUMAN, M.K. (1991). Maya popular culture. In R.B. Browne & P. Browne (Eds.), *Digging into popular culture: Theories and methodologies in archaeology, anthropology and other fields*. Bowling Green, OH: Bowling Green State University Popular Press.

TOERPE, K.D. (2001). Jim Hensen Productions and the Muppets. In R.B. Browne & P. Browne (Eds.), *The guide to United States popular culture* (pp. 441–442). Bowling Green, OH: Bowling Green State University Popular Press.

Anthropology Matters!

Each of the topics discussed in this volume was chosen to provide a glimpse into the world of anthropology and its relevance to contemporary society. The discussions are designed to answer the question: "Of what relevance is anthropological research, principles, and application in the everyday lives of humans?" In part, this question refers to our growing awareness that anthropology, like other disciplines, cannot remain on the periphery. Anthropologists recognize that they must apply their knowledge and insights to find solutions, or at least understand the problems that confront human existence. In this concluding section of *Anthropology Matters!* we will briefly examine the relevance of anthropology in our everyday lives, in the larger context of our community, and the global community.

The Value of Anthropology

Education brings awareness—awareness of the world around us, and the myriad ways that people interact with their environment and other people. Learning about other ways of life can feed our imagination, and challenge our sense of being. As an example, investigating female circumcision and purdah raises the question of whether these practices really promote gender inequality or if this is just a Western perception. From an anthropological perspective, we are encouraged to view these issues through the eyes of the practitioners. The goal is not to change our opinion about these practices, but to come to understand that these practices are not one-dimensional, and that not everyone agrees with the Western perspective. It is incredibly difficult to understand another point of view when it comes to such sensitive topics as gender equality, but this is the true value of anthropology—to expand our minds to encompass infinite possibilities. Anthropology challenges us to question our beliefs and practices—to ask if there are other ways of living as undeniable as our own.

Anthropology is also an examination of self—who we are, where we have come from, and where we are going. Our satisfaction with ourselves and the world around us begins with an understanding of our sense of place and identity. All of us have questions regarding our identity and the identity of those around us. One area where this struggle is particularly evident is in the question of human sexuality and marriage practices. In the discussion on same-sex marriages, the ambiguity and intolerance toward those who own a different sexual identity is clearly evident. Even more relevant to the question of self is the concept of body image—why are humans, especially females, the world over so focused on physical beauty? The medium of television and its impact on our sense of self brings this question into focus.

The Roles of Anthropology

Cultural diversity is a hallmark of human existence. Cultural diversity has been likened to genetic variation: just as species are threatened with extinction if they lose their genetic diversity, the human species is also threatened if we lose our cultural diversity. Cultural diversity provides humanity with the ability to respond to varying environments and situations. Richard Lee (2003) suggests:

> As the world enters the new millennium, the two most press-ing issues are first, how to rediscover "democracy" and "just" society, and second, how to find ways of living in balance with our finite resources. The lessons of the Ju/'hoansi and other indigenous peoples offer insights on both these questions and

challenge the current complacencies. Their new found recognition is a cause for optimism. Let us take heart: ecological and cultural diversity may still have a place on this planet (p. 200).

In a world steeped in modernization and globalization processes, how do we protect cultural diversity and ensure, essentially, our continued existence?

Anthropology helps us to understand that each culture, each way of life, is equally valid in its own right. Anthropologist Bruce Knauft (2005: 4) recognized this fundamental principle when studying the Gebusi people:[1] "The Gebusi were not simply 'a society' or 'a culture'; they were an incredible group of unique individuals." This is why the goals of missionaries are so conflicting for anthropologists: we know that changing the religious beliefs of a cultural group will have a profound effect on other parts of their culture, such as their marriage patterns, leadership roles, subsistence strategies, and so on.

Today, anthropologists are not only studying exotic indigenous groups of people living in distant locales, but also those people and cultural behaviours right in our own neighbourhoods. For example, the "anthropology of shopping" highlights the cultural and behavioural importance of contemporary shopping malls in Western societies. In a similar vein, as the average age of Westerners increases, the "culture of oldness" and the way we view the last stages of our lives becomes more relevant to all of us.

Although the world of anthropology has much to offer, both in knowledge and perspective, the discipline is not without its own challenges. We owe a great deal to the anthropologists who have come before us, who have diligently tried to understand cultural diversity and share it with us. Their interpretations of culture are the building blocks of contemporary anthropological consciousness, ensuring that the field continues to be relevant.

The Goals of Anthropology

The ultimate goal of anthropology is to teach people to *appreciate* cultural diversity, rather than only *tolerate* it. On an individual level, this change in attitude is particularly relevant when we live in a country where immigration from diverse parts of the world occurs. Appreciating cultural diversity makes us more comfortable when interacting with other people who look different, speak different languages, practice different customs, and hold different beliefs.

Many youths travel and live in other cultures—it is one of the most valuable experiences an individual can undertake and in many ways is a rite of passage to adulthood. Appreciation of cultural diversity may enable these travellers to effectively cope with culture shock. On a global level, we face numerous ethnic and religious conflicts; dealing with the inequalities and paradoxes in the world around us is a constant challenge, one that anthropology views from a holistic perspective.

As discussed in the introduction to *Anthropology Matters!* the sharing of knowledge and understanding of cultural diversity is a major goal of applied anthropology, yet anthropologists also help preserve the memory of cultures that have undergone significant change. When asked at a Plains Cree Conference in 1975 what value he attached to his research on the Plains Cree, David Mandelbaum responded that his work provided "for their descendants, some record of their forefathers and of a way of life that many of them would increasingly want to know about. Together with their own oral traditions it could provide that sense of personal and social roots that most people want to have" (1979: 4).

Throughout this book, the importance of understanding someone else's point of view and acknowledging that there are many ways to live has been emphasized. This is what makes anthropology most relevant. Through the lens of anthropology we view other people and the way they live as equally valid and equally deserving of the dignity and respect that we ourselves expect. Although not the answer to all our questions, an anthropological perspective promotes understanding, acceptance, and appreciation of the amazing cultural diversity of our global community.

NOTES

1 See Chapter 9 for further discussion of the Gebusi.

References

KNAUFT, B. (2005). *The Gebusi: Lives transformed in a rainforest world.* Toronto: McGraw-Hill.

LEE, R.B. (2003). *The Dobe Ju/'hoansi* (3rd ed.). Toronto: Thomson Nelson Learning.

MANDELBAUM, D.G. (1979). *The Plains Cree: An ethnographic, historical, and comparative study.* Canadian Plains Studies, No 9. Canadian Plains Research Center, University of Regina.

Glossary

ACCOMMODATION. Recognizing and attempting to address the differing needs of an ethnic group, for example, providing mechanisms for protecting their heritage language.

ACCULTURATION. When two cultural groups come into prolonged contact, the dominant (usually technologically advanced) culture exerts pressure on the other culture to conform to their way of life (e.g., changing religious beliefs or subsistence patterns).

ADVOCACY AND POLICY DEVELOPMENT. Applied anthropologists may become involved in advocacy and policy development for cultural groups, such as assisting aboriginal groups with their land claims or developing immigration policies.

AGE-SETS. A group of people born in the same time period. Age-sets may hold political, military, and economic power as a group.

AGE STRATIFICATION. Unequal access to resources, privileges, and position based on age.

AGING. The biological and social process of growing older.

ANDROCENTRISM. Male-centredness. Usually refers to a male-centred society, where women do not play a dominant role outside the home.

ANTHROPOLOGY. The study of humankind in all times and places. Anthropology is usually divided into four major sub-disciplines: biological anthropology, archaeology, linguistic anthropology, and socio-cultural anthropology. Biological anthropologists study humans as biological organisms. Archaeologists seek to reconstruct human behaviour and lifeways in the past. Linguistic anthropologists study how people use language to interact with each other and transmit culture. Socio-cultural (also referred to as cultural or social anthropology) anthropologists study human behaviour in contemporary cultures.

APPLIED ANTHROPOLOGY. A sub-discipline of anthropology that puts to practical use the knowledge, expertise, and skills of anthropologists to help solve or mitigate societal problems. Applied anthropologists are found in the four sub-disciplines, for example, an applied archaeologist works in cultural resource management to protect heritage sites. Other applied anthropologists work for governments, funding agencies, corporations, law enforcement, special interest groups, and cultural groups.

ASSIMILATION. The absorption of a cultural group into another, usually dominant, culture. Many indigenous groups around the world have been assimilated, thereby losing their own cultural identity.

BERDACHE. Now often called a "Two-Spirit," the *berdache* is an alternate gender (third or fourth gender) documented in more than 100 aboriginal groups in North America. Most commonly a biological male takes on the roles and identity of a female.

BICULTURALISM. A sense of belonging to more than one culture. Often experienced by people, including anthropologists, who have lived in other cultures or regions of the world than their own for extended periods of time.

BLENDED FAMILY. When two adults, each with children, marry and create a new family.

BODY ADORNMENT. Decoration, (e.g., tattoos, jewellery, painting) or modification (piercings, cuttings, and branding) of the human body. Acceptable body adornment varies from one culture to another, and from one generation to another.

BODY IMAGE. A culturally defined image of beauty that influences the way people view their bodies.

BODY MODIFICATION. See BODY ADORNMENT.

BRIDEPRICE/BRIDEWEALTH. Some form of wealth offered to the bride's family when a man asks for a woman's hand in marriage. Brideprice symbolizes the legitimacy of the marriage.

BRIDESERVICE. Similar to brideprice, but instead of giving some form of wealth, the groom works for the bride's family for an agreed upon length of time, either before or after the marriage.

CLASS. A recognized category or ranking within a stratified society based on achieved status. Open class systems allow for social mobility (up or down in class), while closed systems, such as castes, do not allow for social mobility.

CLITORIDECTOMY. A female circumcision ritual, where part or all of the clitoris is removed, as well as part or all of the labia minora.

COMMON-LAW FAMILY. Where two adults are conjugally joined and may have children, but have not legally married. In some state systems, such as Canada, these couples have the same civil and legal rights and obligations as married couples.

COMMUNICATION. Messages passed between individuals that are mutually understood. May contain elements of non-verbal communication (body language, paralanguage, tone) as well as spoken words.

CORPORATE ANTHROPOLOGY/ETHNOGRAPHY. A form of applied anthropology where anthropologists work for corporations to improve productivity, marketability, and so on by employing ethnographic studies of the corporation or consumer.

CROSS-CULTURAL COMPARISON. An approach whereby one aspect of a culture (e.g., ritual) is compared in many cultures in order to develop hypotheses or theories about human behaviour.

CROSS-CULTURAL PERSPECTIVE. See CROSS-CULTURAL COMPARISON.

CULTURAL DIVERSITY. Each culture has its own distinct lifestyle in the form of customs, traditions, beliefs, and language. Cultural diversity is more evident when several cultural groups live in the same society. Analogous with ethnic diversity, meaning that several ethnic groups occupy a given region, and continue to display distinct features.

CULTURAL IDENTITY. The culture to which an individual feels they belong, based on their upbringing, residence, heritage, customs, and language.

CULTURAL IMPERIALISM. Promoting a nation's values, beliefs, and behaviour above all others. Often associated with the Western world inundating other cultural groups with their technology, beliefs, and ways of living via the media, missionism, the military, education, and in particular, economic power.

CULTURAL RELATIVISM. The principle that each culture and their practices is unique and valid in its own right, and must be viewed within the context of that culture, not that of outsiders. Anthropologists use the relativistic approach to avoid judging or interfering with the behaviour of people in the cultures they study.

CULTURE. The shared ideals, values, and beliefs that people use to interpret, experience, and generate behaviour. Culture is shared, learned, based on symbols (e.g., language), and integrated.

CULTURE CHANGE. The process of changing the behaviour, technology, and beliefs within a culture. Culture change is inevitable, and happens in all cultures albeit at different rates. Change may come about through internal changes (e.g., invention, innovation) or external changes (e.g., diffusion, acculturation).

CULTURE SHOCK. A feeling of disorientation, confusion, and irritability that results from living in a foreign environment where an individual is unable to predict the behaviour of others or determine his or her own appropriate responses.

DEVELOPMENT AND MODERNIZATION APPROACH. The theoretical perspective that change, such as the eradication of female circumcision, will not come from outside forces, but rather from large-scale social changes, for example, women becoming more empowered in their communities through access to education and employment.

DIFFUSION. The transmission, spreading, or borrowing of cultural components from one culture to another culture. The most likely cultural components to be diffused are technology, while belief systems are much less likely to diffuse without some form of missionism.

DISCRIMINATION. Distinctions made about people based on gender, age, sexual orientation, disabilities, or ethnic identity that result in differential access to resources and opportunities.

DOWRY. The wealth a woman brings into the marriage, either hers to keep, or to present to her husband's family.

EATING DISORDERS. Psychological diseases that affect the health and mind of individuals through the refusal of food (anorexia nervosa), or overeating then purging (bulimia).

ECONOMIC ANTHROPOLOGY. A specialization within anthropology that focuses on production, distribution, and consumption in small-scale and industrial societies.

EGALITARIANISM. Generally refers to a situation where everyone enjoys relatively equal status and access to resources, such as in foraging bands.

EMIC APPROACH. To consider a culture from its members' (insider) point of view rather than the anthropologist's (outsider) point of view.

ENCULTURATION. The process of learning our culture, usually through transmission from one generation to the next.

ETHICS. The rules or guidelines that anthropologists follow when conducting research. The primary rule is to "do no harm." Anthropologists have an obligation to protect the privacy of their study group, uphold the integrity of anthropology, and meet the needs of their funding agency, which sometimes makes for conflicting loyalties.

ETHNIC BOUNDARY MARKERS. Those indicators or characteristics, such as dress and language, that identify individuals as belonging to a particular ethnic group.

ETHNIC CLEANSING. See GENOCIDE.

ETHNIC CONFLICT. Conflict between ethnic groups that is caused by differences in ethnic identity. Other factors, such as economic power play or religious tension, often play a pivotal role in these conflicts.

ETHNIC GROUP. A group of people who identify themselves as an ethnic group based on a shared ancestry, cultural traditions and practices, and a sense of a common history, thereby distinguishing them from other ethnic groups.

ETHNIC IDENTITY. The identity we possess based on our membership in an ethnic group.

ETHNIC INTOLERANCE. Dislike for a group of people and lifestyle based on their ethnicity. This intolerance often evolves into various forms of discrimination.

ETHNIC STRATIFICATION. Institutionalized inequality with differential access to wealth, power, and prestige based on ethnic identity.

ETHNICITY. A group of people who take their identity from a common place of origin, history, and sense of belonging.

ETHNOCENTRISM. The attitude that one's own culture is superior to all others. Although it is natural to value one's own way of life, ethnocentrism, when taken to extremes, limits our ability to appreciate other ways of living.

ETHNOGRAPHER. An anthropologist conducting fieldwork to acquire descriptive (ethnographic) information on a cultural group.

ETHNOGRAPHIC RESEARCH. The major method of anthropological fieldwork involving the process of collecting first-hand data on a culture.

ETHNOGRAPHY. The end result of ethnographic research. A written description of a people and their way of life.

ETHNOHISTORICAL. An anthropological research method employing historical records, archaeological evidence, and oral histories to reconstruct the way people lived in the recent past.

ETHNO-NATIONALISM. Nationalistic sentiments based on ethnic identity, as found among the Serbs, Croats, and Bosniaks in the former Yugoslavia.

ETHNO-NATIONALISTS. See ETHNO-NATIONALISM.

FAMILY. A vague and complex term that means many things to many people, but generally is defined as people who consider themselves related through kinship. There are two major forms of family: nuclear, containing parents and children; and extended, containing several generations (e.g., grandparents, aunts and uncles, and cousins), as well as parents and children. Today, single-parent families (only one parent in the household) are becoming an increasingly significant demographic.

FEMALE CIRCUMCISION. The removal of all or part of a female's genitalia for religious, traditional, or socio-economic reasons.

FEMALE GENITAL CUTTING. See FEMALE CIRCUMCISION.

FEMALE GENITAL MUTILATION. The Western term for female circumcision, signifying disapproval of this procedure in Western countries.

FEMINIST ANTHROPOLOGISTS. See FEMINIST ANTHROPOLOGY.

FEMINIST ANTHROPOLOGY. A sub-field of anthropology that attempts to view culture from a female's perspective. Feminist ethnography has helped provide a more balanced examination of cultural groups.

FEMINIST PERSPECTIVE. See FEMINIST ANTHROPOLOGY.

FICTIVE KINSHIP. A kinship system comprised of friends and neighbours that is designed to take the place of biological (consanguineal) or marriage (affinal) kin (in-laws).

FIELDWORK. Generally known as ethnography, this anthropological research involves the collection of information describing the lives and behaviour of a cultural group. Fieldwork usually involves living with a group of people for an extended period of time and conducting some form of participant observation.

GENDER. A cultural construct that gives us our social identity, status, and roles in society. We learn our gender identity and roles through enculturative forces, such as parents, peers, school, and media.

GENDER IDENTITY. A socially constructed concept of gender that an individual identifies with regardless of biological sex.

GENDER STRATIFICATION. Usually refers to women who have unequal access to resources, opportunities, and prestige based on their gender. All known societies are patriarchal, and therefore have some form of gender stratification, although in industrial countries, such as the United States, this form of stratification is disappearing.

GENOCIDE. The deliberate extermination of one cultural group by another, usually to gain economic and/or political control over a region.

GLOBALIZATION. A complex process that involves worldwide integration of economies, which has been assisted by global transportation and communication systems and information technology. Globalization has resulted in dramatic rises in inequalities, over-exploitation of the world's resources, and mass displacement of people.

GROUP MARRIAGE. A rare form of marriage where several men and women are married to each other at the same time.

HIJAB. A head covering for a Muslim woman.

HOLISTIC APPROACH. Anthropologists view the components or systems of a culture (e.g., economic, social, political, and religious) as an integrated whole, with each system influencing and being influenced by the other systems.

HOMOGENIZATION. The attempt to eliminate diversity and make all things (usually groups of people) the same.

HOMOSEXUAL. A person who is sexually attracted to people of the same sex.

HOUSEHOLD. Composed of people who live in a co-operative arrangement. Usually composed of family or kin, but may also involve other forms of bonding, such as college roommates.

HUMAN RIGHTS. A vague set of guidelines for the equal treatment of all people, regardless of gender, age, or ethnicity.

IMMIGRANTS. People who have moved to a country where they are not citizens.

IMMIGRATION. Involves the movement of people from one place to another, be it to a new country, from rural regions to urban centres, or from one region to another.

INDIGENOUS PEOPLES. Members of small-scale cultures who self-identify as the original inhabitants of the land based on a long history of occupation. Indigenous peoples the world over are threatened by state powers and economic development.

INFIBULATION. See PHARAONIC CIRCUMCISION.

INITIATION RITE. Rituals, such as circumcision, performed to mark an individual's passing through a significant stage of life, most often puberty.

KEY INFORMANTS. Members of a culture who are knowledgeable regarding some subject, and who supply information to the ethnographer.

LANGUAGE RETENTION. Of the six thousand extant languages spoken today, most are in imminent danger of becoming extinct. Language retention is the struggle to keep these languages alive by teaching them to the younger generation.

MALE CIRCUMCISION. Removal of the penile foreskin, often accompanied by great ritual and status, such as in the Masai warrior society.

MARRIAGE. The joining of two or more people to form conjugal bonds.

MEDIA ANTHROPOLOGY. The relatively new study of media influences on culture.

MEDICAL ANTHROPOLOGY. An applied field of anthropology concerned with all that pertains to human health.

MEDICALIZATION. The tendency to turn normal biological processes into a medical procedure. For example, women now give birth in sterile hospitals rather than at home with their families, and the process of aging and dying is deterred for as long as possible using medications and invasive procedures, regardless of quality of life.

MISSIONISM. The process of converting people to another belief system. Most evident when missionaries from institutionalized religions, such as Christianity, proselytize to indigenous peoples.

MODERNIZATION. The process of making other societies over in the image of the West through changing their social, economic, political, and religious systems. Although officially designed to improve the quality of life of non-Westerners, this seldom happens; indeed, in most cases, modernization lowers the quality of life.

MONOGAMY. Marriage to only one spouse at a time.

MULTICULTURAL. See MULTICULTURALISM.

MULTICULTURALISM. The philosophy that people can maintain their distinctive cultural traditions, values, and beliefs while still participating in mainstream society. The official policy in Canada.

NATION. Traditionally, nation means a cultural group that shares the same language, religion, history, territory, and ancestry, such as the Plains Cree, but today has also come to mean an independent state, such as Canada.

NATIONHOOD. The desire of distinct ethnic groups to receive greater autonomy from states and official recognition as a nation.

NON-VERBAL CUES/NON-VERBAL COMMUNICATION. Forms of communication, such as gestures (kinesics), vocalizations (paralanguage), use of space (proxemics), and touch, that convey messages.

NORM. Expected and predictable behaviour within a given culture.

PANTHEON. A collection of gods and goddesses.

PARTICIPANT OBSERVATION. A research method whereby the anthropologist lives with the study group, learns their language, and develops a rapport with at least some members of the community who may also serve as key informants. The ethnographer closely observes the people as they go about their daily lives and, as much as possible, participates in their daily activities. Participant observation provides a first-hand descriptive account of the way people really live.

PATRIARCHAL SOCIETY. A male-dominated society.

PEDERASTY. A sexual relationship between an adolescent boy and an older man.

PHARAONIC CIRCUMCISION. The complete removal of the clitoris, labia minora, and most or all of the labia majora. These cut edges are stitched together using thorns or other materials, leaving a small opening for urine and menstrual flow. This stitching is known as infibulation.

PLURALISM. See PLURALISTIC SOCIETIES.

PLURALISTIC SOCIETIES. Societies containing several subcultural groups, for example, Canada.

POLYANDRY. An extremely rare form of marriage where a woman is married to two or more men at the same time.

POLYGAMY. An individual is married to more than one spouse at the same time.

POLYGYNY. A man is married to more than one woman at the same time.

POPULAR CULTURE. The culture of our everyday lives, such as television, sports, arts and crafts, fiction, and music.

PROXEMICS. The use of space to communicate messages.

PURDAH. A Muslim tradition of secluding women, either within their homes or beneath concealing clothing.

QUALITATIVE RESEARCH. The use of qualitative data, such as interviews, documents, and participant-observation data, rather than statistics and other quantifiable data. This type of research is most often used to explain human social behaviour.

QUANTITATIVE RESEARCH. The gathering of statistical and measurable data.

RACE. A misleading and inaccurate concept used to place individuals and populations into categories based on broad biological and/or behavioural traits.

RECIPROCITY. The exchange of goods and services between individuals or groups.

REFUGEES. Individuals seeking asylum from political, economic, social, or religious strife.

RELIGION. A belief in the supernatural that offers some sense of control over one's life and answers unexplainable questions, such as what happens after we die.

RELOCATION. The forced removal of a group of people (usually indigenous) from their traditional territory to another region.

RETAIL ANTHROPOLOGY. The study of people who shop from an anthropological perspective.

RITE OF PASSAGE. Rituals that mark important stages in an individual's life, for example, birth, puberty, marriage, and death.

SAME-SEX MARRIAGE. Marriage between individuals of the same sex.

SEXUALITY. Several components make up our sexuality: our sexual identity or orientation, the types of sexual practices considered the norm in our culture, and our interest in having sexual relationships.

SOCIO-CULTURAL ANTHROPOLOGY. A term often used in place of cultural anthropology to reflect the two major schools of thought—social anthropology (British) and cultural anthropology (American).

STRATIFICATION.   Placing people or groups into a hierarchy using various criteria. Those low on the hierarchy enjoy less access to resources and personal freedom.

SUBCULTURE.   Segments of a population that are distinct from mainstream culture, through ethnicity, class, religion, behaviour, and so on.

SUNNA CIRCUMCISION.   Female circumcision where only the clitoral prepuce (hood) is removed.

SYMBOLIC CIRCUMCISION.   A circumcision ritual that does not involve the actual removal of any genitalia, for example, circumcision by words practised in some parts of Kenya.

SYNCRETISM.   The blending of more than one religion; often members of a small-scale society will integrate their traditional beliefs with those of an institutionalized religion introduced by missionaries.

SYSTEMIC RACISM.   Discrimination embedded in the systems of a culture, such as government, education, and economics, that limits access to resources and opportunities for another "race."

TELECONDITIONING.   A term coined by Kottak (1990) that suggests societal behaviour is being modified due to watching television.

THIRD GENDER.   An alternate gender, usually involving a male taking on the cultural roles and position of a woman.

UXORILOCAL.   See UXORILOCAL RESIDENCE.

UXORILOCAL RESIDENCE.   A married couple residing with the wife's relatives.

Sources

Knauft, Bruce K. Excerpts from "*The Gebusi: Lives Transformed in a Rainforest World.*" New York: McGraw-Hill, 2001. Reproduced by permission of The McGraw-Hill companies.

The Canadian Press. "BC Tourney Bars Sikh Soccer Player Over Turban." Article first appeared September 6, 2005. Reprinted by permission of The Canadian Press.

PICTURE CREDITS

Index

abbayah, 158
accommodation, 62, 63, 75
  Canada, 62
  Canadian First Nations, 63
  Czechoslovakia, 62
  definition, 211
  South Tyrol, 62
acculturation, 61, 62-63
  Aztecs, 61
  Basques, 61
  definition, 211
advocacy and policy
  development, 49–50, 124
  aid workers, 50 58
  definition, 211
  and female circumcision,
    107
  refugee camps, 50, 57, 64n3
Afghanistan, 156, 158-59, 166
  patriarchal society, 166
  purdah, 166
age-grades, 132
age-sets, 124, 132
  definition, 211
  Masai, 132
age stratification, 135
  among elderly in China, 135
  definition, 211
aging, 124
  acceptance of age-related
    change, 125–26
  anthropology of, 124–25
  Chinese experience of,
    133–36
  Confucian veneration of
    elders, 134
  coping strategies, 126-27,
    138
  "culture of oldness," xxiii,
    123, 139, 209
  definition, 211
  dementia, 135
  diminished cognitive
    function, 125

discourse of neglect, 129
fictive kin and Chinese
  elderly, 136
"good old age," 126
Ju/'hoansi experice of, 124,
  127-129
mall walking, 38
marginalization of frail
  elders, 135, 138
Masai experience of, 132-33
North American RVers
  experience of, 124, 126,
  136–37
over-medicalization of the
  elderly, 124, 139n1
segregation of elderly, 129
spiritual and emotional
  strength, 126
ties with family and friends,
  129, 131, 132, 134-135,138
wisdom and cultural
  knowledge, 125–26, 138
Yanomami experience of ,
  130–32
aging workforce
  as reason for immigration,
    71
Ahmadu, Fuambai, xx, 107,
  119n9
Ally McBeal (TV show), 194
American Samoa, 21
amusement parks, 36, 38
ancestor worship and magic,
  148
Anderson, Robert, 5, 12
androcentrism, 166, 185. *See
  also* patriarchal society
  definition, 211
Aniston, Jennifer, 93
anorexia nervosa, 97-98
anthropologists
  advocates for the elderly, 12
  and aging 124
  ambiguous relationship
    with missionaries, 144
  and body image, 92
  as cultural brokers, 50

  and culture shock, 16
  and ethnic conflict, 49
  and female circumcision,
    107
  and fieldwork, 4
  and gender stratification,
    156
  and immigration, 70
  and missionism, 144
  and refugees, 50
  and same-sex marriage, 174
  and the business world, 32
  and the media, 192
  as mediators in ethnic
    conflict, 50–51
anthropology, xxv
  of aging, 124
  corporate, 33, 212
  definition, 211
  economic, 32-33
  fieldwork, xxi, 3–12, 21, 59,
    70, 124, 215, 217
  of genocide, 49
  goals, 209
  key concepts, xxvi, xxviii,
    xxix-xxx
  media, 192, 217
  medical, 93, 217
  methods of, xxvi
  participant observation,
    xxvi, 4–5, 34, 70, 124, 218
  relevance of, xxv, 46, 50, 207-
    210
  roles of, 208
  of shopping, 31–42, 209
  of suffering, 49, 63
  value of, 208
applied anthropology, xxv, 11
  definition, 211
Asiatic Exclusion League, 81
assimilation, 60, 61, 73, 75
  definition, 212
Atkins, Dr., 93
Australia
  immigration policy, 71
  same-sex marriage, 182
Azerbaijan, 157

Baker, Victoria J., 11
  experience of culture shock, 17–20
Barbie doll, 94-95
  syndrome, 95
Barnett, Steve, 33
Basques, 60-61
Beausoleil, N, 99
beauty pageants, 93
Bedouin *jalabiyya*, 52
Being Muslim the Bosnian Way (Bringa), 59
Ben-Ezer, Gadi, 50
berdache, 174. See also Two-Spirits.
  definition, 212
biculturalism, 23
  definition, 212
Bill C-38, 173
Blackfoot First Nations
  polygyny, 177–78
blended family, 184,193
  definition, 212
Boas, Franz, xxv, 53–54
Boddy, Janice, 108, 110–11, 113, 117
body adornment, 98, 99
  definition, 212
  Ju/'hoansi tattooing, 98
  North American make-up, 99
  Plains Cree, 95
  Rashaayda Bedouin tattooing, 99
  Trobrianders fashion, 98-99
body beautification, 94–95
body image, xxii, 91, 92, 93–100, 208
  anthropological study of, 92-93
  in Asia, 98
  Barbie doll, 94-95
  connection to power, 93
  cross-cultural perspective, 92
  definition, 212
  dieting, 95-96
  diffusion, 92, 98

eating disorders, 97, 214
  and enculturation, 96
  and ethnicity, 94
  fasting, 93
  in Florence, 97-98
  language, 94
  in Latinos, 98
  marginalization and, 95
  medicalization of racial features, 98
  in Samoa, 98
  in southwestern Nigeria, 97
  thinness, 92–93, 98, 100
  in Vietnam, 98
  Western perception of beauty, 91–94, 98–99
body image distortion, 95-97
Body Image Trap, The (Crook), 93
body modification, 93, 94–95, 98, 116
boondockers, 136
Bosnian conflict, 58–59
Brady Bunch (TV show), 193
Brazil's *telenovelas*, 193, 201
breast augmentation, 94, 116
brideprice, 176, 117–78
  definition, 212
brideservice, 176, 177
  definition, 212
Briggs, Jean L., 5, 7–8, 10
Bringa, Tone, 49, 58
  Being Muslim the Bosnian Way, 59
Britain. *See* United Kingdom
Brooks, Geraldine, 159
Brown, John Seely, 34
bulimia, 97
burqa, 158, 166

Canada, 52–54, 69
  accommodation, 62
  discrimination in, 73, 75-76, 79, 81-82, 85
  harassment of women in hijab, 167
  immigration policy (*See*

Canadian immigration)
  language issues, 52
  multiculturalism, 70–71, 73, 82, 167
  national identity, 73, 75, 85
  same-sex marriage, 181
  segregation of the sexes, 158
  skilled labour shortage, 72
Canadian citizenship, 77
Canadian immigration, 69, 71–72. *See also* immigrants
  Chinese Canadians, 77–80
  discrimination, 75
  Japanese Canadians, 76
  "open door" policy, 85
  points system, 80–81
  Sikhs (*See* Canadian Sikhs)
  Ukrainians, 75
  visible minorities, 76–77, 80
Canadian Multiculturalism Act, 80
Canadian Pacific Railroad, 78
Canadian Sikhs, 80–83
  discrimination, 81-82
  points system, 81
  restrictions on immigration, 81
  right to vote, 81
  taking jobs, 81
  turbans, 52
  turban controversy, 82
censorship, 198
chador, 158
  in Iran, 164
  in Pakistan, 165
Charter of Rights and Freedoms, 80, 82
children
  protection of, 11
  in refugee camps, 58
  in Two-Spirit marriage, 180
  victims of violence, 59
  and violence on television, 199
  woman-woman marriage and, 181

China, 24–27
    elderly (*See* Chinese elderly)
    television, 198
Chinatowns, 74, 78
Chinese Canadians, 74, 77–80
    anti-Chinese riots, 79
    head-tax, 79
    scapegoats for economic
        problems, 79–80
    traditional language, 77
Chinese elderly
    familial care of, 134
    fictive kin, 136
    functions within family, 134
    government support for,
        135
    neighbourhood reciprocity,
        136
    one-child policy, 134
    use of healers, 135
Chinese Exclusion Act, 79–80
Chretien, Jean, 85
Christianity. *See* missionism
Christmas, 76
civil rights, 77. *See also* human
    rights
"civilizing" indigenous ethnic
    groups, 61
Class, 34
    definition, 212
    pharaonic circumcision and,
        113
    purdah and, 157
    and seclusion of women,
        160
    shopping malls and, 34, 40
classroom behaviour
    television's influence on,
        199–200
Clifford, James, 4
climate shock, 84-85
Clinton, Hilary Rodham, 113-
    14
    ethnocentrism, 114
clitoridectomy/excision, 106,
    108, 109, 113
    definition, 212

clitoris as masculine origin,
    111
CNN, 198
cognitive desensitization, 199
common-law family, 184
    definition, 212
communication, 23
    definition, 212
    intercultural, 23
    modern communication
        systems, 75
companionate marriage, 185
conflict of replacement, 56
"conflict of secession," 55
Confucian veneration of
    elders, 134
consumer behaviour. *See*
    shopping; shopping malls
consumer culture, 34
coping strategies
    culture shock, 19-20, 22,
        26–27, 85
    elderly, 126-27, 138
Coronaro, Luigi, 95
corporate anthropology/
    ethnography, 33
    definition, 213
corsets, 94
cosmetic surgery, 94
    in Asia, 98
    in Vietnam, 98
Counihan, C.M., 93
Counts, David R., 124, 126,
    136–37
Counts, Dorothy Ayer, 124,
    126, 136–37
"crisis of the family," 184
Crook, M., *Body Image Trap,
    The*, 93
cross-cultural comparison/
    perspective, xxvii, 46, 92
    body image, 92, 97–98
    definition, 213
    gerontology, 124
    purdah, 156
Crystal Mall, Burnaby, 41
CSI: Miami (TV show), 199

cultivation effect, 199
cultural brokers, 50
cultural diversity, xxv, 46, 49,
    50, 76, 195, 208-210. *See also*
    multiculturalism; pluralism;
    ethnic diversity
    appreciation of, 209
    definition, 213
cultural identity, 23, 112, 164
    definition, 213
cultural identity markers, 164
cultural imperialism, xxix,
    45–46, 200.
    definition, 213
    missionism, 145
    Star Trek (TV show), 196
cultural learning, 22
cultural relativism, xxii, xxvii,
    xxviii, xxix, 9–10, 45, 144,
    185, 194
    definition, 213
    female circumcision and,
        106, 107
    marriage, 185
    Star Trek (TV show), 194
cultural retention, xxii
Cultural Revolution, 94
culture, xxviii, 4, 51, 192
    definition, 15, 214
    enculturation, xxi, 85, 96,
        126, 191, 197, 214
    "learning the culture," 22
culture change, 46, 57, 152,
    184–85
    definition, 213
    from missionism, 144, 152
culture of dependency, 57
"culture of oldness," xxiii, 123,
    139, 209
culture of youth, 123
culture shock, xxi, xxvi, 7, 15,
    16–28, 209
    and anthropologists, 16-20
    coping strategies, 19, 22,
        26–27, 85
    definition, 213
    immigrants, 74, 84

"otherness," 16
reverse culture shock, 22
social support systems, 20, 23
stages, 21-22
symptoms, 16, 19, 21

Darfur, 48
Davis, J., 49
Deep Space Nine (TV show), 195
development and modernization approach, 114
definition, 213
Dhillon, Balteji Singh, 82-83
dieting, 95
diffusion, 32, 46
definition, 214
female circumcision, 108
television, 193, 200-01
Western concept of beauty, 91-92, 98-99
discrimination, 48, 54, 75-76, 78, 85
based on body image, 94
Canadian Sikhs, 81-82
Canadian Ukrainians, 75-76
Chinese Canadians, 79
definition, 214
religion, 82
same-sex marriage, 183
women wearing hijab, 167
displaced persons, 49, 57. *See also* refugees
divorce, 185
djellabah and *haik*, 158
double-income family, 178
dowry, 177
definition, 214
Nuer, 177
Dreaming Law, 146-48
abandoning, 147
incorporating Christianity into, 147
television's effect on, 201

eating disorders, 97
anorexia nervosa, 97
bulimia, 97
definition, 214
economic anthropology, 32
applied, 32-33
definition, 214
egalitarianism, 129
definition, 214
Ju'/hoan, 129
Egyptian *milaya*, 158
elderly. *See* aging
emergency anthropology, 49
emic approach, 51, 160
definition, 214
enculturation, xxi, 16, 85
body image and, 96
definition, 214
elderly as enculturative force, 126
television, 191, 197
Entertainment Tonight, 94
ethics, xxii, xxvii, 11
confidentiality, 11
definition, 214
fieldwork and, 10
medical missionism, 146
in retail anthropology, 34-35
ethics review boards, 11
Ethiopian Jews, 50
ethnic boundary markers, 51, 52-53
definition, 214
food, 52
language, 52
lifestyle, 52
mythology or origin myths, 52
physical appearance, 52
place of origin, 52
religion, 51
religious heritage, 52
ethnic cleansing, 56. *See also* genocide
ethnic conflict, xxii, 47, 48, 50-51, 54-56, 76

accommodation, 60, 62
acculturation, 60-61
anthropologists and, 49-51
assimilation, 60-61
caused by European colonialism, 55
definition, 214
economic, religious, or political factors, 55
genocide, 60-61, 63
imperial domination and, 54
power as underlying reason, 48, 63
relocation, 60-61
underlying reasons for, 48, 63
ethnic diversity, 55, 70, 73. *See also* pluralism
ethnic enclaves, 74
ethnic groups, 48, 51, 52-55, 62-63, 64n2
Bosnian conflict, 58
definition, 214
intermarriage, 58
Kurds as, 60
origin myths, 52
ethnic identity, 51, 52-54, 58, 75, 112
definition, 214
multiple identities, 75
ethnic intolerance, 48
definition, 215
ethnic stratification, 54
definition, 215
ethnicity, 51, 71
definition, 215
discrimination based on, 48
persecution based on, 48
role in body image, 94
ethno-nationalism, 73
definition, 215
ethnocentrism, xxii, xxix, 19i, 114
definition, 215
and female circumcision, 107

in immigration policy, 72
in missionism, 144
Western, 107
ethnographers, 4, 10
definition, 215
ethnographic research, 93, 124, 174
challenges, 6-7
definition, 4, 215
and fieldwork, 5, 12
language acquisition, 6
ethnography, 11, 124
body image, 93
corporate, 33
definition, 215
ethnohistorical, 49
definition, 215
ethnohistorical causes of genocide, 49
EU, 166
immigration restrictions, 72
Europe
immigrants from, 72
immigration policies, 76
European colonization, 55, 148
destruction of matrilineal societies, 160
effect on ethnic conflict, 55
Evenkis, 23

face lifts, 116
family, 174, 176, 183, 184, 193, 212. *See also* marriage
blended, 184,193, 212
common-law, 184
definition, 215
double-income, 178
fictive kinship, 136, 197, 215
single-parent, 184
family entertainment, 37
family-sponsored immigrants, 71-72
fasting, 93
Father Knows Best (TV show), 193
fattening room, 97
Feit, Harvey, 11

female circumcision, xxii, 105, 116-17
age at, 106
anthropological perspective, 107-08
associated with Islam, 113
backlash, 115
choice, 107
criminalization, 115
cultural and ethnic identity, 112
cultural relativism, 107
definition, 215
distribution of female circumcision, 108-09
economic factors, 112
education and, 114-15, 117
ethics, 107
feminist perspective, 105, 107, 111
gender identity, 111
in Guinea-Bissau, 110, 113, 116
health risks, 110-111
historical origins, 110
international aid sanctions, 11
in Kenya, 115
"medical view," 115
performed by women, 112
pervasiveness, 114
reasons for, 111-13
religious grounds, 113
rite of passage, 110, 112
sexual desire and, 113
social factors, 111-12
in Sudan, 108, 111, 112-13, 115
symbolic circumcision, 116
and status of women, 112
types of, 106
Western view of, 111, 113-15
in Yoruba, 113
female genital cutting, 114. *See also* female circumcision
female genital mutilation, 114
definition, 215

female husband, 182
female seclusion, 160, 168. *See also* hijab; purdah
feminist anthropology, 107, 166
definition, 215
on female circumcision, 105, 107, 111
hijab, 161
on purdah, 161
fictive kinship, 136, 197
definition, 216
fieldwork, xxi, 4, 5, 59, 70
constant uncertainty, 6
culture shock, 7, 21
definition, 216
ethics, 10
gender issues, 8
key informants, 5, 11, 34, 70, 124, 217
nuisance problems, 9-10
participant observation, xxvi, 4-5, 34, 70, 124, 218
as rite of passage, 3, 12
First Nations, 53, 61-62
acculturation, 63
Blackfoot, 177-78
genocide, 63
Fondahl, Gail A., 23
food courts, 38-39
food sharing
Ju/'hoansi, 124
North American RVers, 137
foot binding, 94, 158
forced migration, 50
foreign investment, 71
Fox News, 198
France
banning of religious symbols and attire, 167
racist policies, 76
same-sex marriage, 182
Friends (TV show), 194

Gaza Strip, 48
Gebusi, 144, 149-151,174-75, 209

animistic religious system, 149-151
  conversion to Christianity, 151
  cultural loss, 151
  ethnographic challenges, 6-7, 8
  gender inequality, 8-9
  kogwayay, 149
  Pantheon of animal and other spirits, 149
  patriarchy, 8
  sexual behaviour, 7
  sorcery, 150-151
gender, 8, 156, 193. *See also* "hermaphrodites"; homosexuality; Two-Spirits
  in body image distortion, 97
  definition, 216
  "gender variant roles," 174
  research limitations, 9
  shopping habits based on, 37, 39
"gender apartheid," 166
gender identity, 111, 184
  children in same-sex families, 184
gender inequality. *See* gender stratification
gender stratification, 8-9, 11, 156. *See also* patriarchal society; segregation of the sexes
  anthropology and, 156
  definition, 216
General Hospital (TV show), 193
Generation Y consumers, 33
generational culture clashes, 83. *See also* aging
genocide, xxix, 48, 49-50, 56, 60-63
  action genocide, 56
  anthropology of, 49
  Beothuk, 63
  Darfur, 63
  definition, 216

economic or political motivation, 56
gerontology, 124. *See also* aging
  cross-cultural perspective, 124
  multidisciplinary field, 124
ghosts of Iceland, 5
globalization, 70, 75, 195
  definition, 216
  impact on study of anthropology, 70
group marriage, 179
  definition, 216

Hadith, 157
Hamas, 162-63
Han Chinese, 52
"hermaphrodites," 174
hijab, 157. *See also* purdah
  attempts to end, 160
  as cultural marker, 161
  in Azerbaijan, 157
  definition, 216
  educated urban women, 167
  feminist perspective, 161
  freedom from Western gender games, 157, 162
  freedom to choose, 164, 167-68
  harassment for wearing, 163, 166-67
  harassment for not wearing, 160, 162-64
  in Iran, 163-164
  instrument of oppression in Iran, 164
  as liberating practice, 168
  and men's sexuality and lack of control, 161
  Muslim identity, 167
  origin, 159-60
  in Pakistan, 165-66
  in Palestine, 162-63
  as political statement, 157
  as "portable seclusion," 159

resistance to Western domination, 167
  restoration by Hamas, 162-63
  submission to god, 161
  in Sudan, 164-65
  Turkey, 167
  Western forms of, 158
  Western perspective, 155, 161, 166
Hitler, Adolf, xxix, 48
holistic approach, xxvii, 33, 50
  definition, 216
Holmes, Ellen, 21
  In American Samoa, 21
Holtzman, Jon D., 5, 8, 10
homogenization, 200, 201, 214
  definition, 216
homosexuality, 174, 175, 185. *See also* Two-Spirits
  definition, 216
  European disapproval, 181
  stigma attached to studying, 174
  television, 194, 197
Hong Kong
  entrepreneurs, 71, 80
  marginalization of frail elders, 135
household, 176. *See also* family
  definition, 216
human rights, xxviii, xxix, 114, 166
  definition, 216
  female circumcision and, 106, 111, 113
  global advocacy for, 106
human sexuality. *See* sexuality
Hussein, Saddam, 60
Hutus, 55-56

I Love Lucy (TV show), 193
identity
  cultural, 23, 112, 164, 213
  ethnic, 51-54, 58, 75, 112, 214
  gender, 111, 184

national, 73, 75, 85, 198
immigrants, xxii, 71, 195
  adjustment, 73
  African, 69, 72, 77
  from Asia, 69, 72, 78, 81,
  as asset not liability, 75
  asylum seekers, 72
  blamed for welfare costs, 78
  Canada as nation of, 69
  Chinese Canadians, 74,
    77–80
  citizens' attitudes toward,
    75
  definition, 217
  educated and skilled, 72
  employment, 75, 77
  generational culture
    clashes, 83
  investment by, 71–72, 80
  Japanese, 76
  language learning and
    competency, 77, 83
  language retention, 84
  misconceptions, 77–78
  professionals, 72
  recognition of credentials,
    77, 80
  residential segregation, 74
  Sikhs, 80–83
  taking jobs from native
    Canadians, 77–78
  Ukrainian Canadians, 75-76
  visible minorities, 76–77, 80
immigration, 70
  Canadian immigration
    policy, 71-72
  definition, 217
  illegal, 72–73, 76
  multidisciplinary subject, 70
  points system, 80
  reasons for, 71–72
incestuous marriages, 183
India, 160, 198
Indian sari, 158
indigenous peoples, 144. See
  also European colonization;
  names of specific

indigenous peoples
  "civilizing" indigenous
    ethnic groups, 61
  definition, 217
  development-oriented
    missionary work, 145
  First Nations, 53, 61–63,
    177–78
  religious conversions, 144
infibulation, 106, 108, 110, 113
  definition, 217
initiation rites, 110
  definition, 217
integration
  cultural, 75
  economic and social, 75
  two-way process, 74
Inter African Committee
  Against Harmful
  Traditional Practices, 115
international aid, 145
international community, 63
International Conference
  on Population and
  Development, 114
Internet, 75, 156
  cafés, 38
  news sites, 198
  shopping sites, 41
Intifada, 162-63
Iran, 60, 156
  chador, 158
  female seclusion, 160
  hijab, 163–64
  purdah, 164
Iraq, 60
Iraqi abbayah, 158
Islamaphobia, 166
Israel, 55, 62

jalabiyya, 52
Japanese Canadians, 76
Japanese Samurai warriors
  same-sex marriage, 179
Jenness, Diamond, People of
  the Twilight, 12
jewellery, 94–95, 98

Plains Cree, 95
Trobrianders, 98-99
jilbaab, 156
Ju/'hoan elderly
  autonomy, 129
  continuing contribution to
    household, 127
  discourse of neglect, 129
  food sharing, 124, 129
  independence, 127
  living with kin, 124, 128
  regret for inevitable decline,
    128
Ju/'hoansi
  egalitarianism, 129
  ethnographic research, 7-8
  marriage, 177
  tattooing, 98
Junqueira, Aristides, 56

Kapauku, 178
key informants, 5, 12, 70, 124
  definition, 217
  in retail anthropology, 34
Khalsa Diwan Society, 81
khanith, 175
kin network, 177
Klein, N., 35
Knauft, Bruce, 4, 6–10, 149–
  51, 175, 209
kogwayay (Gebusi culture),
  149
Koreatown Mall, Los Angeles,
  41
Kottak, Conrad Philip, xxv,
  192–94, 198–201
Kroeber, Alfred, 174
Kurdish separitist
  movements, 60
Kurdistan, 60
Kurds, 48, 52-53, 59-60

language, 60, 74
  in Acadia, 52
  in assimilation, 60
  as ethnic boundary marker,
    52

in fieldwork, 6, 22
immigrants' learning of
   French or English, 77, 84
influence on body image, 94
North American Jews, 52
preservation, 77
Quebecois de souche, 52
language retention, 77, 84
   definition, 217
Law of the Dreaming. *See*
   Dreaming Law
"learning the culture," 22
Leave it to Beaver (TV show),
   193
Lebleigez, Alan, 166
Lee, Richard B., 7, 8-9, 23, 208
leg-lengthening surgeries, 98
Lewin, Ellen, 182

makeup use, 99
Makkli, L., 57
male circumcision, 110, 116,
   119n10, 119n11
   definition, 217
male-male love, 174
mall junkies, 39
mall rats, 39
mall walking, 38
Mandelbaum, David, 210
Mao Zedung, 94
Mardu Aborigines, 6, 17, 144,
   146-148, 201
   caught between two worlds,
     148
   Dreaming or Dreamtime,
     146-48
   Mission era, 147
   social problems, 147
marriage, 176
   changes, 184-185
   companionate, 185
   as cultural construct, 176
   definitions, 176, 217
   form of social control, 177
   forms of, 176-79
   functions, 176-77
   group, 179, 216

incestuous, 183
joining two families, 177
Ju/'hoansi, 177
Kapauku, 177
monogamy, 177-78, 217
political alliances, 177
polyandry, 179, 218
polygamy, 176, 218
polygyny, 113, 176-77, 183
reasons for, 176-77
same-sex, 174
Two-Spirit, 180-181
wealth generation, 177
woman-woman, 181-82
Masai, 132-133
   age-grade system, 132
   care of the elderly, 132-33
   polygyny, 178
masks, 158, 164. *See also* hijab
Massara, E.B., 93
Mayan people (Guatemala),
   200
media, xxiii, 46
   and anthropologists, 192
   body image, 92-93, 99
   on female circumcision, 105
   mass media, xxvi
   role in Bosnian conflict, 58
   stereotyping features of
     minority groups, 94
media anthropology, 192
   definition, 217
medical anthropology, 93
   definition, 217
medical imperialism, 116
medical missionism, 145-46
   ethics, 146
medicalization, 116.
   definition, 217
   elderly, 124
   of female circumcision,
     115-16
   of racial features, 98
Metis, 53
milaya, 158
Miller, Daniel, 34-35, 40
Milosevic, Slobodan, 58

missionaries, 56, 143
   intolerance, 148
   stereotypes, 144
missionism, xxiii, 143, 144,
   145-52, 209
   conversion for aid, 146
   cultural imperialism, 145
   definition, 217
   development-oriented, 145
   during the Indonesian
     tsunami, 145
   ethics, 146
   and the Gebusi, 149-51
   goals, 144
   involvement with
     international aid, 145
   and the Mardu, 146-48
   medical, 145-46
   proselytizing, 144-45
   social problems caused by,
     147
   in the Solomon Islands, 148
modern communication
   systems, 75
modernization, 124, 132, 152
   definition, 217
monogamy
   definition, 217
   heterosexual, 177-78
moral universe, xxviii
Morsy, Soheir, 115
movie theatres, 38
   teleconditioning, 200
multiculturalism, 70, 71, 73-74,
   82, 167, 196
   day-to-day reality, 71
   definition, 218
   United Kingdom, 73
multidisciplinary approach,
   49, 70, 124
Murphy Brown (TV show), 194
Mustafa, Naheed, 162
mythology or origin myths, 52

nation, 53
   definition, 218
national identity, 73, 85, 198

Egyptian television, 198
unity through ethnic
    diversity, 75
nationalism, 58, 62
    ethno-nationalism, 73, 215
    Kurdish separatist
        movement, 60
nationhood, 48, 53
    definition, 218
Nestorians, 145
9/11, 76
Nolan, R.W., 15, 20, 21
non-verbal cues, 23
    definition, 218
norm, 18
    definition, 218
North African *djellabah* and
    haik, 158
North American aboriginal
    groups
    and Two-Spirits, 180
North American concept
    of beauty. *See* Western
    perception of beauty
North American RVers, 124
    boondockers, 136
    challenging stereotype of
        elderly retirees, 137
    double stigma, 137
    food sharing, 137
    major economic force, 126
    negative images, 137
    sense of community, 137
    subculture, 126
    "Zen affluence," 136
Nuer of Minnesota, 5
Nuer of Sudan, 178, 182

Olberg, K., 15
old age. *See* aging
Olwig, Karen Fog, 70
One Life to Live (TV show), 193
online shopping, 41. *See*
    Internet
"open door" policy of
    Canadian immigration, 85
Ouimmet, Emilie, 167

Overing, J., xxx

Pakistan, 156
    male dominated society, 165
    purdah, 165
Palestine, 156
    ethnic conflict, 55
    ethnic identity, 53
    hijab campaign, 162–63
pantheon, 149
    definition, 218
participant observation, xxvi,
    4, 70, 124
    "borrowed" by other
        disciplines, 5
    definition, 218
    in retail anthropology, 34
Pashtun Afghan *burqa*, 158
patriarchal society, 107, 166.
    See also androcentrism
    Afghanistan, 166
    definition, 218
    female circumcision and,
        107
    hijab and, 161
Peacock, James, *Rites of
    Modernization*, 174-75
pederasty, 175
    definition, 218
People of the Twilight (Jenness,
    Diamond), 12
perfect body. *See* body image
Persian Gulf War, 60
pharaonic circumcision, 106,
    108
    definition, 218
    reinforcing class
        distinctions, 113
physical appearance. *See also*
    body image
    as ethnic boundary marker,
        52
pluralism, 55, 73–74. *See also*
    cultural diversity; ethnic
    diversity; multiculturalism
pluralistic societies, 73
    definition, 218

points system, 71
"politics of names," 114
polyandry, 179
    definition, 218
    fraternal polyandry, 179
polygamy, 176
    definition, 218
polygyny, 113, 176–79, 183
    appeal for women, 178
    Blackfoot First Nations,
        177-78
    definition, 218
    jealousy among co-wives,
        178
    wealth generating system,
        178
popular culture, xxiii, 192, 200
    definition, 218
postmodernity, 200
Prabhataya (TV show), 194
prejudice, 76, 81
Prime Directive, 195
proxemics, 23
    definition, 218
psychology of shopping,
    38–41
    class, age, gender, and
        ethnicity, 40
    teenaged girls, 38
    women *vs.* men, 39–40
purdah, xxiii, 145, 157, 159
    Afghanistan, 166
    attempts to end, 160
    cross-cultural approach, 156
    definition, 218
    emic approach, 160
    establishing paternity, 157
    female seclusion, 157–59
    feminine modesty, 157, 159
    gender stratification, 156
    history of, 159
    India, 160
    as oppression, 160, 164
    Pakistan, 159, 165-66
    Palestine, 162-63
    punishment for breaking,
        165

reasons for, 157
rejection of Western
morals, 157
symbol of status, 157
Western forms of, 158
Western perception of,
155–56, 166

qualitative research, 5, 124
definition, 219
quantitative research, 5
definition, 219
Quebec
harassment of women in
hijab, 167
Quebecois, 52
Quran, 159, 198
on purdah, 157

race, 53, 54
definition, 219
racial features
medicalization of, 98
racism, 72, 78, 82
systemic, 76, 219

Rashaayda Bedouin, 16-17,
165, 178
masks, 158, 164
patriarchal society, 164
segregation of the sexes,
158
tattooing, 99
RCMP turban controversy, 82
reciprocity, 134
definition, 219
neighbourhood, 136
Red Cross guidelines on aid
work, 145
refugee camps, 50, 57, 64n3
culture of dependence, 57
refugees, 48, 50, 56–58, 71–72,
76
cultural adaptations, 57
definition, 219
Ethiopian Jews, 50
Reich, Alice, 4–5

relevance of anthropology,
xxv, 46, 50, 207-10
religion, 48, 143
ancestor worship and
magic, 148
blending of (See syncretism)
in Bosnian conflict, 58
Canadian Sikhs, 81
definition, 143, 219
Dreaming Law, 146–47
as ethnic boundary marker,
51
Pantheon of animal and
other spirits, 149
institutionalized, 143-44
religious conversion, 144, 148,
151. See also missionism
religious freedom, 167–68
relocation, 61, 62
Asinias, 61
definition, 219
First Nations, 61
Jewish inhabitants from
Gaza Strip, 48
Turks, 61
"rescue and civilizational
missions," 115
retail anthropology, 34
definition, 219
ethics in, 35
retail tribalism, 34
rite of passage, 3, 21, 23
definition, 219
female circumcision, 112
fieldwork as, 3, 12
Rites of Modernization
(Peacock), 175
Roma, 52
Rwanda, 48, 55–56

salwar kameez, 159
same-sex marriage, xxiii, 174
anthropologists and, 174–76
Azande, 181
Bill C-38, 173
brideprice, 179
definition, 219

history of, 179
legal recognition, 173, 181–
82, 185
military men with "boy
wives," 181
opposition to, 176, 183
solving economic or social
problems, 182
woman-woman marriage,
181–82
Samoa, Western, American,
21
sari, 158
Saudi women, 159
compulsory hijab, 160
segregation of the sexes, 158,
164. See also purdah
Rashaayda Bedouin, 158
Seligman, C.G., 12
Serbs, 52
sexuality, 7, 174
definition, 219
Shariah law, 75
Sharma, Ashok Rattan, 78
Sharma, Sudesh, 78
Shi'ites in Iran, 60
Shirazi, Faegheh, 164
shopping
anthropology of, 31–42, 209
consumer culture, 34
shopping malls, 35
amusement parks in, 36
anchor stores, 37
charitable organizations
in, 38
consumer experience in,
35–36
decline of, 41-42
elderly people, 38
ethnic specialty centres, 41
exterior aesthetics, 36
family entertainment, 37
food courts, 38–39
geared to women, 39
Generation Y consumers, 33
kiosks or "pushcarts," 37
men, 38–39

public space, 36–37
"sideshows" in, 36
social aspects, 38, 40–41
stratification of shoppers,
39–40
teenaged girls, 38
use of public space in,
32–33, 36–37
Sikh Coalition, 82. *See also*
Canadian Sikhs
Sikh turban (*dastar*), 52
Sikhs of India, 51
Sinhalese, 17
Six Feet Under (TV show), 194
Skarphedinsson, Magnus, 11
soap opera, 193-94
socio-cultural anthropology, 4
definition, 219
sojourners, 71, 78
Solomon Islanders, 144, 148
ancestor worship and
magic, 148
missionary work, 148
Sopranos, The (TV show), 199
sorcery, 150
Sri Lanka, 17–18, 20, 194
Star Trek (TV show), 191, 194-
97
consumerism, 197
cultural imperialism,
196–97
cultural relativism, 194
Deep Space Nine (TV Show),
195-96
Enterprise (TV Show), 197
fictive kin, 197
mirroring North American
ideals, 197
Prime Directive, 194-95
reflection of mainstream
North American values,
194
Star Trek: Next Generation
(TV Show), 195
Voyager (TV Show), 196-97
women in, 195–96
stereotypes

elderly, 126
missionairies, 144
stratification, 39
age, 135, 211
definition, 219
ethnic, 48, 54
gender, 150, 156, 216
of shoppers, 39–40
subculture, 126
definition, 219
Sudan, 156, 164
Sudanese *tobah*, 158
Suduwatura Ara, 18-20
suffering
anthropology of, 49, 63
sunna circumcision, 106, 108,
110, 113
definition, 219
Sunni Muslims, 60
symbolic circumcision, 116
definition, 219
syncretism, 148
definition, 219
systemic racism, 76
definition, 220

Taliban, 166
tattooing, 95, 98–99
Ju/'hoansi, 98
Plains Cree, 95
Rashaayda Bedouin, 99
technology, 184
teleconditioning, 200
definition, 220
telenovelas, 193, 201
television
advertising consumer
products, 198
anti-smoking campaigns,
197
censorship, 198
classroom behaviour, 199-
200
cognitive desensitization,
199
as controlling device, 198
creating national identity,

198
creating public forums, 202
cultivation effect, 199
cultural imperialism, 200
cultural significance, 192
diffusion, 193, 200–01
distorted perception of
reality, 199
Drive Safe campaigns, 197
Egyptian, 198
enculturation, 191, 197
entertainment value, 192
as global medium, 191
homogenization, 200
homosexuality, 194
impact on our sense of self,
208
informative value, 192, 202
national identity, 198
popular culture, 192
as reflection of culture, 191,
193–94
social solidarity from, 193,
202
symbol of culture, 202
violence on, 199
terrorism, 76
screening of immigrants
for, 77
thinness, 92, 95, 98, 100
comparison to religious
cult, 93
third gender, 175
definition, 220
Tito, Marshal, 58
tobah, 158
Tonkinson, Robert, 4, 6
experience of culture shock,
17
fieldwork challenges, 9, 10
Trobrianders of New Guinea,
4
fashion, 98-99
Tucker, John, 146
Tudjman, Franjo, 58
Turbans, 52
controversy, 82

Turkey, 59, 167
Turkish *yashmak*, 158
Tutsi, 55-56
Twiggy, 95
Two-Spirit marriages
  among North and South
    American aboriginal
    groups, 180
  reasons, 181
Two-Spirits, 174, 180–81.

Ukrainian Canadians, 52, 54,
  75-76
Underhill, Paco, 2, 32–35, 36-
  37, 38–39, 41
United Kingdom
  immigrants from, 72
  multicultural policy, 73
  same-sex marriage, 182
United National Leadership of
  the Uprising (UNLU), 163
United Nations, 115
United Nations Fourth World
  Conference on Women, 113
United States, 77
  harassment of women in
    hijab, 166–67
  immigration, 72, 76
  melting pot philosophy, 74
  same-sex marriage, 182
Ury, William R., 11
Utku Inuit, 5
  emotional behaviour, 8

uxorilocal residence, 134
  definition, 220
Vancouver's Chinatown, 78
Vasco da Gama Center,
  Lisbon, 36
veil. *See* hijab
visible minorities. *See under*
  Canada
vodun (voodoo) cults, 148
voice, 11, 51,
  to the elderly, 124
  of women following purdah,
    156
  of women practicing female
    circumcision, 106

Weidman, H., 8
Weight Watchers, 93
Weiner, Annette, 4, 6
West Edmonton Mall, 37
"Western decadence," 198
Western forms of hijab, 158
Western imperialism, 114
Western-influenced
  education, 151
Western perception of beauty,
  93–94
  diffusion, 91–92, 98–99
  negative effect on other
    countries, 92
Western perception of hijab
  and purdah, 155–56, 161,
  166-68

Wika, Unni, 175
Will and Grace (TV show), 194,
  197
Winfrey, Oprah, 93
Winnipeg Telegram, 54
woman-woman marriage,
  181–82
  among African groups, 182
  Dahomean, 181
  Nandi, 182
  in Northern Nigeria, 181
Women's Action Forum
  (WAF), 168
World Health Organization,
  115

Yanomami, Davi Kipenaus, 57
Yanomami people, 56–57
  elderly, 130-31
  genocide, 56
yashmak, 158
Yoruba, 51
Young, William C.
  experience of culture shock,
    16–17
  reverse culture shock, 22
Young and the Restless (TV
  Show), 193
Yugoslavia, 48, 58

"Zen affluence," 136